I0083069

This book is dedicated to
Larkin and Isme

I am thinking back to the time when for us the known world hardly existed; days became simply the spaces between dreams, spaces between the shifting floors of time.

Justine
By Lawrence Durrell

DANCING ON THE MOON IN THE WATER

DANCING ON THE MOON IN THE WATER

Peter J. Gorham

Copyright © 2015 Peter J. Gorham
All rights reserved.

ISBN: 069256425X
ISBN 13: 9780692564257

CHAPTER 1

I first met Susanne in the high school library. I was sitting at a long wooden table looking at a book with glossy pictures of mammals, trying to find the one I'd dreamed about the night before.

She stopped behind me and said, "What are you staring at so deeply? You look like you're studying a riddle." She was German.

I turned towards her and was captured by her amazing blue eyes, a shade of blue I had never seen and a penetrating brilliance that was surreal.

"It is called a 'sloth' " I said.

I had never spoken to her but had noticed her statuesque dignified presence. She was a new student, but she moved with maturity and poise.

"A tree sloth," I added. "Isn't it interesting and beautiful in an odd way?"

"In a clumsy way, yes, it is beautiful."

"Look at its eyes. They are peaceful and gentle and wise and sad too, as if it knows that what is in its heart is something no one will ever see."

"What a nice way to say it," she said and sat down next to me.

"Let me show you other pictures of it," I said, eagerly sharing with her the oversized book. "It's called 'arboreal', which means it spends most of its life in trees. It eats and sleeps and even mates there. When it comes down to the ground, which is rare, it moves slowly like a baby first walking. In my dream the animal had been walking over rocks, lifting its awkward legs high and slowly, moving toward me. To rescue me from something, to take me somewhere that I needed to go before I'd become lost. This picture is exactly what it looked like in my dream."

"Well, wouldn't you expect it to look the same in your dream as it looks in life?"

"Yes I would, but I have never seen a sloth before, even a picture of one. So I couldn't have known how to dream it without ever having seen it."

"Maybe you knew it for another time in your life."

"But I've never seen one at any time in my life."

"What I mean is that maybe it is something that you are *going* to see. We can dream the future too."

As impulsively as she had sat down, she stood up and announced, "I must go now," putting her hand out to me. "My name is Susanne. What is yours?"

It was a harsh winter. The coldest and the snowiest that anyone could remember. Susanne had recently arrived with her mother from Germany. She wasn't adept yet at speaking American English, but she had uncanny insight and intuition. She also had prodigious musical talent.

Over the winter our friendship grew deeper, until we were spending whole days together. Feelings that were in me and had never come forward, flowed out in her presence.

Each morning I awakened before the sun and put on my clothes and hurried to Susanne's house and knocked on her door quietly. Susanne would open the door and say the same thing each time: "So, Michael, you have come for me."

Some nights I had trouble falling asleep because I was so excited that in a few hours I would get to see Susanne again. And then other nights I fell asleep easily, comforted by the thought that I'd see her the next morning. Each night I wrote Susanne a poem and read it to her at the lake, as we waited for the sunrise.

Spring came.

One day Susanne and I were at the small lake near my home watching swans dive for food, moving their graceful necks as if in a dance. I said to her: "Susanne, you remind me of those swans." She laughed and asked me why. I told her that she glides gracefully through this life, as if propelled through water; that she arches her head like the swans and that, like them, no matter how old she becomes or how harsh the winter is upon her, she will always be beautiful. She leaned across the table at which we were sitting and kissed my cheek. She held her lips to it long enough to invite me into her heart. I put my palms gently against her cheeks as if I were holding a priceless ornament and brought her lips to mine and tenderly touched them together. We remained so touching for what seemed like minutes and then we slowly pulled away and looked into each other's eyes and I said something to her that I had never said to anyone before: I said, "I love you, Susanne." For the longest time she kept her eyes closed, not responding, as if she were listening to a celestial sound and savoring its tone and otherworldliness. Then she said to me: "I love you too, Michael."

When she said that, I felt at once a relief, as if I were now at last safe, after a long unending cautiousness. But following this I felt a troubling sorrow: if I should lose this love, my safety would vanish with it and I would be adrift again on the sea of life without defense.

Susanne became stronger. She learned to speak English beautifully. Her laugh grew more spontaneous, stronger, more frequent. The sometimes sad and lonely expression on her face when we first met, changed throughout the spring to radiance. Her white skin tanned quickly to dark brown and her hair became lighter in the sun. She was aglow in beauty.

As her strength and confidence increased, mine faded. I was happy she had changed from lonely and tenuous to confident and strong. But I felt as well that she was drifting from my shore where her ship had stopped only for a while. Furthermore, I felt that she was not mine to encumber.

One orange fall morning at October's end, I went to Susanne's house. I was startled that her mother answered the door instead of her. I asked if Susanne was there and her mother told me that she had to return to Hamburg and might be gone some time. I asked more questions, but her mother was vague and I could see that she didn't want to talk to me about it. I asked for Susanne's address in Hamburg, which she gave me reluctantly.

I wrote Susanne many times. She never wrote back.

CHAPTER 2

Through a network of referrals and hyperlinks too maze-like to remember, I became connected with a company in New Zealand called HealthNet Resources. Its purpose was to gather the names and addresses of healing resources throughout the world concerned with ecological and health problems and to establish a centralized way for them to contact one another.

Christiane was the name of the woman with whom I made an initial contact. The president of her own company, she was forty years old. We talked in the beginning mainly about health issues, and when I told her I was a doctor, she was enthusiastic to have a dialogue with me.

Despite our rather formal attitude towards each other at first, we quickly established a rapport. After our first conversation we agreed to "meet" again at a certain time. I was pleasantly surprised to find her there at the designated hour.

This soon became a daily meeting, and inevitably the talks became personal. As she unfolded to me her Latin American background and mentioned her child and her deceased husband, and told me about her life in New Zealand and her life before that with her husband in Germany, it became obvious to me that I didn't have much personal life to share with her. Work was my life.

I told her that my headaches began two years before, just after a friend of mine had died from cancer. He had wanted to leave the medical profession, which he hated, and start a career in art. But he couldn't, because the profession provided him and his wife with a luxurious and prestigious lifestyle. They couldn't break away from it.

It appeared to me that my friend had "willed" his own death as the only way to escape his situation.

This caused me to question my own feelings and beliefs, and I began reading ideas about sickness which were not traditional. I told Christiane that I was starting to believe that health problems of many people are more profoundly related to their mental condition and their outlook than I had realized. We talked at length about the spiritual dimensions to healing. Some of these discussions opened up new discoveries for me. Christiane obviously possessed, even culturally, a deeper understanding of these things than I, but she let me talk and listened without interrupting. Sometimes, in fact, I had to stop and say, "Are you still there?"

I told her that my headaches moved from an occasional frustration to an almost constant debilitation. Even though I studied, researched, and talked to other physicians about the treatments available, and tried them all, I was unable to control my sickness. In the end I couldn't perform surgery except occasionally, being afraid that I would have to leave an operation prematurely.

Eventually I developed pain in the middle of my back, and began having chronic abdominal pain, nausea, and diarrhea. I lost weight and had no appetite. I thought I had pancreatic cancer, but all of the tests I took were negative.

After months of ineffective and frustrating treatments, I made a choice which for a common doctor was unusual: I chose to stop taking traditional medical treatments and to try to cure myself with whatever "alternative" treatments seemed sensible to me. I couldn't deny that my condition seemed imaginary, but the thinking and reading I had done had helped me understand that many things about illness are just that: imaginary.

I had heard of a woman in the city to whom several doctors had gone rather secretively for help with troublesome diagnoses. It was said that she was able to discern with remarkable accuracy health problems that had eluded traditional methods of diagnosis. No one knew or seemed to care how this was possible, just that it worked. I knew one of the doctors who went to her, and I respected him. He told me she wouldn't see me without a recommendation from someone already seeing her and said he would recommend me.

I called her and set an appointment. I was surprised to find that she lived in a modern brick home in a newer subdivision. Upon answering the door I saw her husband disappear down the hallway. I later learned that he himself was a doctor. The woman had dark hair and penetrating dark eyes and spoke with an accent I couldn't identify. She had a calming presence.

"Why are you here, Michael?" she asked me.

"I am a doctor, and I'm sick. I can't figure out what I have. I can no longer lead a normal life because of it."

She handed me a deck of cards and told me to shuffle them. She had me turn the cards over one at a time and she studied them. She put her hand to my left shoulder and turned me around and gently touched the middle of my back. "There is a blockage here. Do you have pain?"

"Yes."

"This is a nexus, a place where the 'battle' is taking place. You're trying to change yourself. You want to reach the spirit which is buried within you, but the way to do it involves the death of a part of you which you cannot let go of. Is that correct?"

"I'm not sure."

She turned over more cards and laid them next to one another and studied them.

"The strength you must find now will come from faith. From patience. From developing and trusting your intuition. From letting go and relinquishing your need to control. Not from your reason, but from your heart. From listening, not only to others but to whispers from the stillness, voices audible only to your passive, receptive ear. It is a greater strength which you can gain. When you have acquired this faith, the blockage will open up and the pain subside. You will sense an inflow of insight like matter flowing into a vacuum.

"Michael, this will be hard for you. Your illness is the manifestation of the inner struggle you are having. You know there's another way, a life besides the one you live now, and although this life has been good for and to you and was appropriate and necessary, now you need to go beyond it to a higher level of living. But before you can move onward, you must go back to build a bridge to the Oneself you abandoned on the other side of your spiritual journey. At some point in your life, a separation of your self has occurred. You must re-integrate with yourself who awaits you on the other side. I see a boy in your life. Do you have a son?"

"No, I don't."

"In some sense a boy, or perhaps a young man, is in your life but apparently you don't know about him yet. You will, however. He will be instrumental in showing you the way to this inner strength. Michael, this may be you, this boy. Or it may be a boy like you. Maybe someone not directly related, but he's connected to you and to your destiny.

Probably also to your past. If you continue to follow your need to find your self within, this boy will become a fellow journeyman. Are you now treating yourself?"

I told her about my diet and exercise program and my reading and the yoga I'd begun.

"Good. Continue these things. Don't allow dark thoughts and vexatious people into your life. Walk away from them. Bathe your life in all things relating to your spiritual quest. Trust your intuition and have faith. Learn to wait for still urgings not discernible through noise, clamor, and impatience. You will have to release the old way of thinking, which will not work now. Already you are changing, can you tell that?"

I nodded, "I think so."

"There is a girl too."

"What do you mean?"

"I see a girl in your life, whom you are holding onto and have been holding tightly for a long time. Was there an early love for you?"

"Yes."

"You have only let yourself love *her*, have you not? And no one else. But she cannot love as you want and need, and so your life with love is dead. Do you know who I'm talking about?"

"I think so."

"Michael, you have great powers to heal others. That's why you're a doctor. But now you need to heal yourself. You've neglected to provide nourishment to your soul, and it is dying. That's why you are sick. You must care for it now with utter priority. Your body is telling you this. Do not fail to listen.

"You must let go of this girl and the subconscious expectations you have with her. You must grow beyond her. You are unable to free your emotions. They are in prison and dying. It is a vicious cycle. You've invested her with a power which no one can have and since this power is unreal, so is your relationship to her and to your past. This in turn serves to keep you from opening yourself up to others emotionally and keeps you from being hurt again. It insulates you from all types of intimacy which are necessary for your well-being. Did your parents die when you were young, Michael?"

"Yes," I said. I was shocked that she knew these things about me. No one knew them.

"They are also part of this withdrawal you've made with your emotions. Your mission now, Michael, is to open yourself up and allow others to come into your presence and into your heart. Not only do you need others. They need you too."

I felt exposed, the hidden state of my self suddenly revealed not only to her but to myself as well. I felt subservient and dependent. These were feelings I wasn't used to or comfortable with. At the same time I felt a lust to find out more about myself.

"The boy and the girl are connected somehow. Look for the boy. Be faithful to him."

After an hour and a half she indicated that we should stop because she had another appointment.

I asked her how I will find this girl and this boy and she said they are in my destiny, unless I decide to change it. She said this, which disturbed me: "The boy you must see, but the girl...she may just be a memory that you need to release."

She told me other things which were impressive in their accuracy, and helped affirm my overall impression of her reliability, as I thought about her later. She had recorded our "reading" and gave me the disc, telling me to study it. She told me to call her if I needed to talk again.

Finally she said to me, "Michael, you can get better, but it will not be an easy way for you. I'm not talking necessarily about pain, although you'll have some of that ahead too. I'm talking about changing yourself. It will require a radically different method of treatment than you are accustomed to. I think you want to change yourself, which is good, because you will have to change. Illness is often your mind acting as your body, giving you sickness as an opportunity to change yourself into what you want and need to be. I feel that this is the case with you. I have pointed out some signals to you. You need to think about them. And remember the boy, Michael. I see the boy clearly. He looks like you. But as I see him, he is of another world. He is exceptional and kind and understands more deeply than his years."

I left her house feeling both exposed and healed, in a way. Questions multiplied, which were not amenable to reason. She was right, though: I wanted a way out of my identity and a return to who I started out to be, before I was deflected. Things within me would have to die in order for other things to be born.

It took a long time to tell this story of the psychic to Christiane. Each night we met at a prearranged time and I talked from my office while she listened graciously to me. Her person as well as the anonymity of the internet allowed me to talk to her in a way I had rarely talked before. I hadn't spoken about Susanne to anyone, even to myself, for over two decades.

Christiane didn't respond right away. And then she said: "This is an amazing story. My son, Simon, is badly in need of help. Since his father's death, he's withdrawn into silence. He's pulled away from the world and will not come back. He is disappearing. Maybe you are supposed to help him, Michael."

I loved these meetings with Christiane. They became the single most important event of my days and nights. Occasionally she could not meet me (or I her) because of other commitments, and I experienced longing for her, loneliness even. One night I walked home after talking to her. The sun was going down in perfect late summer dusk. I was walking briskly and whistling. I felt peaceful, and as if I would feel just as good no matter where I was - living in the present for more than the usual instant.

I realized I had not felt this way since I was a boy. When I would walk home each night glowing inside with joy. When I would fall asleep in ecstasy and awaken in anticipation. When even the most prosaic detail of my life felt replete.

For the first time in decades I could feel Susanne's presence in the overwhelming way I'd felt it as a boy. I felt a helpless, ecstatic attraction for her again, and felt the same fear I'd had before – that it couldn't last. I also felt another fear: that I had to let go of her finally as a phantom possession I'd hid and horded subconsciously inside of me and which still resided there powerfully, now as an infection to my soul.

CHAPTER 3

I began reading everything I could find about Hamburg, Germany, to feel Susanne's presence again. I got all of the flight information of every airline to Hamburg and penciled the departing flights meticulously on a globe, with the times of arrival at each point along the route. I carefully labeled them and rated them in terms of desirability with regard to several criteria. This project took me days. Ironically, however, it was so impersonal and unrealistic that it allowed me to achieve a protective distance from the event of her disappearance.

I obtained maps of Hamburg from libraries in the city and found the street that her father lived on and by copying and painstakingly arranging the maps together one upon the other, I made elaborate sub-maps of conceivable routes she might take upon leaving the house in whatever direction she might go. Its effect allowed me to successfully feel her presence in some real way.

One day in my obsessive searching, I discovered a European book-store. A very old man with a thick accent came up to me and asked me what I wanted. I told him I was trying to get information about Hamburg, Germany. I said, "Do you care if I look around?"

"Help yourself, help yourself," he said and walked away.

The store was a treasure house of information. I called to the old man as I was leaving and said I would return. "You have a wonderful store here," I told him.

"People don't buy books like these today or read history. There is only the present." I asked him what hours he is open and he said, "Just come by, I am here always." His name was Kurt Seiler. He was German.

I did come by, many times. Although Mr. Seiler was distant towards me at first, after he saw me behave respectfully with an enduring interest in his store and in him, he began to help me. We spent hours together. He was a wonderful teacher and I was his grateful pupil. In the beginning he simply found the things I asked for, about Hamburg in particular. Although he was not born there, he had lived in Hamburg before and during the war and knew it well.

One day I asked Mr. Seiler: "Why did you come to the US?"

He turned and walked back to a bookshelf behind his counter and took out a book and gently handed it to me. He said: "I will answer your question, Michael, but first I ask you to read this book." It was entitled, "The Battle of Hamburg" and was written by an Englishman, a former RAF pilot in World War II who was in that battle. I took it home with me and read it that night.

The book was technical, and yet interspersed among the technical discussions were personal accounts from Germans who'd lived in Hamburg at that time and other pilots who'd bombed Hamburg.

It was shocking. I had no idea the extent of destruction that was done to this major European city during World War II.

I finished the book without stopping. At five o'clock in the morning I looked out my window and it was just getting light in the east. I laid my head on the book and I cried. For the people who lived in Hamburg that summer of 1943, whose faith left them, probably never to return. And for myself, whose faith in love was clinging to life with only desperation. It seemed at that moment that all of this pointless research and obsessive searching I was doing could never bring back Susanne, just like the people of Hamburg could never bring back their destroyed city.

I simply could not confront Mr. Seiler for a long time. Then one Saturday I returned his book. The door was locked, but I knocked anyway. Mr. Seiler answered it quickly, as if he had been expecting me. He told me to come into his office and sit down.

The office felt comfortable and overstuffed, crammed with books and big cushioned chairs and a small cot towards the rear where he took a nap. An old brass lamp with a green shade provided the only light. On the shade was a scene of hunters and dogs in black outline. The row of hills in the background went into a woods. I thought how happy the hunters looked to be together in that lovely billowy scene of nature and how it fit into Mr. Seiler's room.

"It came with me from Germany. I like the light it gives."

Indeed the light was wonderful. Warm and yellow and diffuse but effective, yet leaving the distant places of the room private in semi-darkness. I sat in a corner in a huge overstuffed chair and waited for him to speak.

He took his time. He always took his time. Something about that made me feel as if I had another sense experiencing its delightful object the way smell senses food or hearing senses music or touch senses softness. It was the first time I had experienced patience as a desirable thing, a thing to have as a goal, not dissimilar from pleasure.

"You asked me, Michael, why I came to the US. In 1943 I was in my late forties. I was married and I had two children and Katerina was expecting a third. World War Two was being fought and it did not look good for Germany. The US had entered the war, and their might and the fact that Germany could not reach them the way it could reach England and France, made them a formidable opponent. My father and I owned a shipping company and we lived on one of the most elegant boulevards in Hamburg that overlooks the beautiful Alster lakes. I lived in a house near my father's house with my wife. She had been diagnosed with multiple sclerosis and was deteriorating quickly. We didn't talk about it much but we hoped our child would be born before my wife was unable to give birth. The pregnancy was causing her illness to progress even more quickly.

Mr. Seiler was leaning back comfortably in his chair looking up above my head where the ragged-edge circle of light blended into the darkness. He seemed to be speaking to himself.

"It is hard to describe the beauty and elegance of Hamburg at that time. It was lush and green, magnificent trees in parks everywhere. (Do you know, Michael, in the 16th Century, to cut down a tree in Hamburg was punishable by death!) It was called the Venice of the North, because waterways and canals were threaded throughout the city. There were beautiful old buildings, elegant shops, and fine hotels just near where we were living. There was the Rauthaus, the town hall, which contained 647 rooms, bigger than Buckingham Palace; and the Rauthausmarkt; and the churches. The Deichtrasse, the oldest residential spot, from the 14th Century. Beautiful homes hidden away behind iron fences, canopied in lush tree branches, on quiet brick streets where horses clip-clopped slowly throughout the day until dusk.

"Art flourished everywhere and music was the best in Germany. We were one of the largest seaports in Europe, called 'The Free and Hanseatic City of Hamburg,' members of the Hanseatic trading league going all the way back to the Middle Ages. Hamburg was a paradise little known by the world at large, a Riviera. Our family entertained guests from all over. We were Germans, of course, but we were people of the world. Hamburg was cosmopolitan. We had more negative votes against Hitler than any other city in Germany.

"Hamburg is like the Phoenix from Egyptian mythology that is consumed by fire and then rises – born again! – from the ashes. Throughout its history the city has been destroyed again and again, by fire, flood, and war. Each time the citizens of Hamburg raise it again dutifully - like Sisyphus – to rebuild it and restore its beauty, as if it is their penance to pay over and over.

"I hated Hitler and I hated the Nazis. When they started gaining strength in Germany, I knew we were doomed. This is what happens when people are out of money, they turn to leaders like Hitler and the Nazis who show strength and who are self-assured and who promise restitution. After World War One, Germany was treated badly in the Treaty of Versailles, especially by the French. We were broken. We are proud people, and the treaty made us into beggars.

"I had miraculously avoided military service, because I was working with my father in the shipping business and we were capable of moving armaments from place to place using all of the transportation connections we had, which were many. Each day when the mail arrived I handed it to my wife, because I couldn't bear finding out that I was being drafted. Of course we were mostly silent about our feelings towards Hitler and didn't often talk about them even amongst ourselves, but now and then one of us became angry over some incident and would lose his temper momentarily."

Mr. Seiler stopped speaking. His lips trembled perceptibly and his eyes seemed glazed with moisture. "Saturday, July 24, 1943: it was 27 degrees Centigrade, which is hot for Hamburg. We were outside in the yard talking at a park near a building we owned in Hammerbrook, having a picnic for the workers at our company, except my wife who was with a friend who lived not far away in a lovely apartment. It was almost 8pm. The sun was gloriously bright as it moved through the dusk. It was the color of yellow that it is only occasionally, at just that time of year when it is changing directions, with a tint of green that makes the world one views appear to be behind glass. I can still see it. The day had the feeling of a great impressionistic painting. Sun bonnets and long dresses, children playing croquet and horses dancing in fields afar.

"We were always ready, so we thought, for the worst to happen – an air raid. Hamburg until that time had been free of major damage. The city had constructed elaborate defenses both above ground and below ground, sophisticated sprinkler systems. Laws were strictly enforced forbidding people to use building materials in the upper levels of their homes, or even to store things which were flammable in closets or attics.

"Still, I knew. Something within me knew. We were a major manufacturing city, the most important producer of submarines. Our time would come.

"The sky that evening filled with plane noise. We'd been told that the German Flak air defense was impenetrable, but this sound was fearsome, like a swarm of huge bees. The sirens began and everyone became anxious. We heard bombs exploding off in the distance. The immediate scene became hysterical and panicky. I directed people into the catacomb-like shelters set up beneath the towering brick buildings. I had a bad feeling. Shortly after the bombs started falling near us, I looked at my mother and said, 'Es ist alles aus!' – 'It's all gone!'

"And it was. In one week my home was gone, my neighborhood was gone, my shipping business was gone, my city was gone, and, as it turned out, my wife-with-child was gone along with one of my two children. It took me almost three days to find the body of my wife. My son's body was never found. Presumably it burned up in flames absolutely indescribable in their horror. In just a day my life was over."

He stood up slowly and went to the refrigerator in the back of the room. "Would you like something to drink, Michael?" he asked me.

"Maybe some water," I said, sensing we were coming to a part that would parch my throat.

Mr. Seiler was gone a long time. When he returned with the water I could see that his eyes were red and his unshaven face damp. He handed me the water. He had huge hands, which almost concealed the large glass of water he gave me. But they were fine hands, shapely and sensitive.

I didn't know what time it was, for I was so captivated by his story that the continuity of the day for me had been broken.

"Michael," he said to me, "I'll tell you more if you like, but if you don't have the time or if it is unpleasant for you, please tell me. Because what I have to say from here is upsetting."

"I would like to hear more," I told him, "if you want to tell me."

"It's not that I want to tell you, Michael. I have to tell someone. These things have been inside of me alone for so long, waiting for someone's ears to hear, and I think that you are the one."

"Then tell me, Mr. Seiler, I'll be all right."

He leaned forward and put his hands out to me and I instinctively gave him my hand. It disappeared between his two huge clasped hands. "How old are you, Michael?"

"Eighteen," I said.

"You see, Michael, my son Fredrich, who died that night in the flames, was 19 years old, just your age. Not only did he die, but I never got to see even his body again. He was the younger child who came to us when we were so busy at the shipping office. Many nights I slept at work because I was too tired to go home. As a result Fredrich and I never knew each other. I always told myself that one day I would slow down and get to know my son." He produced a photograph from his desk drawer. "Fredrich is the third from the right."

It was a photograph of his family of several generations. Freidrich was thin with dark hair and dark eyes. He was quite good-looking and seemed to be laughing inside, standing with a rakish and carefree attitude.

"He's very handsome," I said.

"Yes, he was, and humorous and very intelligent too. I think of him every day."

Mr. Seiler took a book from the shelf behind him. "I want to read you something, Michael:

'Vengeance of God! what dread must thou inspire
In everyone who now shall read and learn
Of that which was revealed before my eyes!
For I saw multitudes of naked souls
Who all were weeping piteously, and seemed
Tormented all in varying degrees.
While some were lying supine on the ground,
Others were sitting huddled in a heap,
Or running round about incessantly.
More numerous were those who ran about;
The fewer, those who in their torment lay,
Although they cried the louder in their pain.
Over that sandy waste fell slowly down

Broad flakes of fire, falling measuredly
Like snow upon the Alps in quiet air.
Even as those flames which Alexander saw
Fall down unbrokenly upon his host
From out the torrid skies of India,
So that he bade his men to stamp the earth,
The better to put out the burning vapor
Before it spread into a sheet of flame:
Just so th' eternal heat was falling down,
From which the sand, like tinder under steel,
Burst into flame, the torment to redouble.
Without a moment's rest the slapping hands
Danced frantically on, now here, now there,
To brush away the torture of the flames.'

"Even this 14th Canto from Dante's Hell cannot convey the horror of the bombing of Hamburg," he said.

"It was as if the air was on fire, but the 'flakes' of fire didn't fall in 'quiet' air. It was moved by an awesome force which so voraciously sucked oxygen from all directions that what had been the quiet Hamburg summer night became more like the vortices of a hurricane blowing not air but fire at speeds of up to 135 miles per hour in all directions at once. Even the bricks seemed on fire." He shook his head slowly from side to side as if to clear the dread of recollection. "The Germans feel guilty about this war. And they are guilty, no question about it. For what they did to the Jews and what their arrogance did to the earth. But the world doesn't know of Hamburg and its punishment, the world forgets that there was an oven in which German bodies burned too. Their tongues dried out and cried for an end from the howling storm of fire they could not escape. Hamburg's night sky became within minutes, on the first night of Fuersturm, a hell on earth for which there are no words adequate to describe it.

"Before Hamburg the aim of bombing missions had been to destroy targets which contributed to the war effort of the other side. But the Allied Forces dropped 10,000 pounds of bombs, including incendiary bombs and phosphorus bombs on everything in sight, on residential areas and parks, on historical landmarks, even on the beautiful Hagenbeck Zoo, killing all of the precious animals, as if their goal was to kill and burn to ashes all trace of Hamburg civilization, every creature that took breath and everything that men there had created.

"We were not Nazis, we were ordinary people living life like others throughout the world, with families and friends."

As Mr. Seiler talked dreamily in that yellow-lit room of pillowed chairs and light just right, illuminating countless leather-bound testimonies to man's accomplishments, it flashed into my thoughts – for an instant so brief that I didn't miss a stroke of Mr. Seiler's word-painting – that this was a moment of human sharing between us that few people would ever experience. An 18-year-old boy listening like a therapist to an 80-year-old man talking for the first time ever about the feelings of an experience in his life 35 years ago so momentous in scope that nothing which had happened since or would ever happen, nothing which could even be imagined, could compare to it. The ordinary nature of life and its sense of wishful fulfillment and joyful anticipation would disappear from this man's life at the age of forty. In that way he too had died in late July of 1943, but in another sense he was being reborn in retelling his story.

Ironically, as horrible as the events were which his story described, the process of telling it was restoring something within us both. I am almost ashamed to admit it, that afternoon or evening or whenever it was – I had lost track of the moment - I didn't want our discussion to end.

He continued: "I am over 80 years old. It has been 40 years since those few days in July, but every day – each day of my life since then, more than 10,000 times, one for each bomb that fell and more – before my mind's eye passes a scene of a small girl wandering aimlessly, her clothes burnt off, her face singed, carrying in a rucksack the head of her dead brother; people crawling and screaming, stuck in the middle of the Eiffestrasse in molten asphalt, burning alive, trying to reach the canal's water on the other side; throngs of hysterical people escaping from one inferno beneath the buildings into a greater one above, stepping through the fat of molten bodies on the steps; 1,000,000 people evacuating on foot, like beggars at Lourdes, their hands out for a drink from anyone who might have water.

"These scenes and others visit me each night and have for so long now that I am not entirely sure whether they actually occurred or are part of a dementia that is mine forever. Fifty thousand people died in the firestorm that night, burned to death. Two hundred fifty three thousand – over half – of the residential dwellings of Hamburg were made into ashes. Nine hundred thousand people were made homeless – half of the population of the city. These were mothers fathers, sisters and brothers, your children born and unborn, your grandparents and neighbors and co-workers. Slaughtered, burned to death."

Mr. Seiler talked with the greatest lucidity of these things that had happened decades before, with what appeared to be almost total recall, as if he had prepared for this speech his whole life.

"I gathered my mother and my father and all of the people that were there at the picnic and led them directly to the fallout shelters.

Many others followed. These shelters were built in anticipation of air raids and were tough and strong, but even in their maddest dreams the designers of these shelters could not have envisioned a fire with one-hundred mile per hour winds and heat of eight hundred degrees Centigrade; fire that was visible at a distance of sixty miles and glowed at night for weeks from the coal and coke it set aflame.

"The bombs were falling so massively that it literally rained fire for hours, which generated its own torrential wind and blew the fire everywhere to start new fires. The fire above was literally sucking the oxygen from everywhere it could find it, in order to feed itself. There were probably twenty of us who stayed in a completely dark, window-less interior room for hours and hours, growing hotter all the time.

"When we came up from our cave many hours later, it was daytime, but we emerged not into the light but into the darkness. The smoke from the seven square miles of fire was so dense that it shrouded the sun. Not only that but it took away the oxygen, so that even more people died from breathing only carbon monoxide. We, however, man-aged to live by entering a tunnel I knew that ran beneath the River Elbe and came out in an area that wasn't as smoky.

"For hours and hours we wandered searching for an escape from the city and finally joined the throngs of people heading in every state of shock and madness imaginable, toward the outskirts of town, to find deliverance from the storm of fire. The city was vanquished, gone, dis-appeared, 133 miles of street frontage crumbled to ashes. It was now a ghost town"

Mr. Seiler picked up my water glass and walked to the back room and filled our glasses again and sat down once more in his chair. It felt like nighttime to me. I was tired, along with the minions of wounded having reached safety. He was tired also, I could tell.

"So why did I come to the US, you ask. I didn't right away. I tended to my family that had lived. Just to restore the functions of daily living took much time. I told my parents and my remaining son that I was going to leave and asked them to come with me. I could see in my father's face that his life was over, that he would soon die, which he did. My mother would go with me wherever I went. But my son said he would never leave Hamburg. He was twenty-five years old.

"I never even considered going anywhere except the US. Even though they had bombed us, they had always been friends. The Americans forgive. In fact, they felt guilty themselves and offered immediately to help."

He stood up slowly and said to me: "Michael, I have to stop now and fix dinner. It's getting late and you probably must go home."

"Are you okay?" I asked him.

"Yes, I am okay. How about you, Michael, are you okay?"

"I think so, sir. I'm sorry about what happened to your city and your family."

"I know you are, Michael. You are a good boy, to listen to an old man like me with tales of woe." He put his arm around my shoulder and we walked towards the door. We said goodbye, but first I asked him, "Is your son in Germany still?"

"I think so. I've not heard from him for many years now."

"Have you ever returned to Hamburg?"

"No, never."

I wanted to ask so many more questions. It almost seemed wrong of him to tell me this story and then ask me to leave. But I knew he wanted to stop now. With uncharacteristic boldness I said to him:

"Maybe we can go together to Hamburg sometime and you can be my guide."

I expected him to say he would never return to Hamburg, but then he put his arm around my shoulder again and gently moved me through the doorway, saying: "Yes, maybe someday we will. After I sell my store. Goodnight, Michael. Thank you for listening to me tonight. You are a special boy. There's a reason we have met, you know?"

He started to close the door and I was already walking away down the walkway to the street, lit with old granite streetlights of eight-sided glass and tarnished copper spires.

"Michael," he called after me. I turned around. "Why do you want to go to Hamburg?"

I answered obediently. "There's someone there I want to find," I said softly, almost as if to myself. Standing there alone, I listened to my own words come forth outside of my own control to betray me and give up the secret I had hidden.

He nodded his head. "I see." He looked at me with tenderness and tired, the way one looks when for an instant words have purged the heart, and vision comes directly through the eyes from the soul. "Goodnight, Michael."

"Goodnight, Mr. Seiler," I said and wished that I could take his hand and lead him into a dreamless sleep for once.

"Well, then, Michael. I shall look forward to seeing you soon again."

I turned back to the walkway. The night was pleasant; fall was in the air. Freedom's feeling and release from summer's stifling heat. Window of quiet reprieve before winter's own snowy solemn silence. I wondered what I would have done in such a Firestorm.

"One more thing I should tell you, Michael," Mr. Seiler called out to me as I turned onto the sidewalk in the direction of my home. "This lovely evening reminds me of this, which I should tell you to counterbalance the rest: I left for America in autumn, with my mother.

Something miraculous happened just before we left. You can read about it in books of botany. The bushes and the trees that had been burnt in the bombing, scarred and stripped of summer's life in the Firestorm, suddenly blossomed again in October, completely out of season, and we had another spring in the fall, as if God had forgiven us. The spirit of the plant life, like Hamburg itself, showed that it was indomitable and could also rise again, even out of step with the rest of the universe. Quite remarkable."

CHAPTER 4

I had not heard from Christiane for almost a week. She had said she was doing research and would not be available to talk for a few days. Then an email arrived which said, "I want to talk to you. I have information which might help you." So I sent an email back to her and arranged to meet her that night and talk on the internet.

"I've found and talked to someone who was cured from a condition just like yours," she said. "The same symptoms, the same resistance to conventional treatment. She's a professor at a British university. A fellow professor in the archaeology department gave her the name of a woman in Peru who is involved in ethnobotanical healing. That woman referred her to a shaman in northeastern Peru in the rainforest at the beginning of the Amazon River. The professor traveled there and stayed for a month, undergoing many healing ceremonies. This was almost a year ago and she is now cured, able to conduct her life as before, free of debilitating headaches and stomach issues and other problems. I have talked to her about you. She said it's unbelievable what happened to her. Her life is now entirely changed. She claims that the world she lives in now is not the same world she had lived in before. She said she would be happy to talk to you.

"I know about these ceremonies, Michael. I have had friends and relatives involved in them in one way or another. Under the right circumstances and with the right shaman, they can be effective. However, one shouldn't get involved in them casually because they are emotionally very powerful. Some people aren't ready for that. And just as with medical doctors, one must carefully choose the shaman who will administer his healing. But then I know you wouldn't enter into it unless you felt right about it. I'll get you more information to study."

I didn't want to talk to the woman in England. I now trusted Christiane to guide me. She had proven herself to me as being reliable, accurate, thorough and perceptive. Beyond that, however, I believed that she was a part of the plan the psychic woman had alerted me to and which, if I didn't deflect it, would unfold in my life inevitably. Christiane cared for me and had no motive except genuine concern.

"Will you meet me in Peru, Christiane?"

It was late fall, early winter. The air was crisp and cool with the dark of night coming quickly in the afternoon and bringing after it an eerie spectral eveningtime.

I wanted to be outside, to see the last days of the city's autumn before my departure. So I made myself walk despite my headaches and the pain in my stomach and back. It was so hard at first that I could barely walk a block, but I pushed myself day after day until I began to overcome the pain and could walk longer and longer, miles each day. The experience of freedom which the walking engendered brought an ecstasy almost addictive.

One evening on my walk, I heard a sound behind me and turned around and saw a large black dog a few steps away. He stopped reluctantly when I looked at him. I went on. He followed me. Finally I stopped and sat down on concrete steps while he looked at me as if to say, "Can I walk with you?" I put my hand out and he cowered a bit as he came up to me and sniffed my closed hand. He was dirty. There was blood caked about his shoulder. His eyes had a familiarity.

I put my hand lightly on his forehead then felt the blood on his shoulder. He flinched in pain. I let it go and stood up and said, "Come, let's walk," and he followed just behind me for an hour until I got home. As he stood by my door, we both seemed to understand that it was an important moment.

"I'm leaving in a month, so you'll be alone then again. Is that what you want?" I asked him. "I'll do my best to find someone to take you, but I don't know if I can, and I'll have to make you homeless again." He cocked his head as if he'd understood, and I opened my door for him and he went inside.

I took him straightaway to the bathroom, told him to climb into the tub, which he did, and I gave him a shampoo. His fur was matted and grew irregularly, so I clipped him with my scissors. He was an attractive dog -- part Labrador and surely part Doberman pinscher.

I examined his shoulder. It was deeply cut and had flaklike lacerations, as if he had been shot or scraped by a multi-headed object, a barbed wire fence perhaps. I washed the shoulder and examined it more carefully. There were many splinter-like objects which took me nearly two hours to remove, after which I taped a bandage to his shoulder. "I will call you 'Shaman'."

That night the pain in my stomach stopped. A feeling of well-being I hadn't had for days returned, and I recognized anew how wonderful the homeostasis of good health feels and yet how easy it is to take it for granted and ignore that it is the foundation of one's outlook and mental state.

I slept wonderfully. In the morning the sun was out. The dog was waiting for me. We walked for hours. We did this every day until I left. In the mornings before the sun arose, we walked and watched it rise, and in the evenings we walked through the sunset into dusk. These symbols of meeting the light and saying farewell to it each day became ritualistic and therapeutic. We didn't stop until it felt right, and then we ate together and napped. Shaman's being and mine were a unity in this final stage before my descent into another world.

In between these rituals, I prepared for my trip to South America. I began reading about Peru: the history of the Incas, the conquest of the Spaniards and, of course, the rain forest and its gradual destruction.

It was shocking to discover how little I knew about a country – even an entire continent – directly south of me. The history of the Incas was truly magnificent. They were a superb and superior people, spiritual as well as scientific. Their locus of power, the city of Macchu Picchu, was a breathtaking site at the top of a mountain, accessible only on foot and surrounded by awesome green mountains and formidable rock formations, containing stonework almost perfect in design.

I went to the library and read about Peru and the rain forest. It was the world's largest ecosystem, containing thousands of curative medicinal secrets passed on from native doctors of one generation to the next. However, not only was the chain of knowledge being broken by the seduction of the younger generation away from their pasts, but also the rain forest itself was being destroyed by the profit motives of international corporations. Many plants and animals were on the edge of extinction. Since the medical knowledge and wisdom of the shamans were not recorded or codified, the world was recklessly allowing the obliteration of the most sophisticated native botanists on earth.

There were places in the rain forest that no one had ever been, even the native Indians. It was primeval, with thousands of species of plants and animals and insects, over 600,000 species there. The plants had evolved chemically to protect themselves from the insects and many of the chemicals they produced were also capable of fighting disease in man. Someone wrote that "Whenever you are in the rain forest, you are in the middle of chemical warfare that has been going on for hundreds of thousands, if not millions, of years."

The doctors - shamans - knew which plants could be used to combat any particular ailment, from sore ears to hornet stings to malaria to Hodgkin's disease to ovarian cancer and on and on. These shamans were the original pharmacists, powerful and knowledgeable. But the reality they see is different from other pharmacists. They believe that malevolent spirits are at work in illness. They believe that hallucinogenic experiences are caused by deities that inhabit sacred plants. They believe the reality we live every day is a dream. They believe that a medicine man in touch with the world of spirits can transform himself into a jungle animal.

The night before I was to leave for Peru, I took Shaman on a long walk. We must have gone ten miles. I didn't know how I was going to say goodbye to him. There was no one I wanted to give him to who would understand him the way I did. So I had decided that I'd turn him loose somewhere just before I left. I was having trouble knowing where to do it and was waiting for an answer to come to me from within, but nothing came. So I walked and walked and walked. He was now strong and healthy and spirited. I relied upon his presence and his strength and the comfort he gave me. I felt that he was involved with my illness's remission. I even considered taking him with me, but I was trying to let go of all things holding me.

Finally that night, I was so tired I could hardly stand up, so we went home. Every night before I locked the door for the evening, I let him out into the back yard and waited for him by the door. He always returned within a couple of minutes. I opened the door and he looked at me strangely, as if he wanted to say something. "What's wrong, Shaman, don't you want to go out?" I asked him. I squatted down to his level and he stared at me, then licked me tenderly on the cheek and turned and went outside. I waited the allotted time and then called to him. He didn't come. I walked to the back yard and he was not there. I felt a panic. I hurried down the driveway and to the front yard and looked down the block and in the street. I spent a long time searching the immediate neighborhood in the darkness. Then I waited by the door, but he never returned. I went inside and sat on the stairway, feeling sad. Throughout the night I came down and opened the door, thinking he had returned and was waiting there for me, but he didn't come back.

I felt lonely and alienated. My life from the past was gone. My life in the future was uncertain. Suddenly, I didn't know if I was doing the right thing. To my surprise, my confidence began to wane. That startled me and made me wonder if it had been fabricated in order to hide a desperation now surfacing.

I met Christiane on the internet a last time before Lima. "I'm having remorse about going tomorrow," I wrote to her.

She wrote back, "It's only natural. This is a new experience. Don't worry. When you get there the weather will be nice and the sun will be out and it will feel right to you, I promise. You will love Peru, Michael.

You will feel free in a way you've never felt free, I know it. A burden will be gone from your shoulders as soon as your plane touches the ground."

I wanted to believe her. And the psychic too.

CHAPTER 5

One day in late fall I walked by the bookstore and saw Mr. Seiler behind the counter reading, his eyeglasses low on his nose like Santa Claus. I went inside. He looked up and saw me and came toward me.

"Where have you been, Michael? I was so worried about you."

"I quit college, sir. It didn't make any sense to me and I was bored."

"Michael, college is the way forward for a young man like yourself. You are a smart boy but you need to learn about the wisdom of the past."

"I know that, sir, but I'll still learn on my own. I read a lot. I'm studying German," I said, hoping it would take away his seriousness.

He stood close to me. There were pleasant smells on his body. Not cologne exactly, but cleanliness, shaving soap perhaps, and his dark ribbed sweater smelled old in a delightful way.

"Michael, I hope you will reconsider this move. Is there still time to go back?"

"Maybe. But I want to go to Hamburg with you."

He looked puzzled and then remembered he'd said something about it. I was disappointed he had apparently not thought about it the way that I had every day since I last saw him.

"Michael, even if we went to Hamburg, it could not happen until the store is sold, and no one is yet interested in buying it. I've not even had time to write an advertisement for it or to go around and talk to possible buyers. How could I go to Hamburg? You would waste your life waiting for that to happen."

"I could come to work for you, for no pay, and then you would be free to go out and find someone to buy the store."

"Well, let's not talk business just now, let's talk about other things. I'll think about what you have said."

I was excited. A smile burst onto my face.

We walked back to the room in which our talk about the bombing of Hamburg had occurred only weeks before. It looked different and felt less intense. I could now see the titles of hundreds of books on the shelves and wondered how a person could ever read them all.

Mr. Seiler and I sat down to drink tea. The chair felt good, lush and comfortable, the way a chair is meant to feel.

"So tell me, Michael, how are your grandparents?"

"They're okay, Mr. Seiler,"

"Do they approve of you quitting college?"

"I don't think so, sir. They don't know what to think of me. They can never understand why I am the way I am."

"And what way is that, Michael?"

"Well, sir, they don't know why I'm not just happy with what I have, with the opportunities available to me. To them having a job is everything."

"They grew up in a different time, Michael, things were different for them. There was a time in this country when everyone lost his job and the prospects for life became hopeless, so that having a job was all that mattered. In much of the world people have no work."

"But even then, Mr. Seiler, life must have had more to it than just your job. It is learning. It is music. It is the feeling of having a goal far away and moving toward it until you are there. And then to go on towards another goal, another place. It should be endless like this."

"Well, Michael, maybe you are right in the way you see it, but you need to understand them also. Your grandparents must be near to my age, so I can tell you that the world has changed entirely around them. It does that, you know. And maybe you are the beneficiary of their single-minded concern. Maybe it has allowed you to think beyond them. They have put themselves down like stepping stones for you to use to cross to another side of life that they themselves will not be able to venture to or even understand. For them you are the future and they sacrifice to make it possible for you."

What he said made sense to me. I thought about it a lot in the days to come.

"What happened to your parents, Michael?"

"They died in an automobile accident when I was ten."

"And your grandparents have raised you since then?"

"Yes sir, they have. They've raised me very strictly. They disapproved of many things." I had never talked about these things and felt ill at ease, even guilty, as if I were betraying my grandparents. And yet I hoped that Mr. Seiler would ask me more.

He drank tea and sat silently. I remained silent with him and listened to the sounds in the building: the heat pipes stretching; stockinged footsteps softly creaking the wooden floors above; insulated sounds that occur among books and cloth in wintertime when doors are closed.

Then the front door opened and the Christmas bell permanently attached to it tinkled, announcing a customer. It broke the spell. Mr.

Seiler dutifully moved to get up, but I told him that I would go instead. I went out to the main room and greeted the customer. She wanted a French dictionary. I took her to the spot and stood beside her until she found the right one. She was grateful and told me about her trip to France. She noted what a special store we had, how wonderful to find a place specializing in rare historical books and foreign languages. I agreed with her.

"Does your family own the store?" she asked me.

"The man who owns it is a friend of mine."

"You are so lucky to have a place like this in which to work and absorb ideas from the past."

When she left I looked around me and thought how wonderful it was that Mr. Seiler created an atmosphere like his store. Even the arrangement of the shelves and the two levels elevated by just two steps, store-width windows facing the city street outside, the magazine rack with papers and periodicals from around the world. One had a feeling of living in more than one century at a time, a continuity through learning. It felt like I thought Europe would feel.

That moment began my new job at Mr. Seiler's bookstore.

At first Mr. Seiler would only let me do a few things without supervision, but I worked diligently and responsibly until it was clear to him that I could manage his store while he was gone. Upon learning that, he became a free man, and so did I. Even though it was always he who opened the store in the mornings, after a while he turned it over to me throughout the day, and often I even closed it. I loved this job. He paid me a small salary, but it was all right because I didn't need much, and I saved all of it for my ticket to Hamburg.

One Saturday morning Mr. Seiler put his arm around me and said, "I would like you to introduce me to your grandparents, Michael."

I was shocked. We had only spoken about them once. I didn't know what to answer because I think I was ashamed of my grandparents. They were uneducated. Although my grandfather read all of the time, he was volatile and prejudiced. He was complex and had contradictory sides. I didn't understand him and was a little afraid of him. I didn't know what he would think of my 80-year-old friend.

"Why do you want to meet them, sir?" I asked him.

"Because, Michael, if we go to Hamburg, you will need their blessing, so now is the time to begin acquiring it."

"I'll not need their permission, sir, I'm almost twenty years old and on my own."

"That is not the issue, Michael - how old you are. You need their blessing, not their permission, because they have raised you and will worry about you, especially if you leave the country and leave with an old man they have never met."

It was comforting, in a way, that Mr. Seiler's values were clear, although they felt flexible and permissive. They were consistent. He expressed them not forcefully or dogmatically but from a position that he felt was obviously right, expressed in a way which often persuaded me to embrace them and which assumed that I was good enough to understand what made them valuable.

"My grandfather doesn't like Germans, Mr. Seiler."

"Does he know all of us Germans?"

"No, sir, he probably doesn't know any Germans. He's still fighting the war."

"Well, Michael, then he and I have something in common: I'm still fighting the war too."

Probably neither of them had wanted to be involved in World War II, both feeling estranged from the monstrosity of it and yet forced by fate to take a stance; marked forever by the consequences.

"Michael, I have been through this many times before. I know what it's about, believe me. Your grandfather's opinions won't be new to me. What about your grandmother?"

"She won't be a problem. She gets along with everyone. She's a simple woman."

"So, we have already achieved fifty per cent approval without even trying!"

"Okay, Mr. Seiler, when would you like to meet them?"

"How about next Sunday? Do you go to church in the morning?" I nodded that I didn't go but said they did.

"Well, how about in the afternoon, after 3:00 pm so that I can have a nap and some tea. You tell them I am coming over at three, okay? Say you want them to meet your new employer. That should please them."

My grandmother insisted upon making a meal.

Saturday night I didn't sleep well, wondering if a confrontation might occur. Also I felt that the special relationship I had developed with Mr. Seiler would never be the same after he saw me in my home, for some odd reason. I was ashamed of my own shame as well. So my sleep was disturbed and confused.

It snowed all night and into Sunday morning. The land was white and puffy. Sounds were muffled in the snow whisked by the wind into round and irregular shapes that changed the contours of the world.

The whole city felt the way that Mr. Seiler's study felt, cushioned and comforting.

Mr. Seiler was waiting by the door in his black long coat and hat with ear flaps, wool trousers and galoshes. As a matter of fact, I thought, he looked like my grandfather, only shorter. My Grandfather waited for his callers this way too.

He greeted me and we drove to my grandparents' house. It was an old frame house two stories tall with a big front porch and a porch swing where they sat in the nice weather and talked and watched the cars go by. I loved the house. My mother had been born there. After my parents had died I would lay on the swing after dinner in the summer air in my grandmother's lap and she rubbed my head until I fell asleep. There were two big elm trees on the front terrace. In the back were apple trees and a huge garden where grandma spent her summer days tending and harvesting vegetables.

We parked on the street and walked between the canopy which the trees provided. My grandmother was waiting by the front door, ready to open it at the right instant. My grandfather stood behind her calmly, holding his hands together below his waist. He looked pleased that we were there. For them it was a great event. He wore his black three piece pin-striped suit. He dressed this way commonly at home. I realized for the first time how rare it was for a working man to dress like this. Just as rare for a working man to read Shakespeare and Victor Hugo, as my grandfather did.

I suddenly knew that everything would be all right after all. The heavens had aligned just right. My fears had been unfounded.

Mr. Seiler introduced himself confidently and my grandmother took his coat and put it on the downstairs bed. His German accent was still heavy, and I looked at my grandfather and saw his face was pleased.

"What a lovely home you have!" Mr. Seiler said to my grandmother.

"Well, let me show it to you."

"That would be wonderful," he said.

Together the four of us wandered slowly from room to room. My grandfather explained the renovations he had made since buying the house fifty years ago. Even though I had heard him explain this before, for the first time I really heard it - it meant something to me.

By the end of the tour, they were all friendly with each other.

By the end of the meal, they were friends.

I felt joyous.

They talked throughout the meal and I listened. Finally, as I had feared, the discussion turned to me.

"We're glad that Michael is working at your bookstore, but we think that he should be in college," my grandfather said.

"He should be, I agree," Mr. Seiler said. "But since he's not in college, at least he is in the presence of good literature. Michael is an avid reader and a deep thinker. I have faith that he will turn out well, whether he eventually goes to college or not or if he decides to go later. Don't worry about him. I don't hire just anyone at my bookstore." Mr. Seiler looked at me and winked.

"I simply don't understand why a boy, given the opportunity to go to college, would choose to go to work instead. Michael's mother was the first in our family to go to college. He should go too."

"Well, I don't understand either," Mr. Seiler said, "but that's what he's chosen, and he's a good boy and a smart boy, so there must be a good reason for this. I'm sure in time the reason will appear." I hoped my grandfather would not continue to express his inability to understand me. I liked Mr. Seiler's answer: "I don't understand either, but he has chosen, it is his choice."

"Michael was doing fine until he got involved with that girl from Germany," my grandmother said. "I tell you, she was all he thought about from morning until night. He was usually gone to school by the time we woke up at 6:30. And then we wouldn't see him some nights until after dark. And on Saturdays and Sundays..."

She went on and on about Susanne, talking about me in the third person as if I weren't there. But quickly I tuned her out, for she really knew nothing about Susanne, not even her name. I had hidden my involvement with her from them and from the rest of the world as well. Susanne and I had lived a fantasy. The world we created, the way we spoke, the laughter we engendered with each other, the expressions we made, the performances we became, the places in her mind she took me, the deep understandings we developed, were so entirely ours and ours alone that no one else could possibly ever know what we shared with each other. It was such a rare and fortuitous combination of personal traits, needs, dispositions, mirror-imaged selves reflecting back the light of ourselves upon ourselves. It was magic. It could never be again.

"...And then she went back to Germany..." I heard my grandmother say.

She knew! How did she know? All at once she realized she'd said more than she should have known. She looked at me in guilt.

"Well, we found out about her, Michael. We were worried about you, we knew something was wrong."

I looked at Mr. Seiler. Now he knew why I wanted to go to Hamburg. I was glad.

"You didn't know her, Grandma. I liked her very much."

"But she wasn't good for you, Michael. Your schoolwork suffered when you were with her, and you became isolated."

"She *was* good for me, Grandma. I was always isolated. With her I didn't have to pretend."

I could see my grandfather was preparing to make a pronouncement, but Mr. Seiler saved us from an argument.

"Why don't you and Mrs. Hanchak come by the bookstore next week and see where Michael is working. I think that you'll approve of it, since I observe many books on your wall and surmise that you are readers of books yourselves."

"That's Charles," my grandmother said, "He is the reader in the family."

"Well, Charles, why don't you come by then? I can show you my bookstore and we can make a cup of tea and talk."

My grandfather liked that idea. He forgot about Susanne. We retired to the living room and talked casually for an hour or more. Then Mr. Seiler and I took our leave. It had been a good afternoon. My fears were displaced. Susanne had been introduced. In time Mr. Seiler and I would begin our discussion of her, I knew.

———

It was dark when we left, still snowing softly in the fluffy night. Flickers of light reflected off the falling snow and looked like tiny lights flashing out a Morse code, approving the night with sparks.

The two of us drove silently through the marvelous deserted Sunday landscape. We arrived at the bookstore and I parked outside to let Mr. Seiler out. The normally busy streets were mute and motionless. I had never seen them this way before and realized that even the busiest spots on earth must be secluded sometimes.

Mr. Seiler put his hand on mine. "Thank you, Michael, for a very nice Sunday evening. I liked your grandparents. It is nice for old people like us to find each other. It reaffirms us."

"I could see that they liked you, sir, as well."

"You see, Michael, when one becomes old like us, we are tired of anger and we are tired of all the things which once gave us passion. A good book, a good meal, a good talk, a good sleep. Those are sufficient for our happiness. Our answers don't answer the questions anymore. So when we find someone our age, even if they were once our enemies, they are now our friends, and when this reversal happens we wonder why, when we were younger, we wasted time having enemies at all."

He started to open the door, and then closed it again. "Michael, I sold the bookstore."

To my surprise, the instant he said that I felt anxiety. The dream of finding Susanne was going to happen. It was no longer just a wish; I would reach the goal. Suddenly my life could not continue to idle but would eventually become engaged.

"That's wonderful, Mr. Seiler! When will they take it over?"

"We'll close on it the last day of this year, but I'll have until sometime in the spring to be out of the store."

He talked more about the details but I didn't listen, I just waited for him to mention Hamburg, but he didn't.

I went back and forth, wondering if I should bring it up, first deciding no and then yes. He said goodnight and got out of the car and started walking to the door. I put the car in "Drive" and started to go, but then parked it again. I got out and ran after him and met him at the door.

"Will we still go to Hamburg, Mr. Seiler?"

He nodded his head slowly. "If you want, yes, we can do it. But there are many details to work out about the store and flight reservations and many, many things. You will need to help me with them."

"I'll do it all, sir. You won't have to do a thing."

Mr. Seiler smiled at my enthusiasm. "Well, I know you're a hard worker and a smart researcher, so I'll certainly load you down with things to do. But I am old, Michael, and as I said before, I do things differently than I once did. I am slow. Are you sure that I'm the person you want to travel abroad with?"

"I wouldn't go unless I could go with you, Mr. Seiler."

He laughed and put his strong hand on my shoulder. "Well, then, we shall go. But first I must get some sleep before I can begin to concentrate upon the details of our trip. So you go home and in the morning we shall talk again. Thank you for this wonderful evening. It was delightful. Goodnight, Michael."

He turned to unlock his door. I stood waiting to make sure he got inside and the light came on. Then I walked again down his walkway to the street.

Just a few months before, I had walked away like this, having heard his story of the ruin of Hamburg, and now we were planning to visit his city. What a miracle it was.

CHAPTER 6

I t was nighttime when I left for Peru. I sat alone in the plane preparing for take-off. It was dark except for small lights above a few seats focused on passengers and vacant spaces below. It reminded me of a time when I was young and took a long train trip west with my mother. That trip began at nighttime too and this night's light was evocative of it and the feeling of traveling similar. At that time, like now, I sensed leaving behind something indefinable, which turned out to be a shedding of the skin of my first incarnation, and evolving through it and beyond it until it was not possible to return with the same understanding of myself that I had had before. All that I understood then, actually, was the novel sensation of freedom's upsurge, pulled forward by the mighty train moaning and crying immensely, symbolically, into the massive wilderness beyond the place where I had always been.

I hadn't thought of my mother for a long time. It was strange, I remembered, that in the total feeling of train travel from something familiar merging into the unknown, she had represented both my security and my place from which to escape. I remembered feeling it strongly and not knowing how to manage the conflict of loving her and needing her and wanting her to stay behind. I preferred to be the only witness to my metamorphosis.

Miami was the last stop before leaving the country.

It was dawn when I awoke and looked out of the plane's window and saw the rain forest for the first time. It looked from above like huge green iridescent sponges slurping in the morning sunlight while the fog of plants' breath rose above them and condensed to mist. A canopy of forest spread from horizon to horizon, so dense that I could not distinguish a cultivated acre or a house, a road, a bridge or a village. Nothing but glowing greenery, layers and layers of plant life, trees and plants and vines tangled together impenetrably. There were no power lines or signs or lights, nothing manmade that I could see. I couldn't take my eyes from it. It was a single living thing, a huge Mother of Creation lying down being suckled by all of her creatures at once. I felt as if I were glimpsing back at the Earth the way it was at the day of Creation.

I had read about the rain forest's ecosystem, and staring at its immense unity below me I understood it more clearly. It is called a "closed ecosystem." Many people mistakenly believe the rain forest must be extraordinarily rich soil, but in fact the opposite is true. It is worthless soil, all of whose minerals and nutrients are stolen perpetually, gobbled up by the forest above in its tireless quest for nourishment of the Mothersystem. As a result, cleared land never regenerates because the soil is completely depleted, and the source of richness, namely the plants, is gone forever. So the irony of the rain forest is that the revelation of the secrets that it holds is a condition of its never-being-tamed. In other words, the power is contained in the mystery.

I felt good and I felt wholesome. My sickness felt minimized by the ostensibly awesome universal process of life giving death and death returning life, which I intuited from my vantage point above the forest. I felt that the rain forest would be a good place to die, should one need a place to die.

But all at once we were out of it. The incredible Andes mountain range appeared below us, stretching hundreds and hundreds of miles from Colombia in the north to Chile in the south and separating the rain forest from the coastal desert on the other side, where Lima resided next to the Pacific Ocean. What amazing diversity was visible all at once below me. In the mountains were the awe-inspiring Inca strongholds of Macchu Picchu, Cuzco, Nazca, places of deep mystery and sophisticated ancient culture. The top of the Andes mountain range was flat. A road could be seen which ran from Ecuador to Bolivia. On one side of the mountain range was the most complex rain forest and the longest river on earth. On the other side was a desert hundreds of miles long. And beyond the desert was the Pacific Ocean. The country of Peru was one superlative next to another.

The plane circled above Lima, made invisible almost year-round by fog, garua, the condition obtaining from the desert meeting the sea. Finally it landed on flat dry earth beside the Pacific Ocean.

I knew at once which anxiously awaiting person in the reception area was Christiane. She knew me too, although neither of us had seen a picture of the other. When I first saw her, for an instant I saw her as a little girl, the way she must have looked as a child. Her eyes were black and deep, and seemed as if they were impatiently trying to take in more world than their capacity to absorb would allow.

Her face was pretty, adorned with bright red lipstick that gave an old-fashioned touch to a voguish elegance. She smiled at me and confidently held up a placard upon which she had written in thick black lettering, "Michael, I am Christiane."

"Hello, Christiane, I am Michael," I said holding out my hand to her.

She put her arms around me and said, "Welcome to Peru."

It was hot and humid, steamy. The air in Lima was sensuous and thick, with strong smells, delightful and offensive together, blended into a single aromatic presence around us everywhere.

Christiane drove me through the city, pointing out sites and landmarks of her childhood which happened to be on a route I could not believe was the most direct one.

She spoke with tenderness of her connection to Peru and to the Incas whom she adored and identified with. The prevailing colors of Lima were yellow and red. The vistas were wide and barren. Even the people seemed opened up, as if the geology could reveal their thoughts as it revealed everything else.

There were throngs of people everywhere, incredible traffic jams which occurred and then cleared spontaneously like pressurized water bursting through clogged pipes. It was remarkably efficient anarchy.

The city and surrounding areas were mountainous and desert-like at once, showing the obverse of the rain forest's impenetrable life forms. Gluts of mankind, however, swarmed upon it, obviously demanding more than it could sustain. So it was a fading city with a legacy of Spanish opulence, declining now, dying even, expiring from demands exceeding supplies. Dying the way that cities can die until there is nothing nourishing left or left to nourish, until time's vector moves the forces of life a different way. But one could still see the touch of the Incas. Their spirit remained, I was to learn, to claim in some measure the hearts of the inhabitants despite their inevitable surrender to change.

Christiane pulled the car to the side of the avenue. It was a beautiful street of old Spanish homes, many of them gated with wrought iron. It was private, shaded with sumptuous trees, adorned with tropical flowers and bushes.

"See that house, Michael?" She pointed to the lovely villa in front of which we'd parked. A somnolent gardener attended to the occasional imperfections in the yard.

"Yes," I said.

"That is where I was born. That is where *my* world collapsed for the first time. Right there."

She opened the door of the car and said, "Wait here," and walked slowly to the gardener in the yard where she had lived. They talked and gestured and laughed a few moments, and then he took her to the front door of the house. After a moment, a woman came to the door and they talked a bit more and then Christiane turned toward me and motioned for me to come to her. I walked across the perfect yard and up the limestone steps and could see tiny fossils embedded in the surface. The railing in the center was granite with fitted brass ends. It was wide and substantial and many times denser than necessary for support. At the top of the stairs the servant stood deferentially, presumably trying with his body language to make himself smaller than the rest of us to signify his humility. Christiane stood next to the matronly woman of the house who wore a long reddish-brown taffeta dress that hid worn bedroom slippers that peeked out occasionally. The woman looked at me with an expression of curiosity. Christiane introduced us, and I listened to the two women talk in Spanish, until finally they motioned for me to come inside.

We walked a few steps past the foyer into the living room and then Christiane stopped. I watched her face loosen into reverie as she took in the scene of her youth and absorbed the memories flooding towards her. She looked around the room.

The home was spectacular. Huge chandeliers with hundreds of sun-sparkling crystals centered each room. The ceilings were tall with ornate hand-crafted molding of religious themes. In the foyer was a brown and white marble floor and brass and wooden doors to tall palatial closets. The focus of the living room was the stairway to the second floor with a railing made of shining brass with a glass base.

They spoke more Spanish and Christiane said "Come on," and we walked slowly through the luxurious dining room with cut glass windows looking onto a sunporch outside, which was a magnificent greenhouse of lustrous colors. "That is where I studied my lessons," she pointed and smiled. Then we walked into a dazzling kitchen almost as big as the living room. Chrome and ceramic and fine wood. An enormous island for cooking. A side room with leather booths viewed the greenhouse. Beautiful rounded antique appliances sparkled like new. The whole room was bathed in light from skylights above.

"Look at this house, Michael. Have you ever seen anything like it? I lived here in this palace. Even as a child I knew it was a great privilege to be here. I've managed to separate in my mind this house I adored from some of the awful things that occurred within it."

She spoke at length to the woman in Spanish, then took her hand and thanked her profusely. The woman's face glowed with friendliness. I shook her hand too and we slowly walked back through the luxurious charming home. I was hoping we would go upstairs, but we didn't.

Outside on the lawn Christiane walked me slowly to the car without speaking. When we got to the car she turned back toward the house. Her face looked jubilant.

"I have always wanted to do that. Every time I come back here I drive by this house and contemplate doing what we just did. I needed to do that, Michael. To see that place and have it be more than just thoughts and remembrances. I have always remembered it as something like a howling sanctuary, which contained both danger and protection. But now I only detect peacefulness. What a nice feeling, like healing old wounds at last."

I didn't understand, and she didn't explain, and I didn't ask more.

We got in the car again and drove into the heart of the city. Lovely buildings surrounded statued courtyards, keeping alive a spirit of 1500's Spanish dominance. Thousands of itinerant peasants lined the walkways and sat and lay on grassy areas near their possessions. These were people, I learned, who'd moved to the city and left behind their rural life in search of dreams of prosperity, only to find that there were no opportunities for them and that the life they'd left behind was not retrievable.

"Christiane, tell me about your son," I said.

"Michael, his father died eighteen months ago, and Simon has gone into deeper and deeper depression. For some reason he improves a bit when he is in Peru, as long as I stay with him. But, of course, I have to be in New Zealand for my work, so he goes back with me then or occasionally stays here with his grandmother."

"How old is he?"

"Eleven."

"Was his father Peruvian?"

"No, but he was working for a project in Peru when we met and we married here."

"Maybe that's why your son improves when he is here."

"Yes, I suppose you're right. But Simon is fast disappearing from me, Michael. We were once so close. He was happy and so brilliant and funny and charming. He was like a holy child, with amazing compassion for others and even for animals and creatures of all sorts. Enlightened. He was like light, yes, that is the word. Full of light and understanding. Every day I awoke excited to see him, but now he is gone into a dark place and cannot get out of it, and I cannot help him. He hardly talks anymore. He stays in his room on his bed for days at a time."

"I think he stays on his bed because it is the only place where his father still lives," I said. "He is afraid that if he leaves, his father might leave as well."

"What makes you think that?"

"Because I lived that way too. Long ago, after my parents were killed. After the funeral I inherited my parents' bed and moved it into an upstairs room in my grandparents' house. Off the bedroom, joining it, was a miniature sewing room of my grandmother's which she rarely used by then. In the room was an old wooden sewing machine console with tiny little drawers. Inside the drawers were pictures of my mother as a child and as a girl and then as a woman married to my father.

"After school I would come right home with all my books and tell my grandmother that I was going upstairs to study. But I'd go into the sewing room instead and carefully take the pictures from the tiny drawer and lay them out on the bed and lie on the bed and stare at the pictures for hours. My mother was beautiful and my father dashing and confident. Being in their bed looking at their pictures made them come alive. I talked to them and they talked back to me. It was what kept them in my life. Anytime trouble occurred or I became confused about something, I stoically endured it knowing it could be remedied by laying the pictures out on my parents' bed and lying on it and talking to them. I suppose it was a form of meditation or maybe even a trance which I entered, some sort of primeval, instinctive healing ritual. Their bed was my connection to them and maintained the continuity in my life and my sanity."

"That's interesting, Michael. Simon has all of Tomas's pictures too. I find them placed in different sequences around his bed. I see them and become so sad I don't know what to do."

"You don't need to do anything. He has his own form of therapy which maybe he believes no one else will understand."

"He seems in so much pain."

"He is in pain. Yes. But he has found rituals, just like I did, to relieve the pain. The reality of the rituals doesn't matter."

We left the public streets of Lima and turned into a private housing area many acres in size, beautifully landscaped with flowers and trees I had never seen. We entered through a gate with an electronic opener. There were white residences with gardens and porticos, one of which was to be mine.

Curved brick walkways meandered creatively from one building to the next. Light and openness artistically delineated privacy within an apparent community. It felt safe and substantial to be there.

"This is yours," Christiane said stopping in front of a one-story residence on the curve of the street. "It will be your decision when you want to go to Iquitos and visit your doctor, when you feel right about it. You'll need a day or two just to get rested from the trip. I expect you will want to take longer and acquaint yourself with your surroundings and feel at home here. Whatever length of time is required is okay.

"How much notice does the doctor need?" I asked her.

"There's no way to notify him at all. We'll just go there when you are ready."

"I need to talk to you about this doctor, Christiane," I said.

"Yes, you do. But now is not the time. You must feel at ease here first. It will happen probably very quickly. You should lie down and rest here for a few hours. I have some things to do. I will return later in the afternoon, and we will have dinner together, ok?"

"Before you go, Christiane, tell me about Simon's father."

She laughed. "You are anxious to know everything right at once, eh? I met Tomas in New Zealand. He was there as a speaker at a conference of international doctors sharing new information about epidemic diseases affecting underdeveloped nations. He was well-known as a researcher and a speaker. When I heard him speak I was mesmerized by him. Then when we met I fell in love. He was handsome and brilliant with a mind that could focus like a laser one moment and be light and funny the next. He was older than me, a little older than you, I think. He didn't share much with me about his past, and I accepted that. His parents were dead. I never met them. Or anyone from his family. I knew when I met Tomas that he would be mine for only a short time. Do you know what I mean? Some lights endure like stars, others explode with brilliance but burn out quickly like fires. He was a fire. I knew he would not last, and so I did not demand things of him. He was wonderful to me, brilliant, funny and charming. He and Simon loved each other dearly, like soulmates rather than father and son. Our few short years together were the best of my life."

When I woke up from my nap Christiane took me to dinner in the mountains at a fine restaurant. I was tired but surprisingly I did not feel dispossessed or out of place.

"Christiane, will you tell me about where I am going and who is my doctor?" I asked her again.

"Your doctor is a 'Curandero', a healer." His name is Francisco Alvaro. He was originally from Equador where he studied philosophy at the university. He earned an M.D. degree in the United States. His family were healers. He practices with native people of the rain forest, but he uses Western medical techniques also. He is well-respected by all of the people I have talked to who know of him. He is also a musician and has invented musical instruments from native sources which he uses in his healing ceremonies. He speaks excellent English, but during the healing ceremonies he speaks Quechua, the language of the Incas, or Cocoma or Omagua, rarely English. However, it is not uncommon for participants to claim to have understood everything he said, even though it was in an ancient language. How much do you know about shamanism?"

"I read quite a bit about it, mostly informative things."

"This man is an ayahuasca healer. Like most curanderos, he uses plant extracts which he mixes himself, along with 'icaros,' which is spiritual healing music, power music. The most effective icaros are those learned from natural spirits. They are also used to arouse spirits and structure visions and even re-direct them. It is quite amazing how a skilled shaman can engineer perceptions for participants. Also used to achieve a trance state are sacred rituals called 'arcanos.'

"The curandero is one who can walk between the natural and the supernatural world. And there is a supernatural world. Most shamans consider the normal life we lead to be a lie, an illusion. The real world is the supernatural world. You will see it. It will not be imaginary. Ayahuasca will allow you to see the world of visions and phantasms."

"Have you taken ayahyasca, Christiane?"

"Yes, several times."

"Why have you not considered this cure for your son?"

"Because, Michael, he isn't ready for it."

"Why do you think I can help him? I'm a doctor, not a therapist."

"Maybe you're a therapist too, Michael."

After dinner we went to her apartment. We talked a bit and then I asked if I could meet Simon.

"We could stop by his room, but he'll not speak to you."

I told her I didn't care.

She opened Simon's door slowly and called his name softly. He didn't answer. There were no lights on, so she switched on the overhead light. He was still dressed. I quickly looked around the room for clues. There were several pictures on his headboard but I couldn't see them clearly. A few toys and stuffed animals lay haphazardly on the floor, and books were on the shelf. The room was quite neat and pleasant. Christiane touched his arm.

"No, no, don't bother him now," I said, but she ignored me.

"There is someone I would like you to meet, Simon. His name is Michael."

The light was too bright for him, I felt, so I turned on a weak lamp near me and then switched off the overhead light.

"Hello Simon, I am Michael. I am sick. Your Mother has brought me to Peru to help me get well. I am happy to meet you. She's told me many good things about you. I hope we can talk again. We won't bother you anymore tonight, though. I'm sorry we didn't let you know we were coming." I took Christiane by the elbow and whispered "Let's go," and she said goodbye to Simon and told him she would return and say goodnight to him. He didn't speak.

CHAPTER 7

It was a rare sunny Sunday morning in January, but very cold. Mr. Seiler had closed upon the sale of the store and we were well into our plans to go to Hamburg. I was amazed at how calm he was about traveling to a place he had deserted thirty years before. I myself did not feel so peaceful. I was no longer clear about my own feelings towards Susanne. The length of my separation from her had caused the details of our relationship to become stretched into fantasy and fuzzy.

It was inevitable that Mr. Seiler would ask me about Susanne, and when he did I told him I was in love with her. It sounded odd.

"Let me ask you something, Michael. You said, 'I *was* in love with her,' but it sounds as if you are still in love with her."

"I think I am still in love with her, Mr. Seiler. I'm not really sure anymore what I am. I just know that I have to go to Hamburg in order to understand who I am and what I need to do with my life. In order to draw a conclusion."

"And what if you discover in Hamburg that she is still in love with you?"

"Then I'll ask her if we can be together again. I'll live in Hamburg if it is what she wants. I'll learn German and find work. If she still loves me, I will do anything she wants or needs."

"And what if you can't find her?"

"I'll find her, Mr. Seiler. You'll help me find her, won't you?"

He was silent.

"What are you thinking, sir," I said.

"I'm thinking about what you said. Wondering if maybe there is something else, if maybe it's not as simple as whether she loves you or not."

"Like what?"

"I don't know. I have a feeling that she still loves you, that there is something else."

"She was to me, Mr. Seiler, a savior. She saved my life. And she said that I saved hers."

"Michael, maybe now you need to let go of her."

"I can't let go of her, sir. This story has not ended. It has to have an end. Not an ending which I must guess at. It needs a real ending. Or it needs a new beginning. I need to see her again. It haunts me why she left like that."

"Why does it haunt you?"

"I don't know."

Mr. Seiler looked at me silently with his hand over his mouth, waiting for me to say more.

"I think she might have been pregnant, sir."

"What makes you think so?"

"Because there is no other reason she has disappeared from my life."

"Do you think that this is a reason for her to disappear from your life? That she is carrying your child? That, to me, is a reason for you to be together."

"Not for her. She'll think she's ruined my life and will sacrifice hers for mine."

"Why does anyone have to sacrifice his or her life? Young people have gotten pregnant before, you know, and gone on to lead fulfilling lives. Why not you?"

I didn't answer.

"Yes, I believe now that you must go to, Michael. We will find an end for this story in Hamburg."

"Or a new beginning," I said hopefully.

"Or a new beginning, yes. Hamburg is accustomed to endings and new beginnings."

CHAPTER 8

The next night I saw Simon again. A dim light was on near his bed and he was cuddled into a ball buried in his covers.

"Simon, this is Michael. I just wanted to say hello to you again." His hair was black and his skin was a wonderful healthy-looking light brown.

"I'm here because I know how you are feeling. There is a little boy inside of me your age who feels what you are feeling. He is lonely and wants someone to talk to, but he's afraid no one will understand him. But I think you will understand him. And that's why I have come here tonight - to introduce you to this boy in hopes that you will be his friend and help him. In fact maybe you can help each other. Michael does not want to bother you if you don't want to see him, so he asks if you will indicate to him somehow if he should come back again or not. He is going to give you his picture and put it here above your bed. If you don't want to see him again, you can turn his picture around facing the wall and he will know not to return. He'll come back tomorrow night at this time to visit you. Thank you for allowing us to come and see you again, Simon. Goodnight."

"How was he?" Christiane asked me.

"Just the same as last night. Christiane, I would like to see him tomorrow night at this time if that is all right with you."

"Of course it is, Michael."

"He'll tell me if he wants me in his life or not."

"I don't think he will talk to you, Michael, but maybe he will."

"He might not talk, but he'll tell me if he wants me back. So tomorrow is an important night. If he tells me tomorrow not to return, then I will prepare myself for Iquitos. If he tells me to stay, I will stay until the end."

"And what is the end?"

"The end is when he's better again."

"How will he tell you whether to return or not?"

"I told him a way to give me a sign if he wants us to return."

"Us?"

"Michael and I. Young Michael."

"Okay. Well, you do what you need to do. So you think he will get better?"

"Yes, I do."

"What about your treatment?"

"I'm doing well right now. I feel strong here in Lima."

I felt good again about myself, the way I used to feel when I told patients that they would be all right, seeing the relief on their faces.

The following night after dinner I entered Simon's room. I was a little surprised at my nervousness about how I would find my picture. I noticed that the light was pointing upwards to the top of the bed and in the center of the light was the picture I had given him the night before of me as a little boy. It had been moved slightly to position it directly in the light. Not far from it I noticed another picture in the half-shadow.

"Hello, Simon, we're back. We're happy to see you again." I sat on the bed beside him and began talking about the picture. "When I was that boy in the picture, Simon, I was your age. I remember it felt difficult being that age because although life was thrilling and full of possibilities, it was also full of restrictions.

"The day before the picture was taken my father had bought me a new baseball glove and after Sunday dinner at my grandparents' house we spent hours in the backyard, me pitching baseballs to him. I always felt that I let him down, because I didn't like to play baseball even though I was good at it. I liked music instead."

Simon hadn't stirred since I entered the room. As if he were dead. What amazing discipline he has, I thought.

I noticed the other picture. It was of Simon with a man I assumed was his father. It had not been there the night before.

"Is this your father, Simon? Can I pick it up and look at it?"

I waited, with no response, deciding respectfully not to touch it. I leaned my head closer to see it and my leg pushed against his body. I felt an almost imperceptible resistance against my leg. The beginning of our relationship.

His father was tall but slight, intensely handsome with a playful, almost coquettish look in his eyes and at the corner of his mouth.

I looked back at Simon's half-face lying in the darkness against the pillow. I turned the light a bit to see it better. He was beautiful like his mother. They both had dark hair and long eyelashes. I put my hand on his head gently and stroked his hair a bit. It seemed to encompass my touch as if it were a tissue absorbing affection.

Looking at him I felt his anguish and confusion, and the voice that came from me was from thirty-five years ago.

"My mommy and daddy died and left me all alone. There was no one to talk to. Suddenly I was not a boy anymore, and I was not an adult either. I was nothing. My home always had been full of music.

Always full of talk. Always people around, guests and relatives and people who loved us and wanted to be with us. But when my parents died all of that ended with them. Now people only came with long faces of sadness to give me pity and to wonder how I would ever make it on my own."

Simon's face was flaccid with nearsleep, but I was sure that he had heard me and absorbed my words.

"Thank you, child," I whispered to him.

I touched his hair once more and turned the light back to my picture and covered him with his blankets.

"You were with him a long time, weren't you?"

"Yes, a long time." I looked at my watch.

"But he didn't speak?"

"Well, not words, no. But he indicated he wanted us there."

"How did he do that?"

"I told him to turn my picture toward the wall if he didn't want us back. But instead he put it directly in the light, and put a picture of himself and his father next to it."

"That's wonderful!"

"Tell me more about his father."

"About his past I know very little, as I told you. I adored Tomas, and I didn't care about anything else. Why would I want to find out things that might change my opinion of him?"

"You are an odd one, Christiane. I think you want to live in fairy tales."

"I do. I really do."

"I suppose that's a good place to live if you can do it."

"Can you do it, Michael?"

"Well, as a boy I lived only in fairy tales. As a young man I lived only in reality. Now I sometimes think I don't know what is reality and what is a fairy tale. Maybe I am getting ready to journey back to the land of fairy tales and stay there for a while this time."

"You are a good man, Michael. You'll find the land of fairy tales again."

Each night I returned to Simon's bedroom to talk to him in a great darkness lit just by the light above his bed. Always my picture remained centered in the light, but often he had placed one or more of his own beside it. His father was always in the picture, sometimes with others I assumed were friends or family.

At first I returned with the thought that I was helping him in some way to come out of himself and eventually join us again normally. But as the days went by, I began to see that it was I who was being helped. It was I who was coming out of myself. I was retrieving my past from the darkened corners of my consciousness and the unvisited sanctuaries of my memory.

It was I who relied upon Simon's spiritual presence that I felt so keenly which allowed me to desire my own self-rebuilding. I was not sure what he received from me, but it was somehow meaningful to him because he continued to "invite" me back. So eventually I was not concerned about his outcome or my own.

Every day thoughts occurred to me which I wanted to address that night with Simon. I gathered them to a mental list I repeated to myself throughout the day, sometimes actually writing them down on paper. We came to have a dependence upon one another which we understood intuitively. What was happening to me had the nature of a craving: I felt compelled to return to it again and again because it provided me with soul-substance of which I had deprived myself for most of my life-time, and now I wanted a quarter of a century's worth - my share - as fast as I could funnel it into my consciousness.

It was scary but electrifying - the things that I was allowing myself to call forth from inside of me. It was as if I were traversing my life from a vantage point where I could see it all at once, as the ground from an airplane.

I watched Simon carefully as I spoke. He never moved, not even his eyes slightly or the corners of his mouth. He lay absolutely motionless for hours and hours. It was amazing! Such Spartan resolve alone was enough to make me respect his forceful personality.

There were times when I simply sat in the chair and thought about what I had said. Often it felt as if someone else were mining my soul's earth and raising the nuggets of awareness to the surface of conscious-ness, whereupon I took them into the light like a rescuer in a disaster, returning later to examine them more closely.

It occurred to me in these talks to Simon, hearing like a great mag-nanimous Ear inviting me to partake of its healing receptivity, that upon being rejected by the death of my parents at the age of ten, I had taken a path that had obscured me from the light and had created a dull anaesthetic sameness. In essence, I had died too. Gone to sleep to all things beyond my control. Until I met Susanne.

One night, I began telling Simon a story, that she had made up and had told me:

There was a boy in search of his lost father wandering in the woods away from his home. With nighttime coming and the bit of sky that he could still see changing quickly into darkness, the air was getting cold. Foolishly using the last moments of light, he scurried here and there in a panic. He leaned against a tree and slid down the bark to the ground and sat in lonesome fear, enclosed in sullen darkness with the wind howling. He rolled into a ball and put his face against the earth. The carpet of pine needles poked into his skin, the leaves scratched his face. He grew colder as the night wore on and the earth lost its heat. He heard strange sounds around him and felt tiny creatures crawling on his legs and face.

But after a while his panic left him. The wind slowed down and the tree he'd leaned against gave him strength and support. The bugs upon his body had apparently gone to sleep next to his warmth and hadn't bitten him. The sounds of the forest night had become familiar and predictable and didn't scare him anymore. No big animals had come to get him.

The boy slowly uncurled his body and lifted his torso up to lean against the tree and look out into the flat darkness all around him. He listened intently to the soft cotton-like nothingness of the measureless dark and felt calm.

After an amount of time which he could not determine, the moon rose above the treetops and sent down, through the crisscrossed branches, focused rays of light which illuminated his surroundings like a stage play of the forest.

The next thing he could remember was warmth upon his face and hands, where sunlight funneled through the outstretched arms of friendly trees above him. It was daybreak. He had slept. He felt the pine needles below his cheeks and slowly lifted up and shook them off his shirt and pants. He'd survived the forest's first night.

The boy searched and found the path. Soon the path ended, but he made his own path from there on.

Suddenly the forest opened upon a peaceful lake with a small sunny meadow between it and the woods on the other side. He sat down on the bank and felt the sun's reflected warmth from the lake's mirror-like surface. A turtle slept cautiously on a stump near the shoreline, and frogs chirped from their hiding places where the water joined the land.

It felt so warm and safe to him that he lay down with his face to the sky and fell asleep again. He dreamed a dream that his father walked toward him from the woods beyond the lake's meadow.

Sometime later he awoke to the sound of gentle singing. He rose up to see on the other side of the lake a girl with long blond hair, wearing earth-colored clothing, doodling in the mud with a stick, apparently unaware that she was not alone. He stood up and slowly walked in her direction. When she finally noticed him, to his surprise she acted as if she had expected him all along.

"Hello!" he called out to her as they approached.

"Hello to you, new boy in Pershing's Meadow," she replied.

"Pershing's Meadow?"

"That's where you are. You just came through Halthing Forest, and this is Pershing's Meadow."

"I see. And where are you from?" he asked her.

"I'm from the woods on the other side. Deep into them I live with my mother where we tend a small piece of ground. Every morning early I come to Pershing's Meadow to see my friends."

"Friends?"

"The birds, the rabbits, the otters, all the animals. They're hiding now because they are afraid of you. I knew you were here because when I arrived they were invisible. Usually they are here to greet me. What about you, are you lost?"

"Yes, in a way I am. I was searching for my father and I got lost."

"Isn't that the way it often happens? What is your name?"

"It's Simon. And what is yours?"

"It's Susanne."

I looked at Simon and his right eye was open for the first time since I had met him. For days I had talked to this child for hours and hours and only now he opened his eye. It was beautiful, soft and gentle with long eyelashes. He closed it again slowly as I continued telling the story:

Susanne had a bag beside the water with oranges in it along with tea and homemade bread with nuts inside and honey also. They sat together by water's edge and talked and ate.

"Have you heard of the Highlands?" she asked him.

"No, I haven't," he said.

"It's high above the clouds where the sun is always shining and stars are always out at night.

"It sounds nice?"

"It's very far away. It takes a day to get there, but the trip is worth it."

"What's there?"

"Well, it's on top of Halthing Forest and beyond the river. You have to go through a long and narrow cave which no one knows about but me. I will take you there if you want to go. My father is there. He is the Master Stonemason."

"Oh, I see," the boy said. "It's where you live?"

"No, not I. Just the fathers."

"The fathers? What do you mean?"

"I mean the Land of Fathers is in the Highlands."

Simon shook his head and laughed at his confusion. "I'm sorry, I don't understand what you're saying."

"The Land of Fathers is where all the fathers live. Everyone's father who is gone. It is not just that they are lost but that they are somehow separated from the ones who love them."

"You mean like when they die?"

"Yes, like when they die."

"Do you think my father is there too?"

"Did he die?"

"I'm not sure. He left one day and didn't return. Maybe."

"Then of course he's there."

I looked at my watch and it was late. I leaned over Simon and whispered, "I'm going to leave now, Simon, but I'll come back tomorrow and tell you more of the story."

I slowly rose and reached for the covers to pull up around his neck as I did each night, when I heard him say in a very tender and soothing voice without insistence:

"Don't go yet, Michael. I would like you to finish the story."

The first words.

"Here's what I will do, Simon. This story is very long. I want you now to let yourself fall asleep as I speak more of it to you. I will tell it for one half-hour more or until you are asleep. Then I will leave and sleep myself. But tomorrow I will return and tell you more. First, however, I must tell your mother that I will be here one half-hour longer."

Christiane was asleep on the sofa beneath a beautiful woven Indian rug. The reading light shone upon an open book near her head. She awoke when she heard my footsteps click onto the ceramic living room floor from the carpeted hallway.

"Michael, you have been with Simon a long time."

"He spoke to me."

"He did? What did he say?"

"He said, 'Don't go yet, Michael. I would like you to finish the story.' It's a story Susanne told me a long time ago. I told Simon the story was too long to finish but that I would tell him one more half-hour of it and then continue tomorrow."

I summarized the story for Christiane and then excused myself and went back to Simon's bedroom. I could tell by his breathing that he was asleep. I pulled the covers up around his neck and turned the light away, and left the room silently.

I asked Christiane to join us the next night. I sat meditatively in silence for a few moments to create a mood for listening. Then I continued with the story:

"I don't see how that could be possible - that people die but are still alive somewhere else," Simon said.

"Well, Simon, one thing's for sure: you have to believe in the Land of Fathers in order to be able to find it. Just like you have to believe in the wisdom of animals in order for them to come near and be your friends."

"If my father is there, will he talk to me?"

"Of course he will. But you have to believe in him first."

"I don't know if I can do that."

She put her hands out and said, "Simon, follow me to the Highlands and I'll show you something that will make you believe. But...look at me Simon." Simon raised his head and met her eyes with his. "I want you to believe in this. Believing is not lying to yourself. Believing is just the opposite of that: it is letting yourself see what is there to be seen. You told me when you started through Halthing Forest, you got lost. When you got lost, you stopped believing. And when you stopped believing and became afraid, then you no longer thought you could get where you wanted to go. But then you started believing and set out on the road again, and look where you are now. It is the same thing, Simon, that's what believing is."

"Yes, I'll go with you," he said.

They spent most of the day in Halthing Forest climbing a slow, steady ascent through magnificent huge trees with flowering plants all around. The river she'd spoken of was rocky and wide and fast-moving, its bed formed of rocks from above moving gradually downstream. They climbed and climbed, the sun blazing upon them, until at the top they found an open cavern facing out upon the river. The view was breathtaking and Simon thought he saw the meadow and the lake in the distance beyond the forest they'd come through.

The cavern was comfortable and offered shelter. Around the edges were rocks upon which one could sit and a place to make a fire.

"You can't go into the Land of Fathers except during the daytime because you need all the light you can get. In fact, since this is your first time, I think we should sleep here tonight and go into the cave in the morning."

"Where is the cave?" he asked.

She turned around and pointed and said, "Right there!"

CHAPTER 9

A nd so it was. We were going to Hamburg.

I had found a Lufthansa flight which left JFK at night and flew non-stop to Hamburg, arriving at 6am local time. I told Mr. Seiler it was much more expensive that way, being the only non-stop flight to Hamburg, but he didn't care.

He told me to reserve a room at Vier Jahreszeiten, the most luxurious hotel in Hamburg, on Jungfernstieg Avenue, directly facing the beautiful Inner Alster lake, Hamburg's spot of greatest elegance, luxury, and beauty. I said I would be happy anywhere, that it was not necessary to stay in such opulence. He looked at me sternly and said, "Michael, I am an old man. I don't have many more moments left to experience luxury. You are a young man; it will be a long time before you experience it like this again." He put his arm around me. "So let us enjoy luxury the way it must be enjoyed - without regret or hesitation."

Mr. Seiler was most handsome the night we flew to Hamburg. I was proud to be with him. He wore a dark three-piece suit with a beautiful dark tie and gold tie pin. His white shirt was heavily starched and had French cuffs that shined at the ends where they turned under, and cuff links. His shoes were like black mirrors. His gray hair, still full, was combed stylishly, and he wore a luscious cologne that delighted the sense of smell and accompanied every well-chosen articulate word that he spoke in his German accent that I loved so much, so that his words, in addition to all of the ways in which they were usually important to me, also seemed to smell good. He looked half his age. Somehow he seemed tanned and dark. The corners of his eyes wrinkled/twinkled like twilights of welcome.

"Are you glad to be returning home, sir?"

"Yes. I've been thinking about this return to my home ever since that Sunday afternoon when we went to your grandparents' for dinner. I had never forgiven Germany for World War Two and for the death of my family. I had never once considered returning there. But two things happened: first, through you I saw that it is no longer the same world. The day I told you of the bombing of Hamburg, when you left, I stayed up late, thinking. I had just told my awful story for the first time since it happened, to you, a boy whose people were the ones who had bombed us, and yet you knew nothing about it. You in turn were looking for a German girl who had come to America and with whom you have fallen in love, and you wanted to go to Germany and find her. I realized the absurdity of my position: there is no one left to hate. The sides of allegiance have all changed and the players have re-aligned. The past and its actors are dead. The world has moved on and always moves on like an earthmover, continually changing the familiar landscape into something unrecognizable. That was the first thing. The second was when we went to your grandparents' house and had such a lovely time. I was prepared for them to dislike me, for you yourself had said they don't like Germans. But all was forgotten. Now your grandfather comes into my store every week. We are friends now. So, it is time for me to forgive also. Who besides me loses from my stubborn resolve?

"What about your son, sir, will you find him?"

"I hope so, Michael."

"Do you have an idea where he is?"

"Probably still in Hamburg. He was very independent, so he could be anywhere. But he loved Hamburg. And just as he was fixed in his opinions, he was fixed in all ways: fixed to the place he had always lived, fixed in his loyalty to his friends."

"From his picture I can see that he might be independent like that."

"Ha!" he laughed mockingly. "He was a Bohemian. Half artist and half working man. An artist and a stonemason. Strong body, intense mind. He had his ideas and listened to no one unless they were more persuasive than him. He was a devout reader of philosophy and history, anything to do with ideas. People loved his masonry work. He was in great demand, but his real loves were reading and art. He was a very good sculptor. He was an orator as well - articulate and forceful, argumentative and provocative. Many were in awe of his presence. He had what they call now "charisma". Women were challenged by him, but he was a man's man. He was old-fashioned, born perhaps into the wrong century.

"Horst would take a job and work fourteen hours a day for two weeks. Then he might disappear and no one could find him for another two weeks, and then he suddenly reappeared to finish the job. Because he was so good at what he did, and also simply because he was Horst, people allowed him this freedom. It was embarrassing to us, however, to have to explain to clients who called knowing we were his parents, asking us where he was. Finally we just said: 'He doesn't live here, we don't know where he is.' But inevitably they would say, 'When you see him next, please tell him...' and we would say, 'We never see him...'"

"You didn't see him then?"

"No, not often. Although he sometimes came home and stayed awhile, mainly to be with his mother, whom he loved dearly, but it didn't take long until he and I were fighting again, and he would go off to live in his cabin."

"He lived in a cabin?"

"Yes, he had a cabin in the woods. No water, no plumbing, only a fireplace for heat. He would huddle around the fireplace and read books for days, until he literally went blind and began seeing double. Then he would go to work again."

I liked the description of his son. I wanted to be like him.

"He was constantly inventing things too. Little machines to do this or that. A wind machine to generate electricity; a pulley machine to lift stones to great heights; pumps and motors and levers and devices. He had a great mind for machines, and a fearlessness that caused him to be careless with them and injure himself. Unlike most children, when something hurt him he went back and challenged it. He wasn't afraid of anything. He was born that way. It was obvious when he was only a few weeks old even.

"He also had a dark side. The war didn't frighten him at all. He liked bombs and munitions, the notion of survival, the bareness of instinct and cunning. In a way we were quite dissimilar, in substance that is, but in style we were the same. Perhaps that's why it was a problem for me to accept him. He inherited the style from me but the substance was his own. Do you know what I mean?"

"I think so."

"But, you see, my problem then was that I could only see my life as the type of life he should lead. When I blindly pointed it out to him, he left. Then he returned, hoping, I suppose, that it would be different, but it never was."

"Did you write to him after you arrived in the US?"

"Yes, of course, many times. At first he wrote back but then he stopped. I tried to contact him through relatives too, but he had nothing to do with them. Eventually I gave up. It is a dark spot in my past about which I am not happy."

"We'll find him, sir," I said gallantly.

I asked Mr. Seiler what Hamburg was like when he was a boy. He talked on and on, as if the closed gates of his memory had finally opened up and let him see inside again.

"Hamburg at that time was considered one of the richest cities in the world, primarily because of the Port. The street we lived on, Michael, was the most beautiful street in one of the richest cities in the world. The way it was is gone now. It was like a fairy tale, which is maybe why my memories of that time start out and end on that street.

"It was a 'privileged' youth that I possessed. I didn't have to toil in labor or wallow in ignorance or be hungry at night. Beauty was commonplace, the elegance of music and art were given. Our street was brick and there were huge trees shading castle homes with splendid yards of flowers and ponds and wrought iron fences. It was magnificent.

"It was the turn of the century. The ideas of Karl Marx were catching on. Workers were beginning to become conscious of the injustices done to them. It was not until many years later when I became involved in that cause that I discovered my father had been the first owner of a shipping company to bring about reforms in the way workers were paid and housed, including building extensive housing units with his own money for the people who worked for him.

"Even though I was an excellent student who loved learning and had many opportunities available to me, when I finished school, instead of going on for further studies, I went to work on the docks, unloading ships. Eventually I became captain of a ship which sailed the seas around Europe, Asia, Africa, and the Americas.

"The work was backbreaking, from sunrise to sunset. Each day I awoke with a new quota of youthful energy and by the afternoon I was exhausted with no reserve left except my will. The next morning I would begin the inescapable cycle all over again. My mother never understood why I chose to do this.

"After three years I stopped being a longshoreman, but by then I was a seasoned veteran of the life. I decided to advance myself within this profession. I quickly rose in the ranks and soon was made captain of a ship, and for five more years sailed the ports of Europe. I educated myself. I became a significant member of the union movement that was becoming a huge force in Germany.

"The Port was one of the most important in the world. The population of Hamburg, because of it, doubled in twenty years. Almost unbelievable reforms had taken place in the Port, chief among them being an end to the monstrous privilege of the upper class, of which I was secretly one. My father, bless him, never betrayed me. He never questioned what I was doing with my life. He was a courageous and wonderful man.

"My mother was elegant and aloof. As a boy, she and I lived together on the Avenue a life of extraordinary luxury and beauty with the deepest pleasures. We were rowed by servants around the Alster while feeding swans trailing behind the boat. She told stories of the people in the glistening homes at the water's edge.

"My mother was beautiful. Her hands were long and delicate, dark-colored from summer's sun, with beautiful cordlike arteries near the surface that added depth and mystery and even sensuality to her essence.

"She was an artist and painted gracious watercolor scenes we saw each day: swans on the Alster, giant spreading trees in yards of mansions, sun coming up and going down. The paintings adorned our house and brought the outdoors inside. I remember staring in the winter at watercolor scenes she'd painted of galloping sunnyday horses and dazzling swan-filled shorelines, pastel summer scenes where joy abounded and made the household warm.

"She was a musician as well and played the piano every night before dinner. I listened to her play while I read books in the sunroom as dinner's smells drifted deliciously throughout our house. Each night before dinner she played Chopin's Nocturnes, which were dreamy and slow and mystical.

"Michael, I will tell you something: the life we lived is the way life should be for all people. Despite the world's hatred of the upper class, there is nothing necessarily wrong with this life. Who would not want it except a fool? Why do the revolutionaries become the objects of hatred in the next revolution? Quite the contrary, most everything is right about the life of the upper class except that very few can have it. And there seem to be two types of people who can have it without feeling guilty. The first type is boorish, insensitive and selfish. And the second is like my mother. No one, however jealous or bitter, would want to disabuse her of this life she led - after listening to her play music or regarding her paintings of her beloved Hamburg or recognizing her contribution to the overall goodness of the earth.

"I, on the other hand, felt guilty at once when I learned how most of the world lived. But I contained forever within my soul the feeling of life's potential grandeur instilled in me by the person of my mother.

"I believe now that it is inevitable that some will always be at the top of society, striving to stay there or feeling guilty for their privilege, relinquishing it imprudently, irretrievably, to someone else. Some will be in the middle, heading down or heading up to escape the drudgery of mediocrity. And some will be at the bottom, bewildered and angry about why they were born there, causing one form of revolution or another or else giving up to apathy or regret or some other trapping.

"And then there are those content with who they are wherever they are. My mother was one of them. She would have been content wherever she had been born or placed. So she could not understand why this lovely placid child who I was became a sultry discontent agitator. But I did. One's consciousness is changed by conditions, and I changed my conditions voluntarily to experience the other side of life. But I had the seed of discontent within me from my birth. And my mother did not.

"When I turned thirty, Michael, something happened. I had been a longshoreman and then a ship captain for almost a decade. I had renounced my past of delicacy and tenderness, subtle thoughts and dry humor, historical learning and practiced intuition. I had elected to live beside brutality and coarseness, astonishing physical strengths powered by undeveloped minds, explosive emotions and foolish abuses. I'd substituted the world of women for the world of men. By the age of thirty I knew them both well. I knew which poet was best recited while listening to a Bach sonata, and I knew which ship's sails would survive a western North Sea storm in late December. I had had two lives, two of me, which never spoke to one another. When I turned thirty I introduced them to each other.

"So began a new life. I went to work for my father. Inflation in Germany was staggering. People were starving. But still the shipping line was thriving since world trade was beginning to open up on a grand new scale. My father was getting older and a bit tired and he gradually passed the control of the business to me. I had an empathetic understanding of the situation of the workers and I continued to bring about reforms which he had started, so that soon I had the finest, most loyal and reliable workers on the dock. Everyone wanted to work for us. We had very high standards, set and administered by the workers themselves. Our reputation became known worldwide as the highest quality shipping company. We guaranteed delivery and safety and when there were complaints or problems, we dealt with them immediately. We could charge more and we could pay our employees more. I knew every aspect of the business from dock work to shipbuilding to sailing on the high seas to determining profits and losses and negotiating contracts.

"One day I was working late in my office and someone knocked on the door. I opened it and knew instantly that before me stood the woman who would be my wife. I never had a second thought about it. When I saw her, all at once a large part of the person who I was and had been all my life, vanished and was replaced by another person. I changed like liquid to gas, into another state of being. All this happened before she'd uttered a word."

It sounded exactly the way I'd felt upon meeting Susanne and I told him that.

"But, Michael, there is a difference. Katerina, my wife, had this feeling too and was not afraid to enter into its consequences. Because of that I was secure with the new Kurt Seiler whom she had helped catalyze. But for some reason, Michael, you and Susanne have not been able to make each other feel certain. You have experienced what I have just described, but instead of embracing it, you have run from it."

CHAPTER 10

Susanne and Simon spent the night in the cavern of the cave, which opened upon a most beautiful view of lights sparkling above and below it, stars in the sky and people-lights scattered below randomly throughout the woodland. Here and there were village-clusters of lights glowing communally. Susanne and Simon were balanced in the middle like birds in the air.

They made a fire and ate food from the sack and each lay down on blankets staring at the fire and talking. Simon's first question was about the cave, which he could not get off his mind.

"Let's not talk about the cave tonight," Susanne said. "In the morning is the best time, when we are rested and the sun is out. At night it is best to talk only about cheery things and pleasant thoughts and not try to figure out solutions to problems or ponder events that will take place in the future. My mother taught me that, and it works."

In the morning the sun was out, creeping slowly into the mouth of the cavern where they slept. It moved warmly from their ankles upward. They woke up when it had reached their eyes.

Simon could now see the cave clearly. It was much smaller than he had imagined, barely big enough to kneel in, he thought. Susanne watched him gaze doubtfully at the cave's opening and said, "Ok, Simon, shall we have a little breakfast and some juice and then talk about the fantastic trip we'll take today?"

As they were eating breakfast, Susanne told him first about the Highlands and only later about the way to get there.

"The first time I entered the Highlands, my mouth dropped open in disbelief, Simon. I had never seen such a sight in all my life, even in books and magazines. The way I felt as soon as I saw it was like I was having the most beautiful dream imaginable and didn't want it to ever come to an end.

"There is a waterfall just after you begin walking into the light, and behind that waterfall is a crystal mountain where lights of every color shine in all directions like thousands of rainbows all at once. And you walk towards them expecting to have to stop but instead you just keep walking right through it into the middle, as if there is a tunnel there. But it stays light and bright and rainbowy. You can feel it raise you off the ground as if you are on wings. You realize after a while that you have been coaxed into some other place entirely different, which is not where you began.

"When you realize this you must either relax and let go and just follow into the experience or else fight it and refuse to be taken over by it. If you can let it happen to you without needing to know why, just let go and be taken away, it will lead you eventually to the heart of the Highlands. There is a pink flower which grows there as thick as grass, even on the hillsides. The way you feel in the Highlands is like in your memory when you wish that you could go back to a moment in your past, a perfect moment, like maybe a fall day when you were raking leaves with your sister and laughing and playing and smelling them burn, and hot summer was gone and cold winter wasn't yet upon you. That's what the Highlands is every moment, that's the feeling you have there.

"But first, we need to talk about the cave. As you can see it starts out pretty wide, you can almost scrunch down and walk in it. But it gets narrower. Fortunately, about halfway to the Highlands there's a little room that you can stand up in and take a rest. I leave candles there so we can have some light, because we lose the light after a short while and even though we'll take the flashlights with us, it's nice to see a whole big area all lit up at once.

"The second half of the cave is a little tricky because not only does it curve and have different branches going off in different directions, but there are places where you have to climb upward until you find the correct entrance to move horizontally again. At that point rocks might occasionally fall, not big ones but annoying ones like rain. Once you've gone so far, there is no turning back, because the cave narrows down so you can just barely crawl and you can't turn around and you can't back out. You have to keep going. The only way to come back is to come back from the Highlands."

Simon walked out into the light at the entrance to the cavern. The valley below looked peaceful and calm. The sky above was blue. He told himself there could not be a place like she described, but he wanted it to be true. He wanted to find his father. He wanted there to be magic and a Land of Fathers and more than just what meets the eye.

"Okay, I'll go," he said to her resolutely.

She put her arms around him and hugged him and began to dance, turning him under her and kicking up her heels.

"Okay, here's a flashlight. Don't use it unless you have to, just follow me, I'll go first. Here, take some dried fruit and this bottle of water. I'll take some things too."

She scurried around and got together a bag of her own.

She took his hand and smiled, then stared at him with a serious look which made her seem older than she was. "Come on, Simon, I know that we will *find your father, okay. I promise. The Highlands will be like nothing you've ever seen."*

She ducked headlong into the dark cavity without even turning her flashlight on, still holding his hand, until after a while the cave became too narrow and she had to let go. Suddenly he felt panic at the darkness and the narrowness and the release of her touch. He almost said he was going back, but then he thought of the night in the forest and how it had felt just as bad at first but how it had all changed when he stopped feeling frightened. So he willed himself to concentrate upon the path and to visualize the middle room where he would get some relief.

For quite some time they crawled through the cavity in darkness on stony earth, their heads bowed down seeing nothing but blackness below and ahead of them. The earth smelled musty and wet. Whenever his mind jumped to a scary thought Simon brought it back into single focus upon his vision of the middle room.

At first he tried to talk to Susanne, but her voice was insulated by her body between them and he couldn't understand her, which created a feeling of loneliness. Now and then he reached out and touched her leg or her foot and she would slow down and drag that leg behind her, attending to his doubt, and then she would start out again.

Intermittently he turned on his flashlight just to be able to see her. The tunnel was packed hard with light brown dirt and aggregate stone, wet from years of ground water percolating through timeworn arteries. He wondered where it finally went, if there was perhaps a lake beneath them.

After what seemed like an hour to him, they were still not at the room. He motioned to her to stop and asked her how much farther and she yelled, "About as far as we've come." This was a setback for him. He stopped. Susanne moved forward relentlessly. He called to her but she didn't hear. He flashed his light on her but she didn't see it.

Eventually the same soft feeling came over him that had happened in the forest. He raised his face and reached down to adjust his knee straps, and began again to crawl forward. He counted his "steps" one by one until he reached a hundred and then he started over again. Again and again and again. Nothing was on his mind except the next number going to one hundred. Until he saw the circle of light ahead of him which got bigger as he approached it.

It was the room. The light was from candles Susanne had lit. She heard him crawling and approached the tunnel. She reached for his hand and pulled him into the room.

"By the time I realized you were no longer following me, I couldn't do anything about it. But I just knew you would get here, Simon."

He brushed himself off. His clothes and hers were wet from stale old water in the tunnel. His face was dirty, his arms scratched.

She brushed off his face with her towel and laughed and said, "You are now an experienced caveman."

He laughed with her. They hugged each other.

The room was small but cozy. Susanne had set up what looked like a bedroom with a small cot and some blankets on it. Even some books and magazines. He imagined she'd slept there at times. They sat down and took deep breaths.

"I got scared," he told her.

"What happened?"

"I don't know, I just felt like it wasn't going to end. I had panic."

"I should have talked to you a little about what to do if you get scared or feel lost, but I didn't want to startle you before we began. But you figured it out yourself. You did great! You are the only one besides me who has come back here."

"Really? No one else has been this far?"

"So you sound like you're willing to go on, Simon. Is that true?"

"I guess so, but you have to stay with me. I'm still not comfortable in there like you are. What's the second part like?"

"In some ways it's easier and in some ways harder. It's not as long but there are twists and turns and many places where you can go off and follow a tunnel in the wrong direction. I've got it memorized, but I have to concentrate pretty hard. It's like a puzzle. And there are two places where you have to climb up. We'll have to use our flashlights more, and we can't get separated."

Simon wasn't ready to submerge himself in darkness, so he asked her if they could have one more drink of water and sit for just another minute.

I needed a drink myself and stopped talking. The bedroom was eerie with silent attention focused toward me the actor alone upon the stage. I looked at Christiane and her eyes were wide-open, astounded-looking. I realized I'd been talking without a break, focused completely for a long time, thinking of nothing or no one else except the story that Susanne had told me twenty years before, overseeing thoughts and creations pouring from me like someone sitting idly by a reservoir being drained. It felt the way it did in surgery sometimes when everything - life itself – depended upon my ability to concentrate. Sometimes after finishing an operation, while cleaning up, I couldn't recall anything I'd just done because I had been so entirely focused upon the moment which had needed me. I'd loved that about surgery: it had created a tiny world of perfection which only I was in. It had sometimes felt as if I were dancing with my hands or sculpting alone, aloft, high above the stage upon which I was performing.

I looked at Simon. I realized what an odd intimacy we had established, I and this child whom I only knew as a destiny somehow wrapped with my own, whose mother, my new friend, was sitting behind us in the darkness.

"Do you like the story?" I asked him.

I was afraid he would not answer but would disappear and hide again. "It is a lovely story, Michael," he said in the charming accent. "Will you tell more of it?"

"I will tell you all of it, but I'm tired, Simon, and I don't want to tell it badly."

"Will you continue to tell it tonight until they reach the Highlands?"

I knew it was late, and I was tired, but I didn't want to lose the progress we'd made. He was sitting up, attentive, and I asked a favor of him in return.

"Yes, I'll finish that tonight. But will you do something for me?"

"Yes, I will."

"Tomorrow I'll return and finish the story, but would you have dinner with me and your mother?"

"Yes, I will."

"Good. Then let's go on."

"Can I ask you something first, Michael?"

"Oh course."

"Do you believe the story?"

I answered immediately, "Yes, I believe it. The story is true if you believe, just as the Land of Fathers is true if you believe."

"Then anything is true if you believe in it?"

"Yes. Anything is true if you believe in it."

Before Simon had a chance to ask the next question, I continued with the story:

They climbed into the cavehole on the opposite side of the room. Simon followed Susanne into the darkness as she moved forward, more slowly than before, knowing he needed her near him for assurance. At first she talked to him, but the sound of her voice, filtered through her clothing, hair, and body packing the tunnel, was dampened and deepened and flattened to a single tone without modulation. He could not understand her words but said nothing because her willingness to stay in touch with him was comforting.

Suddenly Susanne stood upright and reached back with her foot and touched him and yelled, "Now we go up. Hold on to my foot all the way."

He liked touching her foot and feeling her confidence. As he raised himself up vertically, suddenly it occurred to him that he was going to make it to the Highlands, where she said his father would be. A chill went down his head and neck and back.

It was hard climbing upward. They had to find crevices in the sides to put their shoes into and to hold onto with their hands. Being below her, rocks began to fall on him and bounce off his plastic hat like hail on a roof.

"I can't help it!" she yelled. "I'm sorry."

They climbed what seemed like fifty feet in the air. He wondered how they would get back down. At the top was a ceiling with several cave holes going into the side walls. She took the middle one which traversed horizontally again.

"Are you there?" she called to him.

"Yes!" he yelled back and grabbed her foot.

"We're getting close, Simon. I'm glad you're with me." Her voice sounded gleeful. He wished he could see her face. He could feel his own face flushing with satisfaction. He was not afraid anymore. He knew he would make it.

They crawled on faster and faster, almost in a gallop. Now and then she stopped until he touched her leg and then she scurried off like a rodent in its burrow. Again she stood upright and waited for him to confirm his presence. She yelled again that the tunnel would change to vertical, just before she climbed like a squirrel up the walls, deftly knowing where to put her feet in the dark sidewalls. He flashed his light behind her to find the footholds.

After a long climb upward, she unhesitatingly chose one of several holes and they climbed fiercely onward. Now without fear, with the goal just ahead, the same monotonous movements of crawling straight ahead in the darkness were no longer to avoid panic but possessed a calmness which seemed in itself gratifying.

The tunnel ended. It went right or left. She chose the right path which began a curving ascent rising gradually higher and higher which he could discern only because he became a bit winded. After a while, however, the tunnel seemed to be going both up and down, depending upon the attitude he took. He liked the uncertainty which gave relief to the unvarying pace of the crawl.

Just as he was beginning to wonder how much farther it would be, Susanne yelled, "There it is! There it is! The Highlands! We've made it!"

He couldn't see anything except her ahead of him, but his heart raced with certainty that they'd reached their destination.

The tunnel began to widen until it would accept them side by side, and together they saw the light ahead.

The circle of the cave's exit into the Highlands was a brilliant blue, tinted like a jewel of amethyst, like iridescent colored light filtered through a prism of transparent metal. He could feel its warm mediating attraction. They stopped simultaneously twenty yards from the mouth of the cave and leaned against the wall and stared at it.

Neither of them said a word. She held his hand tightly.

"This is it, Simon. This is the Highlands. This is my home, Simon. It is the only place where I can be who I am all the time and where things happen like they happen in my mind, like they are supposed to, and where everything makes sense."

Simon stared fascinated at the distant 7-colored chromatic light pass-ing into the mouth of the cave like a multicolored liquid. "It's beautiful," he whispered.

"This is the Highlands, Simon: The most beautiful place on earth. Well, not really on earth." She turned and hugged him. "You made it, Simon. You crawled through the tunnel and trusted that I would lead you here. You are a champion. No one else believed in me." She took his hand and said, "Let's walk into the light together. No more dark tunnels. Now we can see forever. But first I must tell you a few things, Simon, about this place.

"People don't get angry or jealous or compete with each other here. They don't hold grudges for things that happened in the past. That stuff just doesn't work here. I'm telling you this because if there was something between your father and you when he left or died or whatever he did, forget about it. Here he is exactly the person you wanted him to be. Remember that: The person you wanted him to be. You mustn't ask him about the past because if you do he will fade away like smoke. You must contact him here at this moment in the present and appreciate who you can see that he is. If he did things you thought were wrong or if you are confused about who he was to you or you to him or if you think he mistreated your mother or anything like that, this is not the place to bring it up. The Highlands is the place where the essence of each person is alive and obvious, not his faults nor anything else which the world and its demands put upon people. Do you understand?"

"I think so."

"I think you do too. The reason I know about this is because I came here to find my father too, and the first time instead of just being grateful that he was here for me, I began questioning him about lots of unpleasant things, and to my amazement he just disappeared. Now when I see him it is wonderful, because I don't feel the need to revisit those things from the past. They're irrelevant

because they are not a part of us anymore. They are also useless. They don't inhabit the people here.

"It's like this, Simon, which I understand now: We are all okay underneath, we are all good and kind and thoughtful. But we get hurt and we seek revenge or else we just withdraw or become so busy we never have to face up to our responsibilities towards each other. Well, the Highlands is where all people all the time are the way they are underneath, they've shed the other stuff that makes them mean or angry or hurt or whatever. So why try to contact those ugly things? They are gone...dead...they don't live here anymore. Do you see?"

"Yes, I see," he said.

"This is a magical place, Simon. No one believes in magic anymore, but you will see." She turned to the chromatic light-flooded exit, and said: "Is that magic, Simon, or what?"

I looked at my watch. It was past midnight. I was tired and not feeling so well now. For several days I'd been experiencing nausea and was worried about what it meant. I put my hand on Simon's head and told him we needed to stop for the night. I left them alone in the semi-dark room and walked to the living room and lay on the couch. I felt awful. The pain in my stomach was excruciating. I lay on the couch doubled up. When I heard Christiane coming down the hallway, I made myself sit up. I didn't want her to know.

She sat next to me on the couch. She looked beautiful, having spoken to her son for the first time in months. I loved the sound of her voice, the proper English wedded to the earthy Spanish. What a wonderful blending of sounds. She held my arm and stared at me with black bituminous eyes. "Thank you, Michael, for bringing Simon back to me. It's a marvelous story. I can't wait to hear more of it. It has us both on the edge of our seats. I felt like I was in the tunnel with them"

I felt as if I was going to collapse. I began sweating and felt hot and cold at once.

"What's happened, Michael? Is it the sickness?"

Indeed it was the sickness. It was the toxicity of my life oozing out, my suppressed memory of abandoned childhood, my sadness with my life, and my withdrawal from vulnerability. I knew, somehow, it had to be expelled with transcendent power.

CHAPTER 11

I am dreaming. I am sitting in a huge auditorium with grand chandeliers and high ornate curved gilt-edged ceilings. There are rows and rows of seats ascending to higher and higher elevations. I am at the top, sitting all alone. The splendor of the room is so majestic that I gaze incredulously around me for long moments before noticing the stage far below me. When I do I wonder why I've chosen to sit so far away, as if someone had placed me there.

The music begins. A pianist plays so sweetly gently that it almost brings tears and coaxes many images at once, flooding me with poignant recollections. The music surrounds me like clouds supporting luxurious favor up above the world.

I cannot see who is playing because the stage is so far away, but she is wearing a long velvety black dress laced in red which covers even her feet. I can see her body move in a oneness of syncopation with the music that she is creating. When not in contact with the piano, her arms and hands trace patterns slowly and sensitively above the keyboard, describing invisible sensuous circles, as if conducting their own performance. I am enthralled with her. I feel perfect. The sidereal sound in the golden theater. The aeriform ambrosial light. The isolation from the crowd's enchantment. The soft seamless roundness of a moment unsustainable.

I awoke. Morning light came into the plane from everywhere and bathed us in its yellow newness.

Mr. Seiler leaned against the plane's window, staring spellbound at the earth. His hands were angled to his forehead shading the brilliant sun. A few others looked out of the windows and many others slept. He looked like a child seeing the world from above for the first time. His head blocked the entire window.

I left my seat without him noticing and looked out another window and saw the huge city sprawling below. Far in the distance I could see what seemed to be the Elbe River and a myriad of waterways leaving it and threading throughout the near-river city. There was the Binnenalster, the inner lake, and outside of it the Aussenalster. I imagined sailboats upon them and huge ocean liners from all over the world there in Hamburg to transfer cargo and to pour their pleasure-starved stevedores into the cauldron of the city's indulgent nighttime. Even from far above I could see incredible activity at such an early hour. Indeed it looked like ants. What was Mr. Seiler thinking?

An older woman turned around sensing my presence and said to me proudly, "It is Hamburg."

My heart pounded in my neck from the sudden scary realization that the day I'd lived for was here at last.

I went back to my seat and watched Mr. Seiler, apparently frozen to his thoughts. I felt nervous for him too, wondering if he was prepared to see this place again which in a fortnight thirty some years ago had stolen his family and his life.

He had talked all night long. About Hamburg in his youth, the founding of Hamburg in 800 AD, its glorious history, his mother and father and sons, his wife, his business and his home, his friends, the character of the Hamburgers, the Port, the music and art and architecture of Hamburg, the Reeperbahn, Blankenese, the Fishmarket, the nearby town of Lubeck, the swans of Alster. Everything he could think of. I must have fallen asleep listening to him, for I could not recall him stopping.

I watched him stare and stare without moving for maybe twenty minutes. In some place of connection between us I felt his intense feelings as my own. A crescendo of emotion moved within me like an ocean wave to the shore, until at last I felt tears at the corners of my eyes.

The plane circled the city, probably to await a landing assignment, but maybe also in some other dimension of understanding and forgiveness to allow Mr. Seiler time to assimilate the city restored and to place back in his memory the buildings that were gone and to understand the ones which had replaced them, to let him know benignly that the war ruins and all of the other haunting reminders of the city he'd last seen thirty years ago were disposed of properly.

He finally turned to me and said, "Look, Michael, look!"

Mr Seiler was alive with excitement. It pleased me. I squeezed in next to him at the window.

"Over there!" he pointed. "See the water. From here it looks like a huge blue whale. See it?"

How could I miss the Binnen-Alster – the whale's head – and the Auben-Alster, the whale's body? "Yes, I see it, sir. What is it?"

"That, Michael, is the Alster. And at the top, to the northeast, is where our house was, in Uhlenhorst."

"It's beautiful there, green and peaceful. You can't tell that anything was ever damaged."

Mr. Seiler peered out the window again, and then he turned back to me and said, "I was up quite late last night, Michael, thinking about all that we talked about. Memories would not stop. My family, my life as a German and a Hamburg citizen, the question you asked me once 'Why do people do that to each other?' I thought about my life in the United States, the people I left behind here and of course the war. And I decided this, Michael: I don't want to spend my time here talking about the destruction of Hamburg. Not because I'm afraid of it, but because we have only two weeks here, and we have talked at length about it before. Let us enjoy ourselves and be happy. There's nothing we can do about the war except regret it and be shaken by its memory. I don't want that, for me or for you. You are my guest here in Hamburg. I want you to have a good time."

The bus let us out in front of the hotel. Instantly a dignified tuxedoed man requested our bags which he gave to another man. He asked Mr. Seiler our names and then led us to the check-in desk and asked, in English, "The rooms for Herrs Seiler and Langhen?" He was given a key and we followed him to the elevator which took us to our rooms.

Mr. Seiler went downstairs to talk to someone at the desk and I sat in a white high-backed chair with linen upholstery next to a window that looked to the Alster. The swans swimming caused me to finally think of Susanne with some concentration. I felt like pinching myself to see if what was happening was real.

The hotel was not too far from her father's office. His home, presumably hers too, was farther away, though, so I would have to wait to visit it. I tried to organize a plan in my mind. I was a bit surprised that Mr. Seiler had not mentioned Susanne again, because she was obviously the focus of my visit. Still, it was the first day, and there would be time. I knew he had not forgotten. I decided to be patient and let our visit unfold properly and not forget that although my purpose was to find

Susanne, Mr. Seiler was in his beloved Hamburg for the first time in over thirty years, and he had many things to do in order to restore his own world and repair his broken lines of communication.

Just being in the same city with Susanne gave me a sense of well-being, so that I did not feel hurried with panic to find her. In fact, I needed to introduce myself gradually to Hamburg and be accepted by the city a bit before I felt it would be proper to look for her.

Mr. Seiler returned to the room and told me in German that he was tired and would lie down now. I went to my room and lay down too but could not sleep. I slipped out the door of his room where he was sound asleep already, leaving him a note that I'd gone for a walk. I took the key he'd left on the table.

It turned out to be a splendid afternoon. I walked the whole distance from Planten un Blomen southwest through the park all the way to St. Pauli, almost to the Reeperbahn, then back through the city centre, past many old buildings which I had read about: Deichstrasse street, St. Katharinen, St. Nikolai, bridges built a thousand years ago, St. Michaelis church, the Borse stock exchange, and the magnificent Rathaus.

I didn't stop to examine anything carefully because I knew Mr. Seiler would be worrying about me, so I hurried back to the hotel. But I would see it all more closely later.

Chamber music was playing in the dining room of Vier Jahreszeiten. I looked through the doors and watched them play a moment, all dressed formally, dignified.

I turned the key slowly in the lock and opened the door to Mr. Seiler's room, gently and quietly. He was there beside the bed studying the telephone book. He looked up and greeted me and asked me where I'd gone.

"I walked to Planten un Blomen and down to St. Pauli and back through the centre city."

"My God, you must be exhausted!"

I realized that I was indeed tired and that I'd been operating on sheer excitement.

"Did you find your son's name in the phone book?"

"No, there's no listing for him, which doesn't surprise me."

"How will you find him?"

"Well, I'll go to where I knew him last to be. And then begin asking questions. Let's eat lunch, Michael."

We went back down to the dining room. The quintet was still playing Mozart and Schubert. The dining room was not crowded. We sat next to a window overlooking the water.

Like all things in this hotel the dining room was imperial. It was Edwardian style and, of course, palatial, with many fine antiques, old tapestries, gold-framed mirrors above porcelain cherubs.

We ate a luscious meal and listened to the gentle music of the clarinet and strings. It nearly put me to sleep at the table. Mr. Seiler laughed and said, "You go sleep now, Michael. The timeclocks of our bodies will take some days to adjust. But let's not worry about when they decide that it is time to sleep. No doubt we shall feel our peak of energy at three in the morning!"

He accompanied me to the room. He got his coat and hat and put a pen and paper in his pocket and said to me, "Now it's time for me to wander a bit in Hamburg, and time for you to wander in slumber. I might be gone a while, so you sleep as long as you want."

I said goodbye and he walked to the door and left.

I fell asleep and dreamed.

It was nighttime. Ahead of me was a street of carnival lights and cacophony, unnatural greens and reds, flashing lights with zigzag arrows and tawdry moving signs. Loud boisterous people prevailed. On both sides of the street they stood in doorways, reaching for me as I walked by, saying, "She is in here, come this way," while another said, "No, come here, she is here." I felt certain that one of them knew what I needed to know, whatever it was, but it was impossible for me to determine which one. So I kept walking past lanes and lanes of open doorways, alleys of darkness, past throngs of rowdy people, loud music and general confusion. Deep in the middle of this place, I felt lost and hopeless. I did not know how to return to where I'd entered or where to find an exit, so I wandered aimlessly, beckoned by unappealing women and vulgar men. Feeling lonely and desperate, I was prepared to choose whatever doorway called me next regardless of who stood in it.

That next doorway was quiet and dark with no music blaring from it and no garish lights or signs above it. Barely could I see the face of someone inside the shadows motioning to me to come in quickly, which I did. I was disarmed by the smell of her musky entrancing perfume. I heard the bangles on her wrist clink together as she reached down confidently in the darkness for my wrist and holding it walked ahead of me down a candlelit hallway to a descending stairway. I could see in the brighter light that she was gypsy-like, strong and lovely, with dark skin and long hair, wearing a deep red dress with a black and white checkered sash. She pulled me quickly behind her as if she did not want to give me a chance to think about where I was going.

The stairway curved like the stairs of a lighthouse, down and down far below the ground, spiraling around the circumference of a central cylinder.

The light became dim again until we reached the bottom, whereupon the mood became different. Hushed and peaceful, absorbent of sound. She led me across a dark green stone-tiled floor to a massive wooden doorway on the other side, flanked by heavy ornate antiques carved of black wood. She knocked gently upon the door, then let go of my hand and held hers beneath it as it fell to my side. She brushed the small of my back with her other hand with tender assurance, as if to say, "Don't be afraid," and then disappeared behind me noiselessly like a bird from a branch.

I waited by the door, prepared again to accept whoever came to it. But no one answered. I did not knock again. I waited and waited. Finally the door opened slowly and standing there in front of me was the most beautiful boy-child who looked like Susanne in ways and in ways like me. His tall body was lean and dark. His eyes were deep and knowing yet tender too. His cheekbones were high and angular. His lustrous black hair was combed across his forehead. I sensed that even though he was young, he understood the world in some mature way which made him older.

He turned and walked a few steps away from me and said softly down the hallway in a voice of affection and in German, "Mama, it's Michael. Come and see him, Mama."

Soon I heard her slippered footsteps shuffle down the hallway whisking the floor like handmade brooms. I felt profound excitement at seeing her again but was distressed by the sad slow compliant sound of her footfalls; energyless, unlike I remembered her.

But when she entered the room at last, it wasn't Susanne at all. It was someone else whom I had never seen. How did she know me? How did the boy know me? Why was I there? Who were these people?

"Hello, Michael," she said. She pointed to the boy. "This is your son."

"Hello, father," he said.

He must have been ten years old, but how could he be mine! I was only nineteen.

The woman walked toward me and took me by the shoulders and turned me toward the mirror on the wall. I was shocked! I wasn't twenty years old! I was much older.

"Where is Susanne?" I asked her.

She moved close to me as if proximity would facilitate understanding.

Then I was awakened by the sound of Mr. Seiler returning from his walk. I lay in the darkness of my bedroom and listened to him slowly move around the room outside of mine. I lay there motionless, waiting for understanding to emerge clearly from my muddled thoughts which had located me in two places at the same and different times, confused. The image of the boy, the woman, and the grotto-like room faded quickly, leaving a residual sense of reality, until I knew it had just been a dream and I had been asleep. It felt so real, so portentous, that I tried with all of my might to bring it back exactly as it had been. But I couldn't. It slipped away, as sleepthoughts do in the presence of consciousness.

I lay there a long time trying to apprehend the full import of the symbolic dream which brought back cascades of feelings I'd simply hidden from so long. Huge lonely craters of doubt and misunderstanding loomed in my mind at what seemed to be a crossroads of my thoughts.

CHAPTER 12

I was sick in bed for days, acceding to a foggy painful weakness. Humor, clarity, enthusiasm - all of the things of consciousness which make life enjoyable - were stolen from me, so that I was suspended in a middle world waiting distressfully for rehabilitation, mindless waiting for inevitable slow pardon to occur.

During that period Simon came to me and lent me his tenderness to help soothe the condition of my purgatory. I remember hearing his voice, his matchless manchild speech that comforted me throughout my self-disappearance.

Someone rubbed my head afternoons and nights – the worst times - either he or Christiane or both of them, finding, I recall thinking, the exact blueprints of my cerebral afflictions, kneading them with mercy in just the right places with just the right pressures, as if their hands were laser-guided.

The powerful yet gentle intuition that they both possessed in nursing me back to health made me think later of why I had loved medicine so much. At its best it partakes of the privileges of healing: to humbly behold the mission; to reverently accept the calling; to pay fealty to the power of resurrection that one is blessed to conduct; to expertly know how to translate the dialogue between intuition and knowledge.

Healing is a primal art form, the most necessary, the most basic. The power of it is the humbling irony that it is a gift and nothing else, like a powerful right arm or perfect vision or a voice that sings celestially. But it is the King of gifts.

———

After several days I awoke like a sleeping elephant, prepared to live again. It is a unique benefit of these episodes that when they are gone one has an experience of well-being unlike any other. Colors are a greater intensity, sounds contain an inner chamber of sensation usually reserved only for elite soundsmiths. Happiness inheres to all of life itself. Humor is in everything. Energy abounds. Enthusiasm returns as adolescent purity. I would take advantage of it.

When I finally arose, beside me was Simon sound asleep, purring like a kitten, curled foetally in his childmode. The healer, the healed. The child, the man. Which one was which?

I lay watching him, sunlight entering the room only between tilted slats of window blinds, projecting orderly rows of illumination onto the bed where he slept. A tear in the tape of the blind allowed the sun to shine an anomalous erratic pattern on Simon's shoulder like a bright abstract amulet.

Christiane came into the room with tea and morning cookies. Then Simon awoke. The three of us, like a family at a picnic, spread ourselves out casually on the bed and welcomed the new day, happy.

"How are you, Michael?" she asked me.

"I'm wonderful, like a new person," I said.

"Oh, I'm so glad. You were delirious, Michael. We were scared for you."

"You made me healthy again. I was aware of you doing it."

"We rubbed your head, Michael, first Simon and then me, and he brought cold cloths for hours to put on your head. He told you a story too, Michael."

"He did?"

"Yes, it was a lovely story. I think you liked it."

"I'm sure I did. What was it about?"

"Tell him, Simon."

Simon looked serious with huge black eyes and a formal face.

"It was not a story, really. It was more of a setting which I created for you to feel better. A beautiful theater like the ones in Germany and London where we went with my father sometimes to hear the most beautiful music. I played for you a piano piece from my mother's phonograph in the other room, the one I love the most, and turned it up so that you could hear it. And I described for you this lovely room and placed you high above in the top row where the sounds were prettiest and where no one else was near. It wasn't a story really, just a setting."

"What a wonderful and ingenious thing to do, Simon. I remember hearing it now, heavenly music which seemed to accompany your hands touching my forehead. I remember it. It was like sunshine penetrating darkness, like hope."

"I'm glad it helped, Michael. I was wishing it would."

"Thank you both for staying with me and helping me."

"You seemed to be in another world, Michael."

"Yes. They are bad, these episodes. Very frightening because I don't know what to do and have no power or will. They come from nowhere. I thought they had an organic origin. A tumor perhaps or a brain aneurism. Epilepsy or some other neurologic connection. But nothing tested positive. So my conclusion is: a wounded soul."

"Don't kid about such things, Michael. It can happen, you know."

"I know, Christiane. I know."

We lapsed into silence for a moment but only for a moment before Simon made his request.

"Do you feel well enough to continue the story you were telling, Michael?"

"So where were we?" I asked.

"They had arrived at the Highlands and Susanne had said, 'This is a magical place, Simon. No one believes in magic anymore, but you will see.' Then she turned to the colored light and said, 'Is that magic, Simon, or what?' and Simon said, 'Yes, it seems like magic to me.'"

I couldn't believe that he had remembered the exact words where we'd stopped. I sat quietly a moment to still the air for new thoughts and to meditatively prepare myself to tell more of the story:

Susanne and Simon sat staring at the entrance of light. Neither of them felt like moving.

"Do you know, Simon," she whispered and held his hand tightly, "the first time I came here and saw this I knew at once that this was where everyone wants to be, the spot of silence they retreat to, the picture they have of the future which will become wonderful, the nostalgic memories of their pasts. It doesn't matter here what is true. There's no such thing as true. It's so different here, Simon. The hardest thing about being here is leaving and going back to where they do all those stupid things all the time."

"Why do you leave, then?"

"You can't stay here, Simon. It's like this: you can come here for a visit, even a long visit if you want, if you are in need of a reminder of how things should be. But you have to figure out how to be permanently the same on the outside as you are on the inside before you can be inside permanently. It's like

you have to know already how to be the way that people are here before you can be a person here all the time."

"What do they do, just tell you to leave after they think you have been here long enough?"

"No, no. It's not like that, Simon. People don't act like that here. No, it just goes away."

"What?"

"The Highlands."

"You mean it just vanishes?"

"Yes, suddenly you just can't see it. You aren't here anymore."

"You're kidding! You mean you don't even have to go back through the cave?"

"No. If you're still here when it's time for you to leave, all of a sudden you're just back where you started. There are riddles here, Simon. You will be thinking about them for a long time"

"Let's go in," she said.

They moved through the entrance. It took his eyes a moment to adjust to the different light, but when they did Simon saw everywhere the most beautiful white and pink flowers hugging the ground and climbing the sides of the hills on rocks.

Then he saw the waterfall Susanne had mentioned. There was a path which led directly from the cave to it. The path was made of small stones all laid carefully side by side in mosaic patterns creating pictures of natural scenes.

"Are you ready?"

"I guess."

"You're ready, Simon. I know you are." She took his hand and moved toward the waterfall. Into it they went. It felt as if they were riding on the wind, on the back of a huge bird. The vapor of the falls drenched his face and tasted cold and earthen like well water. It swirled together into a rainbow mixture

of colors. He could sense the difference in textures between them, as if they had different identities. He thought to himself: 'How can this be happening. This can't be real,' and instantly he was standing before the waterfall again, holding Susanne's hand. He looked at her and she looked back with disapproval.

"You stopped believing, Simon. That's what happens if you stop believing. It ends. You were believing up until then. Let's go again. And this time...just let it happen, Simon."

"Where does it take us?"

"Who knows? You are in control. It takes us where you want to go."

"I don't know where I want to go."

"Maybe that's why it was like a roller coaster," she said laughing. "You don't need to 'know.' You just need to let yourself go. Yourself knows where it wants to go, just stay out of its way. Are you ready?"

"Okay."

They walked into the waterfall again, and again the air picked them up and carried them beyond their vision. But this time the water didn't blind them nor did the multicolors swirl. This time the ride was slow and steady and the direction clear, just above the treetops where the heather stopped blooming and the rare air stood still. This time the feeling was not phantasmagorical but fantastic.

"What a sight!" Simon yelled laughing with uncontrollable joy.

"It's the Highlands, Simon.

"Where will it take us," Simon asked her.

"How about to the Land of Fathers?"

"Yes, that's where I want to go."

"Then let's go there."

Birds were singing happily everywhere and Simon heard the sound of slowly moving water over rocks that caused a gurgling sound.

It was peaceful and quiet and nearly soundless. There were no engines. Morning birds cooed and crickets chirped as peaceful music could be heard coming from a nearby village. Sheep did graze, he saw, on the sides of heather-filled hills. Simon heard the music louder and saw it coming from a round six-sided stand. They stopped to watch ten musicians playing.

The village itself was spotlessly clean. The homes and cottages were charming, as if from a fairy tale. The streets were made of bricks and there were no cars anywhere. Everyone walked or rode a bicycle or a horse. There were no signs advertising anything, no telephone lines or commercial obstructions. The trees were full and round, providing wonderful shade. The temperature was perfect in or out of the sun.

Susanne said, "You wait here, I'll be back."

When she returned she was with a handsome man with a beard and a long-sleeved red and black shirt. She was holding his hand as she approached Simon.

"Simon, this is my father, Jacob."

Simon scampered out of his chair and stood up.

"I'm very happy to meet you, sir. You have a beautiful town here. I couldn't stop listening to the music they are playing."

Jacob leaned over to him and whispered, "Only a few of them ever played music before they arrived here. But all of them had wanted to play, and that is all that is necessary – just to want to play. It's true that some people have greater natural talent than others, but it's not true that all people cannot be good musicians.

They walked through the enchanted village of white picket fences and delightful residences. At the outskirts of town they followed another stone path between two short walls. That path went down a hill and up another and there at a plateau in the middle of the next hill was a magnificent structure made of stone, half-completed, several men at work constructing it.

"*Is that the archives building you told me about?*" Susanne asked.

"*Yes. Where we'll keep our records and histories of who is here and where they are. Also a research library and reading rooms.*"

"*Sir,*" Simon said, "*Do you know if there is a man here named Johnathan Stillman?*"

"*Yes, I think so.*" Jacob went to a table behind him and opened a huge book. "*Here he is. He's only been here a short time. Is he your father, Simon?*"

"*Yes sir, he is.*"

"*I think I know who he is. He is the woodworker that everyone is talking about. Would you like to see him?*"

"*I think so.*"

"*He is making furniture in Oldham. Have you been to Oldham yet?*" Simon shook his head.

"*I can take you tomorrow if you like. It is just a short walk from here.*"

"*Why are they talking about him, sir?*"

"*Because he's making astounding things of wood and turning them out so fast no one can believe it. He is more like an artist than a woodworker, they tell me.*"

"*Yes, that's my father.*"

Jacob accompanied them on a small tour of the village and then took them to their rooms where they would spend the night, promising to meet them in the morning.

When Jacob left they talked. "*Simon, you look so glum? What is wrong?*" He was silent.

"*Simon, speak to me.*"

"*I'm afraid that if I speak I'll return to the waterfall.*"

She moved to the chair beside him and took his hand. "*Nonsense, Simon. You're not going back. You haven't done anything wrong.*"

"*I'm having bad thoughts,*" he said.

"About what, Simon?"

"About seeing my father."

"That's only natural. I had bad thoughts too when I first saw my father."

"But you said he disappeared as soon as you had those thoughts."

"No, not then. He disappeared when I confronted him about the way he'd treated my mother and some other things too. Because there was still poison inside of me. Until I started seeing things differently and letting my father be who I wanted him to be, not forcing him to be what he'd been. It's a matter of realizing that a person's potential is what is real and that what happened is gone now, has disappeared into time past."

Susanne put her arms around him. "Don't feel bad, Simon. You'll find your father. I promise you that."

The morning was bright and sunny again. The temperature of the air was perfect. Simon had slept a dreamless sleep from the time he laid his head upon the pillow until he awoke to the new day. He was full of energy.

Susanne's father picked them up and walked to Oldham town, past the Archives Hall being built and on beyond into rolling meadows and hillsides clung with heather and cattle grazing calmly.

"It feels old here," Simon said.

"It is old, Simon. Your father is working to restore the past. He's very gifted, they tell me."

As they approached the main street Simon could feel his father's presence everywhere and see the elegant touches of his hands. He felt the graceful wooden lamppost, examined the way that the tongues of the porch's handhewn woodboards joined the grooves of the next board to create the effect of a single piece of wood. Each swirl of the woodgrain of each board matched perfectly with its partner board on either side.

His father had shown him how to do this and how to recognize shortcuts craftsmen take. He had felt it was dishonest to do something imperfectly simply because most people could not recognize its inferiority. "One should use the standards of the greatest artisans to judge one's own work," he had told Simon. "That is how to become a great artisan too."

They walked on. No one was on the streets.

Everywhere he saw creations that looked old and stately, dignified, belonging to a time of architecture's artistry, but which he felt had just been created. They blended consonantly with the style and the character of this old town of Oldham, set in the peaceful valley and cradled in heathered hills.   Simon walked ahead anxiously in search of the next clue on the trail to discovery of his father. Susanne and Jacob slowed down and let him be drawn ahead by the enchanting possibility of self-knowledge.

In the middle of the empty town a door to a building stood open. He heard the sound of fine sandpaper on wood and the noises that cobblers make, and wood nails driven by a wooden hammer. His father did not use metal with wood. It spoiled it, he'd said. Like a splinter lodged in flesh, the wood becomes pained and withdraws from the nail. But wood on wood creates harmony, bringing woods together in the same key, so that two woods together embrace each other and become one in healing.

He walked into the open doorway while Susanne and her father stood away and watched and gave him freedom. The light in the main workshop was intense, natural, flooding in from skylights and open windows.

He saw his father's back, leaned over from his aproned waist, applying pressure to the piece that he was working upon. Simon looked around and saw his father's creations everywhere. Finally, he thought, he's found a place where he can pour out his gifts upon the earth and open the floodgates within him that he had kept closed.

There were huge ornately finished wardrobes, rocking chairs, desks, cabinets, cribs, every furniture imaginable. There were sculptures of individuals and whole groups of people captured in moments of their lives: a mother holding a baby, a father chopping wood, a child playing and laughing, a family at dinner, a congregation at prayer. And also abstract concepts and ideas in wood whose meaning was inherent in their beautiful design and craftsmanship.

Simon sat down across the room and inhaled the fresh woodshop smells he'd loved and missed, the warm perfume of fresh cut wood.

As his father turned to place a piece he'd finished on the table behind him, he saw Simon. He stopped. They both froze. For an instant time past and present flowed between their sets of motionless eyes, as if a spiritual transformer had first to step down the voltages between them so that they could interact together in a new force field.

"Simon, is that you!"

"Yes, father."

His father's face changed gradually to reveal the feelings taking hold of him, like ice melting slowly in the presence of a flame.

He walked fast to his son and without hesitation put his arms around him and picked him off the floor and kissed his cheek as if he were an infant.

"I've missed you, Simon! I've missed you sitting silently with me in my shop watching me work. I've missed your eyes upon me making me want to do my best for you. You were my inspiration."

The two of them stayed embracing tightly. Simon smelled the crumbs of fresh-scraped wood entangled in the shirt fibers on his father's shoulder and the dust of woodwork on his neck and hands and in his days-old beard.

"I hoped you would come here, Simon."

"I told mother I was going to find you. I met a magic girl who brought me here. Her father lives here too. Are you doing this work alone?" Simon asked his father.

"No, I have help, I am the architect and also a worker."

"Have you been here long?" Simon asked.

"I don't know, Simon. It seems that I've always been here. Time's not the same here; it has no feeling the way it does outside. It doesn't feel urgent or delayed or as if it's run out or taking too long or any of those notions. We do what we do with a different commitment. Time is not a prison guard here. Time is not a yardstick or a line that stretches forward and backward with memory or anticipation. It's is not a measurement of accomplishment or failure. It is not a boundary at all. Time doesn't rule us here. Simon, help me finish this piece I was doing."

They went back to the shop and his father pulled another chair beside his for Simon to sit upon, and he started to work again. He explained to Simon what he was doing and how to do it, and then he handed him the beautifully crafted piece of wood he'd been working on and said, "Okay, you finish it, and I will get ready for the final operation. Then I'll show you how to do that operation too."

His father had never even let him enter the shop unless he was there to supervise. He'd never been allowed to touch anything. He was uneasy.

"Don't be afraid, Simon," Johnathan said, "You know how to do it now. Just do as I explained. Don't think about it. It will work out fine."

Simon took the small carving set his father had put beside him and chose the tool his father had advised. He had watched his father work with wood many times, for hours, so the skills to do it himself must be in him somewhere, he thought.

His hesitation at first led to crude mistakes. His father patiently explained what Simon had done wrong, and then said this to him: "Don't let your mind and hands act separately, because if you do your mind will win and your hands will follow. But your hands already know what to do because your mind has told them previously. Your mind will be like a meddlesome parent, however, if you let it be. So only let it be the silent invisible template in which your hands work faithfully."

Simon went back to work and let go of his fear and his expectations of himself. He created superb work. Upon finishing a piece he took it to his father and beamed with pride when his father said, as he did each time, "Perfect!" or "Fantastic!" or some similar shout of the highest approval.

The day slipped by like moments. His father taught him the other operations involved to complete the project. He'd never known his hands were so capable.

When the sun was setting and the workday was done, and the project was complete, they sat together at the workbench admiring their co-creations. Simon had never been in the presence of his father with such a feeling of pride, accomplishment, and equality.

As his father cleaned up and prepared to go back to the village, Simon walked around the shop looking at the pieces his father was working on or had completed and admiring their quality. The door to his father's office was open and the light was on. He went in. He noticed a sculpture behind the door covered with a sheet. It was not wood but clay. While he was staring at it his father came in.

"Is this something you are doing for yourself?" Simon asked.

His father didn't answer but instead lifted the veil from the sculpture.

It was a bust of Simon's mother. He'd never seen his mother more young and beautiful, sylphlike. Her eyes were untroubled and compassionate and her smile was brilliant like sunshine. Her hair was elegant and flowing and lustrous. He felt it to see if it was real.

"This is Mother as you see her?"

"That is Catherine as she is."

Simon couldn't stop staring at the sculpture. New understandings and new questions came into his mind at once. He finally spoke:

"Why did you leave us, father?"

Suddenly the lights flickered, as if he'd closed his eyes for just a second.

He was at the waterfall again. He sat down, stunned, on a rock outcropping. He put his head in his hands and took a deep breath.

"Oh, no. Where is Susanne?" All that he could hear was the rumble of his own dark thoughts admonishing him. Fear swelled in his head, leaving him powerless.

He looked outward. Even though it was getting dark, the sunset was glorious. The last birds of the day were singing farewell to the sunlight. The reflection of the yellowness of day's end from the pink and white heather on the hillsides created a greenish color to the atmosphere that made him wish it would last forever. It was a beautiful spot to be. There was nothing threatening.

Certainty came to him in the form of Susanne's image. He knew she would figure it out and come back for him.

Nighttime came but the earth retained its heat. Simon folded his jacket into a pillow and leaned against a sunwarmed log and looked up at the sky growing dark.

Just as he was falling asleep, Susanne appeared and sat down beside him and stroked his hair gently.

"I knew you'd come back for me, Susanne."

"And I knew you'd be here, Simon."

"Do you want to go back to the Land of Fathers?" Simon asked her.

"We can't go back, Simon."

"We can't?"

"No, we can't."

Simon nodded apprehensively. He looked at her carefully, memorizing every detail of her face and her body.

"I know that you feel different about things than you did when I first met you, because of what you have seen. You know what believing can do now. Don't forget it, Simon." She took his two hands and said again, "Promise me, Simon."

He looked at her face. Strands of golden hair blew past her bottomless blue eyes. He held her hands tightly and whispered carefully and unequivocally to her: "I promise, Susanne." As he did, she leaned forward to him and kissed his forehead.

As if those times had never happened, as Highlands memories start to fade, he finds himself alone again in Pershing's Meadow, Halthing's glade.
The nightbirds chirp, the crickets chitter. Sky's agleam with starry night. The lake's breeze drifts the cattails' cotton. Alas, the world seems almost right.

CHAPTER 13

I got to know the boy and his mother together. Jointly they constituted a whole from which I later could not imagine being separated. I saw them both differently now, as if she was in him and he in her in indivisible proportions.

The three of us together in this lifeinstant were an unlikely but agreeable blend of child and adult. I had not known my own childness, just my adulthood. And Christiane was full of childlike innocence. Simon was both an adult and a child at once.

The window of time between the story that had awakened Simon, and my pilgrimage to Iquitos to retrieve my soul, was a time for me, and I think for them too, gratifying and full of happiness. The memory of it is a source of radiant inner light and love.

We wandered through Lima attending the restaurants, sampling the foods and drinks, laughing, and sleeping until afternoon. We went wherever our steps took us. To the richest spots of Miraflores. To the artist's colony of Barranco and the seafront village of San Isidro. To the sad poverty of the barriadas and the stark beauty of the seaside against the desert sand and treeless hills. The feeling of joy that I had in Peru at that moment in my life was indescribable. I was like a child, yes. But as a child I had never felt that way, so in a sense I was not reliving my childhood but living it for the first time backwards in a mode of adult-as-child.

We were transparent in trust and invisible to each other, permeable to love and to laughter, to sadness and to vulnerability.

I adored the music of Lima: sounds from stringed instruments I'd never heard before. Hand-carved woodwinds like flutes and clarinets together. Small guitars made of dried animal skins. Organ-piano-accordion sounds mixed, combined with saxophones accompanied by fascinating percussions. Instruments with names like sintetizadores, toyo, quena, charango, bajo, bateria, zampona, cromatica.

There was a song I kept hearing which claimed my attention for days and wove thorough my thoughts like an obsession. I hummed it and asked Christiane and Simon if they knew its name.

"It is 'El Condor Pasa.' It means 'The Condor Flies Over," she said.

"I love this song," I said. "It starts out like a church prelude and then becomes a proud march and then a battle and finally a glorious celebration of victory."

"The condor is the symbol of Peru. It is a magnificent awesome creature. In Macchu Picchu it flies over the mountains like an ancient Inca seer. To see it is breathtaking. Its wingspan is three and a half meters and it lives sometimes to be 30 years old and stays with its mate a lifetime. They fly like airplanes, 8000 meters above the earth, and soar in the deep canyons of the Andes. In the early morning, like 5:00 am, I've seen them fly like angels over the Colca Canyon in Arequipa. But now they're almost gone from this earth. There are only maybe a hundred of them left. I think that one should not pass from this life without seeing these magnificent creatures."

"Let's go to Macchu Picchu," I said.

Simon grabbed her arm and said, "Yes, let's go, Mummy. Let's go see the condors before they are gone."

She laughed. Simon laughed with her.

But I knew we would go to Macchu Picchu and see this glorious bird flying above us at the place where the holy Incas worshiped in the early morning sunlight. I felt it.

"Michael," Christiane said to me. "You just got up from your bed. You're still not well. I think it's time for you to look after yourself and begin planning our trip to Iquitos and seek healing."

"But Christiane, you yourself said one must not leave this earth without first seeing the condor fly over –'El Condor Pasa.'"

She smiled back at me. "No. One should not, it is true. But you have not left this earth yet. There is plenty of time before you do."

"But Iquitos may remove me from this earth."

"Iquitos will not remove you from the earth, Michael. But it will show you how to soar high above it with the condors, so that on the ground they'll point and say, 'Michael, El Condor, pasa.' They will say, 'He must have been to Iquitos to learn how to have such a great wingspread!'"

We began our journey to Macchu Picchu the following week. I had been to the Rocky Mountains as a boy and remembered the gradual ascent into them which later had yielded a magnificent view of the Continental Divide. But in the Andes it seems as if one goes from sea level to twelve thousand feet instantly. And in no time one is viewing 360 degrees of the world at once.

We took a bus from Lima to Matucana and from there we took mules on a romantically ridiculous few miles to the next mountain village. From here we took an unbelievably crowded bus to Huancayo, whereupon Christiane persuaded a man to drive us to Cuzco, near Macchu Picchu. I would learn that Lima was the capital set up by Spain, but Cuzco was the Inca capital. They were nothing alike.

The trip by mule, while quaint, was unbearable. We stopped every few minutes to rest.

On the top of the Andes is the most glorious view imaginable. There is the desert and the ocean to the west and towering snow-capped mountains to the east, the tallest in the world outside of Asia. There are nearby gigantic precipices of granite rising almost perpendicularly for thousands of feet. Beyond that is the Amazon rain forest.

We saw huge gorges and narrow valleys, some with rivers and streams. Hidden always on the side of uninhabitable cliffs were tiny dwellings with paths going straight up and down the mountains. With the scarcity of oxygen at that altitude it was amazing anyone could do more than just sit quietly all day long without talking.

The trip took us days. Our driver's name was Tingo Chico. He knew people everywhere and had to stop constantly for a variety of reasons. We spent whole mornings or afternoons on porches or in houses of strangers who spoke languages that even Christiane had never heard. But in some mysterious way we were friends with them by the time we left hours later, laughing and embracing. Tingo was a great ambassador.

By midday, Tingle, as we sometimes called him, needed to stop frequently for what he called "chicha" (home brew) at a pena or bar. However, they were not really penas but houses belonging to his mountain friends. By nightfall, sometimes before, he was asleep in the back seat with his head on Simon's lap snoring while Christiane or I drove over the barely visible roads on the crest of the Andes.

The nighttimes were otherworldly. I felt like an astronaut above the earth in a rare ether between two worlds. I drove or Christiane drove and we talked about everything and anything. Talking openly and transparently to a dear person in a location such as this is intoxicating. At the end of these evenings when we lay down somewhere to sleep I felt as if mental garbage in my life had been purged or cleansed. As if I was detoxified of debris impeding my life's free expression. Made whole again.

An addiction took place between me and Christiane whereby we could only experience this invigorating freedom in the presence of each other. We craved it. Simon was the catalyst that needed to be present for this experience to take place. It was heady.

The mountain night air was cool and brisk so we put our blankets together and lay as one with our arms around each other. I told her how much she meant to me and how momentously my life had changed for the better since knowing her.

She kissed me. Amorously. I felt a deep affection for her at that moment but I could not go on.

"I must tell you something, Christiane." I had never told this to anyone. "I am impotent. I have only made love to one person in my life. To Susanne. I have never had a relationship of love with anyone else since her. It is true what the woman told me: something inside of me is impaired. It is part of why I am here – to find what is lost, the thing for which this is a symptom. I care for you, Christiane. I have feelings for you, but I can't express them that way. Please understand and continue to care for me."

She caressed my forehead with the fingers from both of her hands at once and assured me: "It's not a problem for me, Michael, because it is not the reason I care for you."

We fell asleep face to face with our bodies close, breathing each other's breath.

I awoke to a smoke smell of fire-blended woods and frying foods. Potatoes and onions and meat. Tingo was showing Simon how to cook. Simon was crouched low over the fire, pointing and speaking quickly in Spanish. Tingo was gesturing like a man of the stage.

The day began slowly. Most of my days in Peru began this way. It was an entirely different way to live than the way I'd lived, pursuing precise goals with tight schedules. This way the days were fuller and longer, without the segmented, metered effect that mini-schedules and goals impose. Pleasure was richer. One was never quite sure what the goal was or even if there was a goal. Enjoyment was not something that accompanied achievement but the fabric of each day of life itself. It was simple, as it should be. I felt as if I had discovered a temporal treasure which most of the people I'd known were not aware of and would not have known how to acquire. It was usually the simple people with nothing who possessed it, I discovered. Ironically, I felt possessive of this truth, which was not even mine yet and which, like all truths, cannot be possessed exclusively.

After breakfast Tingo drove us back to Huarocondo and on to a town called Oliantaitambo. He stopped the car and told us to get out and follow him. We walked behind him quickly for a long time. Then he climbed a large rock outcropping and went to the top of it and sat down.

It was an unobstructed view of forever. There was no trace of civilization, only mountains and forests as far as one could see. He sat quietly a long time and we knew that we were not to speak either. The morning cool air and warm sun, the azul sky, the night's rest and the morning's breakfast, along with the enduring noble sense of our mission, raised the moment to a splendor which we all sensed would be broken with speech.

Finally Tingo said to Christiane in Spanish, "Este es el lugar donde condor viene por tranquilidad. Espera que el llegara." She translated for me: "This is the place where the condor comes for peace. Wait and he will arrive."

We sat for a long time in silence and then Tingo put his hand on my knee gently and squeezed and smiled at me pointing: "Miro! El condor pasa."

Suddenly I saw it. A condor floating effortlessly like a hanging dirigible, banking gently into the wind changing directions. It looked like a huge prehistoric glider held up by equal forces from above and below, a slow graceful old dancer dancing on the invisible floor of the sky.

We all watched it speechlessly, agape. And then it disappeared, as if Tingo had asked it to become present just an instant for us, his friends, to see. We sat a few moments in silence waiting for its return, and then he stood up and said, "Vamos."

"Isn't he coming back?" Christiane asked him.

"No," he said. "You'll see him again." And he walked back to the car.

How bewildering, I thought. I got up and followed him and so did the others.

"There is another way to Macchu Picchu," Tingo spoke, with Christiane translating. "We can avoid Cuzco and go directly to Macchu Picchu. We will arrive before others come, at sunrise, and you can be alone and watch the condors. We can go to Cuzco after that, if you want."

"He says that it will be a little difficult to climb, but it's worth it," Christiane said to me. "He likes us, Michael. He doesn't have to do this. He could earn his money and go home. He is showing us something that no tourist knows, only knowledgeable mountain people, and they don't share things easily."

"I'd like to do it, but are we prepared for climbing?"

"Yes, yes," he insisted and enthusiastically began driving in a new direction, taking us off the well-traveled road and eventually into a jungle thick with glorious orchids and tree ferns and amazing voluptuous beauty.

Macchu Picchu is the lost city of the Incas. It was not discovered until 1911, although for five hundred years adventurers had searched for it by the name of Vilcabamba. They knew there was an Inca refuge of the royal family somewhere in the Andes above Cuzco in the valley of the Urubamba River and hoped to pillage its golden treasures. But what they found always were impenetrable jungles, uncrossable waters, and sheer unclimbable cliffs, in addition to poisonous snakes and pestilence.

In 1534 the Spaniard, Francisco Pizarro, an uneducated, greedy, brutal thug by all accounts, conquered the Inca empire which numbered thousands of people, with only a few hundred soldiers. He was able to effect this coup because the Incas were gentle, peaceful, and trusting people whom he deceived and ambushed. He did it with rifles, which they didn't have, at a supposedly peaceful meeting the Inca leaders had called to resolve an issue between them, namely what to do about the priceless artifacts which the Spaniards had been stealing from them.

The secret mountain city of Macchu Picchu, shrouded in fog and obelisk mountains and beautiful beyond description, to which the Incas fled from the Spanish conquerors, was the only thing the Spaniards did not steal, because they never found it.

I quickly saw why. There were granite cliffs with snow-capped peaks rising vertically for thousands of feet above the roaring Urubamba River and beside it the dense forests of the Amazon.

"How can we possibly climb that," I said pointing to just one of the huge monolith mountains all around us.

"Tingo can do it," Simon said, "I know he can." Then he spoke to our guide in Spanish and they laughed and Christiane laughed too.

"What is it?" I asked.

"He says: 'It is very simple: you just have to change yourself into a condor!'"

We were able to drive the car surprisingly far along a dirt road at the base of a mountain. It eventually ended, though, and we began walking. I was also surprised that the path was well-worn since there was no other sign of life. The ascent along a line separating two mountains was gradual and winding and went in and out of dense forest where we lost sight of where we'd been and were going. Everywhere there were creatures, insects I'd never seen before, and at one point flies were thick as a cloud. Glorious flowers bloomed beside other glorious flowers – poinsettia, bougainvillea, climbing roses, and tropical trees – in an orgy of attractiveness.

Tingo carried the water, I carried the food. We had to stop frequently for one or the other. We didn't say much, perhaps not wanting to know much.

Tingo had become a spiritual part of us and melded with the vaguely-understood purpose of our mission.

We walked a long time and then the path opened up into a clearing and Tingo stopped and waited silently a moment. Just beyond the clearing was a small house made of stone where people obviously lived. We stopped again and waited until a man came out of the house, and upon seeing Tingo, came to him quickly and embraced him warmly. They spoke in Quechua and occasionally he referred to us by gesture. Finally they came over and Tingo introduced us to his brother. He was small and strong but with a delighted look of tenderness and mischief on his face. He shook my hand weakly but held it a long time. We went inside the house and had something to drink and the two men talked while we were silent.

After a while Tingo explained to us that his brother had two mountain mules which he would loan to us in order to reach the summit beyond which was Macchu Picchu. Essentially it was like entering the city from the back, the west instead of the east. The usual way was to come over the suspension bridge from Cuzco and by way of the "Great Speaker," the Apurimac River.

At the summit, Tingo explained to Christiane that we could camp until early morning and then reach Macchu Picchu shortly after sunrise.

Simon took my arm and held it up and said, "I'll ride with Michael."

We gathered the things together that we would need, including blankets for nighttime, and were off within an hour. Our mule had a saddle with stirrups which Simon let me put my feet into as he wrapped his arms and legs around mine, which helped me to tolerate the bumpy ride. But what helped even more was the whole sense of being in a place that was first of all truly ineffably beautiful. And sharing it with only a small group of dear people. And also the hallowed feeling of being in the midst of a whole ecosystem belonging to just the animals and plants which made it up. We were not even their guests but trespassing upon their reality, so it was with a deep sense of responsibility and even reverence that we all proceeded. And even a certain fear that our trespassing would not be allowed.

As we climbed higher we could see more in the distance. Sometimes I thought I was hallucinating because the colors of the faraway mountain ranges were seven or eight shades of blue and then different shades later. The patterns of erosion through the ravines created shapes I'd never seen, on which were flowers or cactuses growing haphazardly, as in a lunar landscape. There were ancient trees with snarled, exposed roots as big as the trunk, growing in rocks and spreading out tentacles for twenty feet or more to find water. There were cliffs thousands of feet high and the powerful Urubamba River rushing less and less noisily the higher we climbed. At one point we were above a valley of iridescent green fields and wild potatoes which bloomed on the side of the mountain next to bamboo trees with parrots in them. It was like a travelogue painting of all the beautiful scenery on earth at once, irrespective of logic. Being untouched by humanity it also felt surreal because, ironically, it was haphazard and random, unorganized and unexpected. Just beyond this warm inviting almost pastoral scene was a gorge of desolation, lonely and lifeless and unapproachable, another contribution to the canvas of eternity.

Night was approaching. We were tired in a nice way. The mule ride required our bodies to constantly change centers of gravity in order to maintain balance and continually required us to use atrophied muscles. But also it was tiring to endeavor to take in with our eyes all of the astounding, ever-changing beauty available throughout each moment of our ride and at the same time keep our balance. And then, it was even more special for me to have Simon holding me tightly, believing I would protect him like a father.

Tingo pointed above us and said something to Christiane in Spanish which I understood. I was becoming literate. He said it is not much farther before we stop. Just above us.

I looked below us. I realized I could no longer hear the river except as a vague whisper. I could barely see it. We had ascended what looked like miles by interfacing between mountains which shared the Urubamba valley.

We finally reached the resting place in the late afternoon. The sun was low and with diminished late day light shining into our faces. Our dormitory was a dug-out flat area inside of the mountain that provided plenty of room for all of us to sit and also to comfortably lie down. We ate.

The sunset was an amazing story in itself, including all of the wavelengths - Indigo, violet, blue, and green - mixed in strange unforeseen permutations of the sky's palette, changing all the time, like a kaleidoscope. We ate silently, recognizing the moment's tranquility. The external world and our internal worlds seemed united in a collective moment of mediation.

After a while, I looked over at the others in the unutterably translucent amazon light of night. I realized that the Great Speaker had fallen silent. All of them except Simon were asleep on the floor of the mouth of the mountain, bathed in the light of the moon. I covered them with their blankets. Simon's face was placid, as if he were being kneaded, but he was alert.

"I miss my father, Michael," he said sadly. "All the time."

We both stayed silent, and then he said this: "Why do you think he took his life, Michael?"

I was shocked. I didn't know what to say to a young boy about to fall asleep on top of a strange mountain, having just told me his father committed suicide.

He was quiet then. I sensed that he would give way to slumber the way children can do instantly. It seemed like an empty place to end the night, so before he drifted away I said to him, "I don't know, Simon. But, Simon, I love you. We can talk about it tomorrow, okay?"

When the child was asleep a few quiet moments later, I walked to the mouth of our mountain nightroom and sat on a lip of rocks to stare at the unbelievable South American panorama. There was Bolivia over there. There was Brazil. Somewhere within view the Amazon River, rolling tirelessly to the Atlantic, justified its million species' will to live through its own inexorable quest for the sea. Iquitos of the night reached out its subtle command to me to bring forward in time by dark passage, a new awareness. Somewhere where Andes mountains encountered rain forest, at that black edge of history's blend into formlessness, there the present changed back into the past to re-claim a greater purpose and to re-enact a higher form of being.

The air smelled fragrant like roses or oranges or lemons. I turned back to look at this group banded together somehow for my sake alone, lying innocently asleep at the top of the world under the aegis of a phosphorus moon. Yes, indeed, they loved me. Why was I so lucky?

Trust was upon their sleeping faces, resplendent in purity and goodness without guile. Suddenly a line came to me from the poem "Macchu Picchu" by the Chilean poet, Neruda, whom I had read intently before leaving for South America. It was written for this moment:

And the air came in with lemon blossom fingers to touch those sleeping faces...

CHAPTER 14

It was still dark when Tingo woke us up. We walked on the moon-lighted path whose gradual ascent changed abruptly vertical around daybreak.

We had to stop frequently. Tingo often bounded ahead of us and then returned to tell us what was coming. Eventually we reached the backside, the northwest side of Macchu Pichhu. It was still quite early in the morning and the sharp mountain peaks surrounding the ancient city had pierced the eerie fog lying low above the clear vacant city below. Occasional rays of sunlight focused circles of light upon the stone city, which looked like theatre stages. It would not have seemed out of place to suddenly see Inca actors step into the spotlight and re-enact the dramas of 1500 A.D.

In traveling to ancient cultures one is often struck by the feeling of the past and the present, side by side. However, in Macchu Picchu I was struck by the past and the present together as one. I could not separate them in my mind or in my feelings. The city, though dead, was still alive. Though hushed and unused, it still felt vibrant and pur-poseful. Not just a spirit was there but indeed a spirit which still took breath and was over the land there like a countenance impossible not to perceive.

My feelings were confirmed later in the morning as tourists filed into the holy city. Upon entering, they stopped. They stared. They grew silent. "What is it?" I could see them ask themselves. I sensed that some of them might have felt it appropriate to lower themselves to their knees in reverence as if in a church or to take their shoes off as if in a Buddhist temple.

But on this early morning we were there alone, a group coalesced perhaps by predestination. How else to explain our unlikely union? With a similar veneration, we wandered together and separately throughout the city. I watched the realization come over Simon that this was a sacred place indeed which esteemed the life that once was there.

"These are houses," he realized. "People used to live here. What happened to them?"

I explained the story of the Incas and the Spaniards.

"Which one am I?" he asked.

"Which one do you think you are?"

"I speak Spanish, but I am Inca."

I had a diagram of the city in my pocket that I'd torn from my book in Lima the night before we'd left, and Simon and I walked through the organization of the city, starting with the formal entrance to the Lower City. The location of Macchu Picchu, as beautiful as it was, was obviously chosen for defense. Even though we had come to it by a back route, that route would have been not only inaccessible to an invading army but also easily defended, offering obvious visual warning from afar. Actually, there was only one formal entrance to the city and it was protected with formidable resources. First were retaining walls, then a dry moat, then heavy wooden gates. Everywhere else there were sheer granite walls falling thousands of feet to the Urubamba River.

There were many private dwellings and also public buildings, all exhibiting Inca stonework still unparalleled anywhere on earth. The massive stone blocks, weighing thousands of pounds, were fitted together so precisely (without mortar) that not even a knife blade could be inserted between the joints. The dwellings were windowless, also to protect against invasion.

Beside the formal entrance were long irrigated terraces for growing food. They and the city itself were irrigated from a central aqueduct which fell sixteen steps, thus irrigating and providing water to every place in the city needing it. In essence, the Incas of five hundred years ago had running water.

There was the main Temple, the Temple of The Three Windows, the Inti-huatana (Hitching Post of The Sun), the Sacred Plaza, and the Huayna Pucchu or Watchtower.

We walked with our map to the Upper Level with its Mausoleum and cemeteries. Beyond that was the south wall and beyond that the outermost wall from which we viewed the splendor of the Vilcabamba Cordillera mountain range way off in the distance.

I sat down with Simon to rest. He was moved by Macchu Picchu, I could see. It had touched something within his soul, as it had also touched my soul. I asked him how he liked it.

"It's quite lovely, Michael. I can feel something here which feels like - what should I say? - it feels like the people are still living here and have just left for a while but will be coming back. I feel like I should not touch anything because it is like being in someone else's home. I like it here, Michael. If I had been an Inca, this is where I would have lived. My father would have loved it here, Michael. I wish he could be here with us."

"Maybe he can be here with you, Simon. Maybe he is with you now. Maybe you just need to learn how to find him, the same as Simon in the story did." I wished more than anything at that moment that I had the power to transport him to this world of dreams and hopes and reality as true as it was fanciful. I could tell the story, but I could not provide the wings.

I put my arm around his shoulder and we walked back to the view of Vilcabamba Cordillera where Tingo and Christiane were sitting on the wall talking in Spanish. The sun was behind us illuminating the near mountain spires and raising the fog back into transparency, like a sheet lifted up from the bed of the arisen.

We did not interrupt the others' conversation but instead went off to a rock formation a little to the east but still in view of them. Their Spanish voices provided a pleasant background sound to my thoughts which focused upon the odyssey I had taken from a very orderly and predictable life as a doctor in North America, and the things incumbent with that role, to sitting privately at morningtime in the ancient city of the Incas, contemplating magic. I was astounded at the changes that had taken place in me in a relatively short time. I remembered the psychic woman telling me that my journey would be hard, not painful as much as hard because I would have to change myself radically in order to bring about the conditions for my own health. I had done that to some noteworthy extent.

As I was recounting to myself the steps which had led me to this moment, and as the boy sat beside me deep in his own thoughts, a small shadow encompassed us as if the sun had gone behind a small cloud. Quickly it grew larger. I turned and looked up and just above our heads some fifty feet in the air was a giant condor floating like a helicopter, its wings spread out full like a canvas tent. The tips of its white feathers beneath its roof of wings twitched slight adjustments to maintain equilibrium, while its feet paddled the air powerfully for uplift. I could see its fearsome head and beak and sense its arrant eyes aimed upon us as if we were its prey. My skin tingled with a sense of the supernatural.

I heard Christiane scream warnings in the distance but I could not take my eyes from the condor, not entirely because I was afraid of him but also because I was entranced by something other than his ferociousness. He seemed to hover above me, seemingly hoping I would comprehend the meaning of his presence.

I was overwhelmed by the sheer size of his nearby airborne presence and reached out to touch his foot, something I ordinarily never would have done. I heard the others yelling from afar but I was so focused upon the bird that it was just a gaggle of noise unable to affect me. I knew intuitively that this ornithic warrior was not there to hurt us. I stood upon the rock to get closer but still I could not touch him. I reached for Simon and picked him up on my shoulders. The bird could not keep his stable position any longer and flew away. To my shock, however, he came back to us after gaining control of his flight and returned to Simon's outstretched hand, hovering awkwardly above it, ratcheting down slowly with his massive wings beating the air erratically while pumping with his feet, creating vacuums and torrents of wind forces that nearly blew us over, until his talon finally touched Simon's finger and then my own for just an instant. Then he flew off.

I expected his claw to feel thorny and rough and repulsive, but on the contrary it was soft and warm like a finger or a palm. For just a moment he had wrapped his claw around my finger in what felt like assurance.

I put my arm all the way around Simon's shoulder, touching his chin with my hand. I pulled his ear close to my lips and whispered, "Maybe that was your father."

Christiane ran up to us, terrified, yelling, "Are you crazy, Simon? You could have been killed! That condor could have grabbed you and taken you up into the sky and let you fall to your death!"

"He would not have done that, Mummy. That was not why he came here."

"Simon, my God, what are you saying! They do that all the time to small sheep and animals. They are predators! You are their food!"

"I was okay, Mummy. Michael knows, ask him."

She turned to me with an angry look. "You should know better than that, Michael. You're a doctor. Use your head! These birds are nothing to play with!"

I saw Tingo behind her, his face showing a look which told me that he too had recognized communication between the bird and the boy. In his world I knew it was not regarded as abnormal for one to think that such relationships exist. However, the instinct behind Christiane's anger was protective motherlove, which could not afford to experiment with the possible special relationship between a vulture and her small son.

She pulled him away by herself and talked to him with great seriousness. I hoped he would not tell her we suspected the bird was his father.

I looked at Tingo. He looked back at me and smiled playfully and said, "El Condor Pasa, Pietro!"

I smiled back at him. "Si, Senor Chico. El condor grande pasa...otra vez...gracias. El era el mismo condor."

He smiled broadly, thrilled that I would speak in Spanish. Thrilled as well that I knew it was the same condor. "Si, Pedro, el mismo."

Christiane forgave us quickly. Anger was not an attitude she embraced tightly or which was at home with her. It left her immediately, because it never found a place to linger within her gentle nature.

The four of us moved swiftly forward into the day and never discussed the awe-inspiring encounter with the condor, which must have affected them like it did us.

The tourists began wandering into the venerable city and with them came an inevitable bias towards the secular, which we knew would corrupt our ancient monastic morning if we stayed much longer. So after curiously watching them for a few moments come into our city and make it theirs, we covertly returned to the mules by the hidden path that we had forged on the other side of the mountain. We began our descent to the house of Tingo's brother.

It is a sad fact that immense happenings in one's life lose their tone of significance as time passes. They become supplanted with more salient happenings which are perhaps ultimately not meaningful at all but which are present rather than past. So one mistakenly thinks that the contemporary things are more alive and thus deserve more of our attention, when in fact they are often only more obtrusive.

It was also true that the purity and magic of our solitary Macchu Picchu morning could not be sustained for long after re-entering the modern world with its defilements. By the following morning our attention was not upon Macchu Picchu where we had been, as perhaps it should have been, but upon Lima where we were going. As such, Simon and I lost the compelling need to talk to each other about the event of the condor.

We said a sad goodbye to Tingo Chico, begging him to spend at least a night with us in Lima, but he said he had to go. It was not hard to see that he was out of place there, without the same self-command he possessed in the Andes. We exchanged addresses, believing we would stay in contact, and said goodbye sadly.

Early one night, long after we'd returned to Lima, I was lying in my bed reading when I heard a knock on the door. It was Simon. I asked him in and asked what I could do for him. He wasted no time getting to the purpose of his visit. "Michael, why did you say to me in Macchu Picchu, 'Maybe that was your father.'?"

It caught me by surprise. I thought about it a minute and then said, "I don't know. I just felt that way at the time."

"Do you still feel that way?"

"You mean do I still wonder if it was your father?"

"Do you think it was my father?"

"I don't know. It could have been, if you believe that people can become animals."

"Do you believe people can become animals, Michael."

I had a hard time answering that, not knowing what my honest feelings were. "I don't know. I'm only beginning to understand these things, Simon. I'm trying to believe it."

"And another thing, Michael. When my father had a job to do, no one could stop him. The look in his eyes at those times was like the look in the eye of the condor. Do you know what I mean? They never blinked. They looked straight ahead. There was nothing else in his mind except the thing he was doing or wanting to do. When he became like that it felt like he was someone else, almost like another person. It made me feel lonely. He wasn't there for me or anyone else when that happened. His friends called him Azor. That means 'hawk'. He had eyes like a hawk. The condor in Macchu Picchu looked like that, like he was looking through me to the ground below."

I was impressed with his observations which matched my own. He needed to talk. He told me his father had two distinct natures, one of them very kind, loving and playful, and the other like he described, formidable and driven. He said that he could never synthesize them into one image and so still his father remains for him two non-allied people who in a way cancel each other out.

"Complex people often have this multifaceted nature," I told him. It is sometimes hard to visualize them as a single person."

"Do you think my father was more than one person, Michael?" he asked me.

"I didn't know your father, Simon. I've just seen his picture, and in his picture I see a man who is very intelligent and humorous, whose face is handsome and clear with innocence and kindness. Like you, Simon. I don't know what was inside of him, but I don't think it is unusual to have more than one person inside of you."

"You don't, Michael?"

"No, I don't."

"Are you more than one person, Michael?"

He was bending toward me like a branch toward light. Perhaps he wanted me to be many people too, like his father, like perhaps he knew secretively that he was too.

"I think so, yes."

"Do you like all the people that you are, Michael?"

I was impressed, as always, by the depth of his questions.

"I don't know. Let me think about it, but I think that I do. I don't think there is something about myself that I dislike."

"Are there things about you that you don't understand?"

"Yes, probably, Simon."

"What are they, Michael?"

I was amazed at how little I understood myself when questioned in this way. Whoever asks another such questions?

"Let me think about it, Simon, and I will answer you another time, okay? When I feel like I know the answers. Are there things about you that you don't understand, and do you like all the people you are, Simon?"

"No, I don't like them all and yes, I don't understand some of the things that I am. They confuse me."

He was sitting close to me. I was flattered that he chose me as the person to hear these personal questions which he had perhaps never asked before. Our arms were touching and I could feel a youthful warmth radiating from his upper arm. I put my hand around his back and upon his waist and pulled him to me while he collapsed with no resistance, welcoming my overture of affection and caring. I kissed him on top of his head. His black hair smelled musky like natural perfume.

"Well, let me tell you this, Simon. You're a very fine person and however many people there are inside of you, I think that I would like them all. Accept them for now as part of yourself, and try your best to understand them. They're not different people, really, they are sides of the one person that you are. Be kind to yourself. One day it will be clearer to you who you are and are to be. Maybe later we can talk about this more. I would like that."

"I would too, Michael." He snuggled up beneath my arm like a puppy in a basket. He looked up at me and added: "I love you, Michael."

"I love you too, Simon."

"Michael, can I go with you to Iquitos?" he asked.

I had considered that myself, since he was clearly an integral part of my own development. But I didn't know if Christiane and/or the curandero would approve, nor did I know what role he would have. Would he take ayahuasca? Was it morally correct to introduce an eleven-year-old boy to an experience like that? Or, would an eleven- year-old boy actually be better able to handle the elements of fantasy incumbent to the ayahuasca experience?

I wanted him there with me at Iquitos. I didn't know what things were inside of me to be brought to light with the hallucinogens, but I didn't want to face them alone. I knew that having the two of them with me would be comforting.

"I'd like that, Simon. But your mother must approve and my doctor must approve as well. And I would request that if either of them does not approve, you will accept that. Will you?"

"Yes, I will. But I have already talked to my mother and she said I could go."

I was pleased with that. I would talk to her later about it.

"Do you know what happens at these ceremonies?" I asked him.

"Yes. The people there take San Pedro."

"And do you know what happens to them when they take San Pedro?"

"They have visions. Many strange things happen to them. Sometimes they fly. Sometimes they become animals and their problems turn into odd faces which the doctor helps them understand."

"Who told you these things?"

"My father told me. He and my mother attended a ceremony together."

"Was he sick at the time?"

"He had sadness. 'La Tristeza,' he called it."

"What made him sad?"

"I don't know. That's what I don't know."

I didn't feel at ease continuing the conversation about his father's sadness and thought I should find out more from Christiane before I did.

"Did your mother say you could take San Pedro also?"

"No, she didn't."

I had suggested in Macchu Picchu that we go to Iquitos by land, which I learned later was absurd. Even though by airplane Lima is only 600 miles from Iquitos, before air service the only way to get from Lima to Iquitos had been to go from Lima's port, Callao, up the Pacific coast to Panama, through the Caribbean, down the Atlantic Ocean and up the Amazon to Iquitos. That trip was some 7000 miles! The land between the east side of the Andes and Iquitos is so remote and inaccessible that no one really even knows what is there.

Instead we went to Cajamarca first and then flew to Iquitos. I wanted to see the place where Francisco Pizarro started his 1300 mile journey with only 150 soldiers on August 11, 1533 and ended up in Cuzco November 15th of that year, conquering 40,000 people from perhaps the greatest cultural empire the earth has ever seen, ending that culture forever and replacing it with bullfighters.

Cajamarca, high in the Andes, is an enchanting Spanish colonial town. But we didn't stay long.

The night before we left we sat next to a man from Ecuador in the dining room of the hotel. I related to him the story of our trip to

Macchu Picchu and told him how much I loved Peru and that I had come to Cajamarca to see the spot where the Spaniards began their trip in 1533. At first he was offended, thinking I was there to eulogize the Spanish Conquistadors, but when I told him that, on the contrary, I found it unforgivable what they had done and unbelievable that such a thing could have happened, he told me a story of his own.

Apparently there is a man who was raised in the Ecuadorian Amazon to missionary parents from the West. He lives in the no-man's land between Ecuador and Iquitos, where nothing is mapped, where no one lives, where most of the ground that one can step on has never before been stepped upon by another human being since the beginning of the world. This man makes poison curare for hunting, fishes for piranha, speaks all of the languages of the indigenous peoples, can make medicines from Amazonian plants, and is at home among the numberless species of plants and animals there. In addition, he has a western education, including two years of college at an American university, before dropping out to return to the only life he knows – the Amazon.

He lives in a place called Zabalo with 120 indigenous people of the Cofan nation. Although the Cofan people have no government or social hierarchy, in a way he is their leader because he can communicate with two radically different cultures, theirs and the rest of the world's.

In 1967 Texaco Oil Company discovered oil in the Cofan territory. They drilled 350 oil wells and blasted thousands of miles of exploratory trails. They built a pipeline which broke constantly, spilling millions of gallons of oil and toxic waste into the rivers and streams of the rain forest, ruining the fishing and bathing and drinking water and subsequently putting the local people into poverty and malnutrition. The land was devastated and the Cofan nation had to move east to Zabalo and start over.

The man said: "Consider, then, that Texaco Oil, called 'The Company' by the Cofans, is the equivalent of the Spaniard Conquistadors of the 1500's, who stole the Inca heritage.

"In 1991 The Company showed up at Zabalo, prepared to do the same thing there. However, the Cofan Nation decided to face them down. They captured the oil crew and told them they would *not* drill for oil there. They besieged every other crew which came behind them until finally Texaco pulled out of the country. They were no match for people who could hide with the tapirs and howler monkeys, the long-nosed bats and conga ants, the stingrays and the 6000 volt electric eels, as well as piranhas and jaguars, and make curare from 50 different indigenous plants, one drop of which can be used to lethalize the tips of a 1000 arrows.

"However, another oil boom soon happened and The Company was back, this time demanding from the government that no indigenous people be allowed to stop them. Since The Company accounted for fifty per cent of the country's revenues, what could the government do? The Company started to cut roads and dynamite trails as before, but the western-educated Cofan man discovered that the Company had illegally drilled a well, and he sued them. The man was able to influence newspapers, lawyers, and others who helped them and embarrassed the Company worldwide until finally it abandoned its oil drilling expedition around Zabalo.

"It was the first time an indigenous people had beaten The Company. In the end they were able to secure title to 200,000 acres of land to be set aside as a preserve which can never be invaded by the oil companies.

"The Cofan Nation is the equivalent of the Incas," the man said. "Justice, however inadequately proportioned and however long it endures, has in some small measure finally been achieved by the Incas.

Francisco Pizarro has been turned away this second time! Except that now it is the Incas who had only 200 soldiers and Pizarro who had thousands."

That story warmed my heart and helped prepare me to go on to Iquitos.

CHAPTER 15

After three days in Hamburg, I still had not made an attempt to find Susanne. I had had a wonderful time with Mr. Seiler going from place to place seeing things most tourists might never see. We spent two days at the shipping docks and at the Port walking the amazing labyrinthine causeways in and around the Elbe River. This eventually took us to residential river areas of Altona and Altstadt and farther west to the charming old fishing village of Blankenese with its hilly seaside landscape and twisting private roads. On the way back from Blankense we passed an area called Palmaille. It had broad boulevards and towering trees. Beautiful old homes, thickspread in greenery, sat far back from the road behind tall wrought iron fences. This, I knew, was where Susanne's father lived, on a street called Hoheschulstrasse, not far from where we were driving. I didn't say anything to Mr. Seiler, however.

On the third day he took me through the old city with its grand, magisterial architecture and explained the history of that part of Hamburg. We drove through the edge of the Reeperbahn and he said, "We shall come back here later."

On the fourth day Mr. Seiler decided to begin looking for people from his past, and invited me to come along with him. It was touching to see him reconnect with people he had probably thought he would never see again. In Uhlenhorst we found not only the avenue he had lived on but also the home he had lived in, outstandingly restored to its original condition by its present owners who'd researched the public records and copied photographs in order to reconstruct it the way it had been. And the avenue itself was as beautiful as Mr. Seiler had described it to me on the flight. Even the trees had grown tall again.

On the fifth day, Mr. Seiler took me to the Reeperbahn.

The word "Reeperbahn" means "ropemakers." It is where the ropemakers of old used to wind ships' ropes. Now the Reeperbahn is a place of sex for sale, any sex one can imagine. Ironically, the Davidstrasse police station is at its entrance and keeps tight control on crime, and in the middle of this "babel of sin" is the Catholic Church of St. Joseph, built in 1718, which survived the bombing. The Reeperbahn runs for blocks and blocks in each direction, hundreds of hotels, inns, regular bars, gambling houses, striptease joints, homosexual bars, transvestite performances, male strippers, extravagant sex theatres, brothels, massage parlors, peep shows, pornographic modeling, sado-masochism clubs, tattoo parlors, and every other imaginable service of pleasure. The center of the area is the district of St. Pauli, ironically named after the moralizing Apostle Paul.

Originally the Reeperbahn served the sailors and seamen from the Port. But now people from all over the world were there, particularly from Europe. Only males were allowed to enter the Reeperbahn.

There was something alluring about it that frightened and attracted me at once. I tried to imagine Susanne working there. Even though I was sure she did not participate in the life of sexual favors, I could see when she told me about it that something fascinated her about it too. I couldn't get the Reeperbahn out of my consciousness for a long time after we left it, and it was this which finally re-ignited an intense desire to find Susanne. By the next morning, it had become desperation.

I realized suddenly how I had missed her. For months and months I had diverted my longing for Susanne into other activities, like selling the store and planning the trip and learning about Germany. But now at this moment as I lay in my sumptuous room in Vier Jahreszeiten, the real reason for the last year of my life, the goal of it, the only reason I had lived it even, was now before my eyes clearly: to see Susanne again.

I decided that in the morning I would suggest to Mr. Seiler that we each go our separate ways and meet again at nighttime, allowing me freedom to plan my investigation. However, immediately after saying "Good morning" to me, he said, "Michael, I'm going to try to find my son today. Will you come along?"

"Yes sir, I'd be glad to," I said. I knew he needed me with him or else he would not have asked me that way, and so I delayed my search.

Someone had told Mr. Seiler that he had seen Horst within the year and believed that he lived near the docks in the south part of the Centre City. We spent a long time searching and asking people if they'd seen him. We found people who had heard of him or knew him, but no one knew exactly where he lived.

Mr. Seiler remembered him last living in a Bohemian area of artists and musicians, so we went there. Finally we found someone who knew him, who said that Horst had left the area and that no one had seen him for months.

"Does he maintain a house here still?" Mr. Seiler asked him.

The man laughed sarcastically. "I don't think 'maintain' is the proper word to use. But yes, his shack is near the Elbe. You will never find it without a map. I'll draw you one."

"Is he still a stonemason?"

"He will always be a stonemason, but his love is sculpture. And, of course, gambling."

The man went to get some paper to write upon. Mr. Seiler looked upset as I had not seen him look since we'd arrived.

I touched his forearm and asked him if he was all right.

"Oh, yes. I was hoping he was different now, but still the same I am afraid."

The man returned to us holding in his hand a metal sculpture which looked like an angel. It portrayed a curvaceous attitude of flesh. The head was long and thin and expressive by the simplest lines of curved metal, conveying pain and pride simultaneously with an economy of material.

"This is Horst's," he said, handing it to Mr. Seiler, who took it lightly in his hands and examined it carefully a long time before putting it gently on the table.

The man finished the map and gave it to us, explaining the complications of the route. They talked idiomatically and laughed and Mr. Seiler shook his hand firmly and put his hand on the man's shoulder, and then we left.

"Michael," Mr. Seiler said, "you need to find Susanne."

I was happy that he had finally confirmed my purpose in coming to Hamburg. I needed for him to do that.

"Yes, I do, sir, thank you. But you need to find your son too."

"Well, I know it'll not be easy finding Horst. He disappears like that. He has vices and is pulled by them. It might take the rest of our time in Hamburg to find him, and in the end he may not be here at all. I don't want you to waste the time you have left on a fruitless pursuit. In addition, if we find him, Michael, it may not be a pleasant experience. I'm tempted to devote only a little more effort to it. Involvements with

Horst are often complicated and time-consuming, frequently taking on completely different schedules than originally envisioned, at entirely unforeseen places. There's no plan to his life, he just makes it up minute by minute. An hour might stretch into three days and a weekend into a year. There are many more things for me to do and we must find your Susanne. We've been here for five days."

I knew that whatever he said to the contrary, it was important that he find his son.

"We could spend the rest of the day looking for Horst," I said, "and if we don't find him, then tomorrow you could look for him on your own and I could look for Susanne."

We ambled along in the pleasant empty morning which gradually filled with activity, changing, as near-summer mornings do, from cool deserted stillness to hot crowded frenzy.

"I believe that eventually you will need me to help you communicate with Susanne's father. If he's a doctor who lives in the Palmaille, it's likely that it will not be easy for you to transmit your feelings and thoughts to him. Also, I didn't tell you that the first day when I went for a walk, I went past the address you had given me for his office and it seemed that it wasn't open. Nor was it listed in the telephone directory. His home phone number wasn't there either. Perhaps he's retired or only working occasionally. In that case, you may have to go to the Palmaille to find him, and that's an area which is private and guarded, from which the public is excluded. Let's follow this map and find Horst's house and assess the situation when we are there, okay?"

Even with a map Horst's house was hard to find. It was on top of a small hill above the river on a terrible dirt road with huge holes in it. We parked the car we'd rented and walked the last distance.

There were tall trees surrounding the house, which made it seem non-residential and forest-like, even though there were other houses nearby. From a distance of perhaps 100 feet we could see what looked like a junkyard, but as we got closer we saw it was the yard of a collector. There were piles of stone and sand and limestone for mixing mortar, several ancient hand-turned cement mixers, many trowels, shovels, levels. Tools were everywhere, as if a garage sale for craftsmen was about to begin. There were old truck bodies and engine parts and a couple of cars as well. Some of the things in the yard I could not identify, but most of them had to do with machines.

We went around the back of the house and I saw a garden of sculptures rusting in the open air. All of them were strong pieces of work, some completely finished, others abandoned.

We walked behind these sculptures on a path which led into a secluded clearing on the other side of the trees in a sunny meadow spot. There we saw a bronze cast sculpture ten feet high of a powerful mythical figure with pointed ears and big horns. It had the face and upper body of a man, with legs and hindquarters of a goat. It appeared to be dancing. Its torso and head were reared back in mock surprise and its flowing long hair seemed suitable to the look on its face of merriment. Mischief was in its eyes. The body on top was inordinately strong with huge biceps and deltoids, and the lower body was smaller, more delicate, with sleek fur-covered legs and slim animal hips delicately poised to dance. Its left hand, which it held above its head, was curled nimbly in a gesture that signified a carefree spirit, with the index finger pointing out almost flirtatiously.

The tools used to fashion the sculpture were on the ground beside it rusting in the open air. Also some clothes and a radio which was dead. Empty beer and liquor bottles lay on their sides in the tall grass mixed with weeds. On its base was a plate with a peach pit still on it. Mr. Seiler walked near the sculpture which towered above him and he touched it. "My God. This is beautiful," he said caressing its surface. He walked all the way around it and ended up standing next to me. "Why is this here? It belongs in a museum. It should not be here like this. Who can see it but the birds?"

He stared at the sculpture a long time and then turned and walked to the house. After getting no response to his knocks, he turned the knob of the unlocked door and went inside. I followed him. The small house had but two rooms and no bathroom. Outside was an outhouse. The bigger room was a living room and a kitchen together. The other room was tiny, with only space for a bed and bookshelves. The bed was gorgeous, handmade from handsome dark brown wood. It was impossible to be in the room without being on the bed. It seemed almost more like a nest than a bed, as if the resident were bedridden with infirmity. On the table beside the unmade bed, on the mantle of the bed, and on the bed itself, there were perhaps twenty books, marked or opened, all of which were apparently being read at once. Several pairs of reading glasses were among them. Hundreds of books lined cobbled shelves on two sides. There was not even an aisle between the bed and the walls of books. Several empty liquor bottles were on the floor. There was a picture of Horst and a woman on top of his bed next to ashtrays overflowing with cigarette butts. He was wearing levis and a brown tweed sport coat with a blue turtleneck sweater beneath it. His posture was erect and his countenance was confident and commanding. He was wearing hiking boots and his graying straight hair was long. He was very handsome.

In the middle of the bigger room was a small stone fireplace, functional it appeared, but unfinished. There was split wood piled near it and ashes on the floor in front of it. Several old chairs were around the fireplace, as if it were a meeting spot for communal warmth. Bottles and glasses were on the floor beside it and several more open books.

The room's small refrigerator had very little food in it. Unwashed dishes were in the old sink and things were everywhere: tools, books, clothes, kitchen items, projects being worked on, projects abandoned, paintings, sculptures complete and incomplete, portraits, electronic equipment. No surface in the room was free of clutter.

I could see from his face that Mr. Seiler was aghast. I tried to ameliorate his obvious dismay.

"A typical artist's house," I said.

"Hmm," he grunted his non-acceptance. "This is a typical bum's house."

"I don't think that's fair to say, Mr. Seiler. Look at his work. Doesn't it tell you he is not a bum?"

"It tells me he doesn't care, that he is throwing away his talent like he has always done."

"I don't think he's throwing away his talent. He's expressing his talent. He just doesn't have a need for others to see it or for it to be organized the way you would do it."

"Michael, this is ridiculous. Look at this," he said sweeping his arm at the whole situation. "Being an artist is not an excuse to live like this. I have known artists."

I had not seen Mr. Seiler behave so intolerantly. Usually he tried to understand people's differences and in fact he'd always seemed to me to have wisdom in regard to the world's diversity. Clearly other things were influencing this situation having to do with their past relationship.

He was angry. He turned and walked quickly away from Horst's house. I followed behind him all the way to the car and got into the passenger's seat beside him.

"Let's go, Michael. I have seen enough. Tomorrow we shall look for Susanne. Let's hope she doesn't live like this."

He started the car. I reached over and turned off the key. I held his wrist and looked in his eyes and said, "Kurt, listen to me." I'd never called him Kurt before. It sounded odd but pleasantly familiar and appropriate. "You need to find your son. I know this and you know it too. You must forgive him. He's your son but he's not you. He has his own life which is not yours. It's not a reflection upon you."

He looked stern. He started the car and drove off, back through the Bohemian village and the old city to the hotel. We didn't speak. After we parked he told me he was going to walk a bit and would meet me later in the room.

He walked east from the hotel while I sat in a small park across the street and watched him disappear around the southeast curve of the Binnen-Alster and head north, walking slowly.

It was the first disagreeable moment of our trip. I felt sorry for him. I knew that he should find Horst, but I felt that there would be a confrontation when they met. Still, I decided the next day should be devoted to a search for Horst, and we should keep searching until we found him.

Suddenly it occurred to me that while Mr. Seiler was walking I could go by Dr. Ludendorff's office just to determine if he was there or was coming back. I knew exactly where it was.

I ran the whole way to Deichstrassse, passing streets and buildings I had read about in books I'd found in Mr. Seiler's shop. My legs flew instinctively like the wings of a carrier pigeon. I looked at every girl I passed on the streets thinking one might be Susanne on her way to her father's office.

Deichstrasse Avenue curved along the waterway. Beautiful old buildings, once residences, stood several stories tall, joined to each other in rows facing the water. Most of them were now shops or offices. The number of his office was 412. All of the buildings were tastefully painted in colors which blended into the color of the water and the land.

As I walked closer my heart pounded. I cleared my throat obsessively like a thespian about to go on stage. I rehearsed the German I would speak to whomever I saw in the office. It sounded thin and weak as I spoke it to myself and all of a sudden I was afraid that I would fail to say what I wanted to say. I almost turned back, but then I was in front of the door.

A light was on. I opened the door. The bells attached to its window tinkled cheerfully as they had done in Mr. Seiler's store. No one was visible so I sat down in a chair in front of the reception desk and waited. Still no one came. Again I almost walked out. I was terrified and had no confidence in myself. A tremendous feeling of significance occurred to me as I realized that I was now almost within the moment I had imagined for a year. Before I could grasp the implications of that, an older man came out from the back room.

He was startled by my presence. He looked like a professor. Half-spectacles hung low on his nose and he looked at me from above them. His coat was off and his striped shirt cuffs were rolled up. He held in his hand a thick book. He was tall and dignified and serious-looking.

"We're not open today," he said impatiently in German.

"Can I make an appointment for tomorrow?" I asked him, using the German word 'meeting' for 'appointment'. He didn't understand. I tried to use another word and then another, but I could see that he was getting annoyed.

Again I wanted to leave, feeling helpless, when he said, "Are you English?"

"I'm American," I said, so relieved to speak a common language.

"What is it you want?"

"Can I make an appointment for a physical exam?"

"This office is not open to the public anymore. We do research here."

"Are you Dr. Ludendorff?"

"No. Dr. Ludendorff is dead."

I was shocked. "Dead?" I said to myself. "How could he be dead?"

"Do you know his daughter, Susanne?" I blurted out.

"Why do you want to know that?" he asked suspiciously.

"I'm a friend of hers."

"I thought you were here for an appointment."

"No, sir, I'm here to find Susanne."

He came around the desk and took me by the arm and escorted me to the door saying, "You need to leave now. We are not open."

"Please listen to me," I pleaded. "I need to see Susanne. I'm a friend of hers from America and I've come all this way to see her."

"She is not here."

I pulled my arm away from his and turned toward him in a standoff. "How can I find her?"

"Young man, the police station is just nearby. I'll get them if you do not leave now."

I turned and left.

"Oh my God," I thought. Every plan I had devised to find her had contained her father. I felt anger at his death instead of remorse.

I walked back slowly, looking at no one, knowing she would not be among them. How quickly things had gone from hopeful to hopeless.

Mr. Seiler was in the room and greeted me warmly when I came in.

"How are you, sir?"

"I am fine, Michael. I went for a long walk and thought about what you said. You are right. I must find my son, so tomorrow if you still want, we will look for him. Michael, you don't look good."

"I went for a long walk too, to Deichstrasse, to Dr. Ludendorff's office."

"Did you find him?"

"No, he is dead."

"Dead?"

"Yes."

"How do you know that?"

"A man working there told me."

He exhaled a deep sigh and walked next to me and put his arm around my shoulder. "It's okay. We shall find her still."

"This city has two million people in it."

"That's okay. There are other ways to track her. We haven't even begun yet, Michael. We shall look for her first instead of Horst."

"No, no. I think we should do as you said tomorrow. I need to think about it."

He put his head close to mine and said in his deep comforting voice, "Let's do this, Michael. Let's have a bite to eat at the hotel and after that let's drive to Palmaille and just do a preliminary investigation. I think it will make you feel better and you'll find it will be easier with an old man like me as the translator. An old man in Hamburg can open many doors." He smiled. I couldn't help but smile back.

"Okay?" he asked again.

After dinner we drove again through the old Centre City on the route that we had taken before. It was nearing sunset. I had thought that finding Susanne would not be the hard part. Trying to tell her my feelings and understanding hers would be. But now I wondered self-pityingly if perhaps it might end like a tragedy where I would not find her after all.

Neither of us said a word until we were almost there. We turned north from Palmaille Boulevard just before it became Elbechaussee. At once we were in a privileged world of luxurious estates. Each home was like a personally designed castle on acres of gently rolling land beautifully tended like a park. All of them were inaccessible to the public, some actually guarded at the gate. Most were not even identified by a number.

"Do you have the address, Michael?"

I pulled my address book from my pocket and read it to him.

"That's a long way from here," he said and turned at the next cross street. I was impressed that he knew his way in this Garden of Eden.

He stopped the car at a gate and got out and talked to the guard and returned and said, "It is just up the way a few blocks."

We drove deeper into unbelievable opulence which for me had a temporary hypnotic restorative effect.

Mr. Seiler stopped. He asked me for the address again and I handed him my book. He took it and talked to another man behind the bars of a gate, a gardener perhaps. The encounter between them looked like a prison visitation.

They pointed several times to the adjoining mansion and then Mr. Seiler returned to the car.

"That's the doctor's house." He pointed to the hillside full of magnificent trees. I assumed the house was behind them.

"The caretaker said that no one has lived there since Dr. Ludendorff died. I asked him if any of the neighbors would know where the doctor's daughter is. He said that Dr. Ludendorff was a very private person who associated with no one. However, there is a caretaker who comes on the weekends who might know. We shall return then, okay?"

"Yes," I said. But I was not satisfied. "Are there public records which would tell about who handled his things at death? And would you please accompany me to the doctor's office again to talk to that suspicious man? He must know. Maybe you can convince him that we're respectable people. Maybe he can at least tell us where to go for information."

"Those are excellent ideas, Michael. We shall do that in the morning. Hamburgers are by nature very private. They don't volunteer information to strangers, sometimes not even to their own family. There is a distinct upper class here."

"We need to look for your son in the morning. Let's do it after we find him."

"You are more hopeful than I of finding Horst. I know him, Michael. I think it will take longer than just tomorrow. But we shall see. So tonight we shall forget these misgivings and I will take you to a dining pleasure at the Alsterpavillion. No more playing detective tonight."

"The Alsterpavillion was first built in 1799," Mr. Seiler explained from our vantage point beneath the arched café entrances. It was just east of our hotel, on the lake. "It has been rebuilt six times, the last time after World War Two. It's typical of Hamburg in that sense: destroyed, rebuilt, destroyed, rebuilt." He laughed.

Huge swans glided by in front of us. Boats came and went through the bridges nearby. The table settings were elegant. Pure white linen below heavy ornate silverware and delicate wine goblets.

"Katerina and I came here every Friday night for years and ate dinner and danced."

A small orchestra played waltzes from the center of the open café. The sound distributed itself perfectly, and people danced on a hardwood floor in front of the orchestra. A few danced near their tables.

"Those were wonderful times, Michael. Life could not have been better."

We spent the rest of the evening talking and laughing, listening to the music, and watching the dancers. The experience restored my enthusiasm and my optimism.

As we were about to leave an old man passed our table. He moved very slowly, hunched over like a turtle, with the aid of a cane. He was dressed nicely in a brown suit and was handsome but crippled with arthritis. Suddenly Mr. Seiler stopped talking and stared at him. The old man also stopped upon seeing Mr. Seiler staring at him.

"Johann?"

"Yes, that's my name. Who are you?"

"Johann Barlach?"

"Yes."

"I am Kurt Seiler."

It seemed as if the Alsterpavillion stopped moving for a moment, that the music paused in deference and the dancers stopped dancing, in order to pay respect to two old friends reuniting after 35 years apart.

Mr. Barlach dropped his cane, as if he had received a miracle at a shrine, and hobbled to Mr. Seiler like a child on new legs. The two of them embraced.

"Kurt, you have come back here to Hamburg," he said with a tear in his voice.

"I have, Johann, I have."

"I knew you would come back someday."

Mr. Seiler put his hand on my shoulder and said, "I could not have come back without the help of this young man."

Then he introduced the man as his oldest friend on earth. They had known each other since being young children. They'd been in school together and even worked on ships beside each other. Their families had worked together and they had attended the same church. All of their children had been friends.

"Do you know what, Michael? This is the last person I saw when I left Hamburg. He took me to the airport. He was with me the night that Hamburg died, in the shelters below the buildings."

They had accommodated me until then with the use of English, but suddenly they began speaking German. I could follow enough of it to know that the subject they discussed was the war. Name after name was brought up. I concentrated for minutes on the conversation but after a while it was too difficult, so I drifted away in thought.

How to find Susanne? I felt the obsession taking me over again, and it felt good. I also thought of where I was and how I'd gotten there, like a miracle indeed. Already in less than a week I felt stronger as a person and capable of doing anything. I no longer felt like a boy. I was taking control of my life.

"Listen to this, Michael! Johann saw Horst a few weeks ago. He is staying with a woman in Stadtpark, north of the Alster. He says that some of Horst's sculptures are displayed in the park. Quite an honor!"

"That's wonderful. Do we know her name?"

"Not only that but he told Johann the name of the school where she teaches, so we can start to find him there." He was beaming with excitement and I felt it too.

Mr. Barlach asked me some questions about myself and my ambitions.

"He's going to be a doctor!" Mr. Seiler said proudly.

"Ah, that is good indeed. Will you go to medical school in America?"

"Yes," I said. I said it out loud for the first time: that I would be a doctor. Even though I continued carrying on the conversation automatically, I didn't hear anything else that was said after that, because at that moment the silly hope of Mr. Seiler – that I should become a doctor – materialized and took a place in my mind next to solid facts and possibilities.

They talked and laughed as two boys again. I watched them proudly, knowing that with unconscious intention I had brought about their reunion within a galaxy of possibility I somehow shared with them.

The night went on past midnight, until finally the three of us walked back to Vier Jahreszeiten. The Conditorei was still open so we had an ice cream.

"I'm going to walk Mr. Barlach to his car, Michael. Shall we meet in the room in a while?"

I shook Mr. Barlach's hand and the two of them walked away.

Had the itinerary of our trip involved nothing other than this evening at the Alsterpavillion with Johann Barlach, I knew that Mr. Seiler would have regarded the trip as successful.

"But we shall make it more successful than that," I thought. "Tomorrow we shall find Horst."

The only thing that could have made the evening more nearly perfect would have been if Susanne had walked into the Conditorei at that moment and had said to me, "So Michael, you have come for me." The way she used to say it when I'd go to her porch just before the sunrise, and we'd walk hand in hand to the round silver lake where the graceful swans danced on the moon in the water. And we'd watch them unfold while the slow night elapsed as it linked to the dawn of next day.

CHAPTER 16

Most modern medicines are originally derived from plants in the rain forest, and it is certain that there are hundreds more to be discovered. The rain forest seems to contain a cure for literally everything. However, the irony is that to discover and use these plants as medicines, other than just locally, requires modern systems of manufacturing and transportation, including roads, which are "the cancer of the rain forest." In other words, to harvest the rain forest's bounty on a large scale is to destroy it forever.

The best shamans, the richest source of knowledge about medicines and cures from Amazon plants, have not codified this information. It has been passed on from one to another for thousands of years. Now, however, not only are species becoming extinct, so are the shamans. Both the natural medicines and the natural doctors are disappearing at once. When one of these shamans dies, it is like "a medical library going up in flames."

I learned these things from an American biologist I met in Iquitos. There are an amazing number of scientists and fellow travelers in Iquitos wanting and trying to study and save the rain forest. There are an equal number of people simply wanting to experience it before it will inevitably disappear. (It is thought by some that the rain forests of the world will be gone within 50 years.) There are people like me, believing with greater or lesser conviction that they can be cured of their sicknesses in a different way from Western medicine, which in one way or another has failed them. And then there are the bio-pirates, scientists who want to get rich by finding herbs with medical properties and selling them to drug companies. Alongside them are the loggers who decimate the rain forest just ahead of the legislation designed to make them cease and desist.

———————

We huddled together in Iquitos like three immigrant waifs waiting for naturalization orders. We were supposed to meet the man who would take us to the shaman, but he didn't arrive.

It was so hot and so ugly where we stayed in Iquitos that after two days we decided to hire a man to take us into the Amazon on his boat for a preview.

After about an hour we were merged with the jungle, hearing strange and beautiful birds, one which sounded like an entire symphony. A single bird would inspire another one until the forest was screaming with a thousand voices at once.

Christiane asked our pilot to stop and let us get out and listen, but he didn't respond. He was not Tingo Chico, unfortunately. He had the attitude of a native in a town of tourists.

Still, it was wonderful to be away from the city in the middle of a crushing advance of nature. Our trip was just a few hours, but when we got back to Iquitos we were revived to our original spirit, knowing then what awaited us.

We knew the name of the village where Francisco Alvaro practiced medicine. It was not on a map, so I couldn't tell how far away it was.

However, we decided to spend another day or two getting accustomed to the area and then find a boatman to take us to the village.

A village could be ten or twelve huts only. One had the feeling that self-governing, autonomous and even unknown villages abounded in the rain forest. In fact, I read of one such village on the border of Brazil and Peru. The village consisted of about two hundred people, hunter-gatherer Indians. They were discovered by a group of French journalists who were able to record their first-ever contact with the outside world. It is said that in the past, such newly discovered groups had died from measles and flu which they contracted from outsiders, because they had no immunity to modern diseases.

By the fourth day we were ready to leave. Simon was inordinately quiet. I feared that he was slipping back into withdrawal. Something was on his mind.

I found a boat leaving in the morning, taking others to various places, and persuaded them to let us join them.

That night Simon went to bed early and Christiane and I stayed up and talked.

"Something's wrong with Simon," I said.

"I know."

"What is it?"

"He's a thoughtful boy, Michael. He disappears into his own head sometimes and is not available. He has special qualities, as you know. He can sense things that others cannot. Feelings and intuitions. Sometimes I know that he has received messages or insights about what is going to happen, even in the form of pictures, and they haunt him. He has told me precisely what's going to happen in the future, and it has happened."

"Do you think he's afraid?"

"No. Not for himself anyway. I think he's worried for you. He loves you, Michael. He wants you to get better. He doesn't want any harm to come to you."

"Do you think there is harm coming to me?"

"No. But this is powerful stuff, Michael, and it was not long ago that he lost his father. He's probably afraid of losing you."

It was the right time now to talk to her about his father. Iquitos seemed at last familiar and friendly on this final night, and we were alone, I realized, for the first time in a long time.

"Christiane, tell me about Tomas's death."

She looked scared and uncertain.

"I know that he took his own life. Simon told me. You don't have to tell me anything if you don't want."

She started crying and I felt bad that I had caused it. But what I really wanted to know was why she had not told me that they had visited a shaman themselves.

"I don't know why he took his life, Michael. As I told you before, his childhood was not good, but I don't know exactly what it was. He wouldn't talk about it. I tried several times. He had serious episodes of depression. I would know when he sensed them coming because suddenly he would start working like a madman, for two or three days without stopping, until he collapsed. It was his way to keep from being taken under. When he first became a doctor, he worked with the mentally ill because he sympathized with their condition.

"I didn't tell you this, but he and I attended several healing ceremonies in Lima. They helped him. But they also made him more aware of what was bothering him. Lima is not the place to undergo this type of treatment, and the conditions were not right, so he stopped doing it. I believed that he was at the doorstep of an understanding of himself which would eventually have led to inner peace for him. But he stopped. His work always came first. However, I think he was not able to look inside of himself completely. And I think the suicide was his final act giving up to failure.

"Everyone adored him. And wanted to be like him or at least be around him. But none of them knew that inside he didn't want to be Tomas. He wanted escape from the things which tormented him."

"How much does Simon know about this?"

"Simon knows almost everything. He has questioned me lots."

"Is he afraid this will happen to me?"

"Maybe."

"It won't."

She looked at me and smiled with tears running contradictorily, vulnerably, down her checks to the corners of her lips, dripping from her chin onto her shirt. I wiped them off with my shirttail. She put her arms around me and hugged me and said, "Thank you for saying that, Michael."

"Do you think Simon sees something ahead which disturbs him?"

She didn't answer. I patted her hair and whispered, "Don't worry, Christiane. It will be okay. I came here because it called me, remember? It would not call me to harm."

She nodded, "Yes, that makes sense to me."

In the morning we waited with others for the boat's owner to arrive. He was late. Some of the people waiting were botanists studying plant species in the area. A few were simply riding the boat for an adventure, and one couple was going to the same village as we. They were married and in their early thirties perhaps. He had a long red beard which didn't fit the formal clothes he was wearing. He was a farmer, physically strong, and seemed quite nice and childlike in a way, naive. She was a psychologist at a university in the United States, emotionally stronger than he, it appeared.

Finally the boat owner arrived and spoke in Spanish to us. Christiane became the translator, telling the captain where each of the people onboard wanted to go. Our destination was at the end of the line, the same as the young couple, the four of us hoping to see Francisco Alvaro. The woman knew more about him than we did and she spent the first part of the trip discussing him. It was nice to finally have a concrete feeling about who my doctor was, and a bit comforting as well to have people with us who were going to the same place, thus confirming that it was going to happen after all. Her name was Mary and his was Richard. She had an almost worshipful reverence for Francisco Alvaro and could not stop talking about him.

The further we traveled away from Iquitos, the better I felt. The sounds of the Amazon have no parallel. Where else is there a place where plants and animals are kings, free as they never are in civilization, unconstrained by roads and human development? Where else could they live so loudly, without their noises curtailed by the overpowering sounds of humanity? Where else could they behave exactly as they wanted, exactly as their instincts told them to behave, exactly as their genetic codes licensed them? Exactly to the limits of their own free will. Where else could they enact their lives in a perfectly natural undisturbed ecology?

I knew that I was entering a pure and primeval domain unlike anyplace I had ever been. It was not the way the earth was at the moment of creation. It was the analogous evolution of the kingdom of creatures, coterminous with the evolution of man's kingdom outside of it. It was the place to which creation had evolved without the membership of man. I knew positively that one day what I was seeing would be gone, because to even be aware of the rain forest was to invade its sanctity. And I knew that if I was there as an American doctor, just having opened my eyes to its existence, it would not be long until everyone was there exercising his own newfound awareness of it.

The concept of ecology, until then only a popular word to me, would take on a vast personal significance in the Amazon. Under the influence of ayahuasca, I would feel its frightening qualities of predestination, survival, and symbiotic adaptation of strength and weakness and common need that would protrude into all of my awareness.

We wandered farther and farther down the Amazon.

Simon came alive again seeing the hundreds of creatures all around us. His glee was re-evoked by screaming macaws and parakeets, millions of frogs croaking at once. Nature as we knew it seemed almost hilariously akimbo. He laughed at the strange insistent sounds.

The forest became almost silent. Then one bird squalled and another screeched, then another, until the entire woods talked competitively at a volume which ascended to an uncomfortable level until our ears were on the verge of pain and our nerves jangled with fear and excitement. Then, as if an invisible conductor somewhere in the middle of it all had dropped his baton to insinuate sotto voce to the orchestra of animals, the voices dropped off one by one until there was merely a hush.

In front of the boat swimming not ten feet from Simon was a giant tortoise. A frog with bright red, yellow, and blue stripes sat in solitude upon a giant water lily ten feet wide. Parakeets and iridescent butterflies swooped at the edge of the water. An alligator waddled in below them.

Simon grabbed me again and again to point out an animal, then a fish, then a bird or an insect.

The boat moved slowly through wonderland, farther away from civilization and its monstrous import. In time there was no human trace, no path or boat dock, not a piece of litter or Twentieth Century noise besides the muffled purr of the undersized boat engine moving us along slowly through the meandering Amazon.

I had no idea where we were or how to get back. The excitement of the group had changed to quiet reverence and awe. I lost track of time.

We'd left behind us traces of recognition. All of us moving slowly down the Amazon knew that we were maneuvering inexorably towards greater self-realizations of one kind or another. What a fitting place in which to find uncharted worlds inside of ourselves - in a world itself uncharted.

The bright sun was hoarded by the first dense layers of needy plant life below it, and being a suppliant for solar nourishment, the dark, layered rain forest had little light left to give the passengers which the boat emptied one by one onto its black shores throughout the long delightful day.

I stood next to Simon and Christiane at the rail of the deck. Together we enjoyed the final hours before our arrival at a village somewhere ahead, unbeknownst to us. I stood between them and put an arm around them each.

"I love you two. Whatever is ahead for me, I feel grateful and confident that you are with me. My life has never been so full of wonderful things as it has been since coming here and being with you."

I put my arm around Simon tightly and he put his arm around my waist.

"Simon, you asked me some questions when we returned from Macchu Picchu. And I said we would talk about them later. Do you still remember them?"

"Yes, I do. I asked you if you are more than one person. And I asked you if you like all the people you are."

"What an amazing memory you have, Simon!"

"I can remember some things forever if they are important," he said.

"Well, I've thought about them, and I know this: I'm more than one person, for sure. I'm not sure that I even know who they all are. One is a little boy. I think he doesn't like himself too much. I am a successful doctor who likes himself pretty well because others tell him he is wonderful. Another is a man who is completely undeveloped as a person and is only beginning to understand himself. That man has to develop himself in relation to the boy, because he is the boy. However, the boy remains unfinished somehow, so it's hard for the man to develop. There are probably other people inside of me, but that's enough to think of for now, don't you agree? The person that I like the most is the man, and do you know why, Simon?"

"No, tell me, Michael."

"Because he is free to be who he wants to be. He's happy and full of curiosity and adventure. He's a man who is still a boy. He's like you Simon, and he is who I like."

"Cuchari," the captain whispered. There were several small homes almost to the river's edge which I could see as the boat's engine stopped and we paddled the last small distance to shore. The homes were built on stilts, presumably to keep them above the river's rising. It was dark but the moon shone graciously on the small village.

We stood watching the distance shorten between the shore and the boat until finally we were there. The captain got out and invited us to do the same.

A tall thin man wearing a lightweight white gown emerged from the forest and said, "You have come to see Francisco Alvaro, I presume."

"Yes, sir," I replied in the dark, barely able to see him. "Can you direct us to him?"

"I am Francisco Alvaro. You have traveled long and you are tired. I'll take you to your residence and in the morning we shall talk." He turned and walked into the forest.

He walked like a deer, slowly with long strides, swaying rhythmically from side to side, his feet touching the ground weightlessly without making noise. Before he had turned to walk away, I had seen a light reflected in his eyes, which otherwise I could not have seen in the darkness.

Simon and Christiane took my hands and walked beside me, behind him. I could feel their excitement.

We walked blindly into the darkness. Finally our leader stopped at a small hutlike cabin and went inside and lit a kerosene lamp and beckoned us inside. There were two small rooms with open screened windows and with one large cot in each of them.

Now I could see his face as he walked toward the door. It was peaceful, quiet and gentle. His English was perfect. None of us was presumptuous enough to ask him a question. I discerned that he could command others with few words and with the smallest amount of movement.

So here we were, at last. Living what had just been an idea a few months before. I was a neophyte to this new awareness, to be sure, stumbling with small faith, no doubt, but convinced that I was ready.

CHAPTER 17

A band was playing crisp and loud in front of Vier Jahreszeiten. It was a parade. Hundreds lined the terraced sidewalks and stood on high perches viewing the pageantry and becoming part of the crowd's single character. The marchers moved in synchronicity, their uniforms elegant and pressed sharply. Their tall white and blue hats made them look like animated giants to the gleeful children following playfully behind them and in front of the bands that came after.

The day was beautiful and the bustling city was settling down into happiness because it was spring in Hamburg. The air was dry and unobtrusive. In the sunshine it was delightfully warm and pleasantly cool at once, like hot fudge-covered ice cream from the Conditorei. It was a holiday.

Mr. Seiler and I watched and listened from the graceful lobby of Vier Jahreszeiten. The many hotel windows that faced the festive street provided an excellent viewing circumstance from comfortable chairs. No one blocked the windows even though many people in the lobby watched the celebration. It was Hamburg. People were polite. All was in order.

"Let's take a taxi today, Michael. We shall hire a driver for the day and not be bothered with the traffic."

Mr. Seiler went to the desk and returned and we sat silently for some time listening and watching. It was a grand moment.

The driver, Karl, found us and offered his services. Mr. Seiler instructed him that we had only a general idea where we wanted to go and not a clearly defined destination, so we would need his services "on call" for many hours.

Karl drove us through the crowded parking lot in back and onto the large avenue that Mr. Seiler had walked the day before on the southeast side of the Alster.

Mr. Seiler looked wonderful. He was dressed casually in an off-white cotton sweater with dark blue trousers. He wore a suede Irish hat. He was handsome and smiling. I told him he looked good.

He took my hand and said to me, "Do you know what, Michael? Last night and the night before, I slept the entire night without waking up and without having a dream. It's the first time in thirty years I've not dreamed of the bombing of Hamburg. I feel marvelous. I feel like I have been given a new beginning." Even though we had agreed the night before that our objective that day was to find Horst, I think we both wanted to take our time. Mr. Seiler loved the early morning because, he said, if one arises before the sun, his enterprise is rewarded with an extra portion of energy to extend the time before weariness sets in, before crowds take over the landscape and noise silences the birds and the breezes. He said that early in the morning one can "re-share for an instant the nectar of youth in nature's purity."

We went above Auben-Alster midlake, through Uhlenhorst, and followed the Alster River above Stadpark. Mr. Seiler told the driver to stop at a scenic wooded glen near one of the river's lakes and we got out and walked. Karl stayed in the car but Mr. Seiler turned back to the taxi and motioned broadly to him saying, "You come too, you need a walk."

Karl followed behind us, but Mr. Seiler hooked the driver's arm in his own and brought Karl forward. The three of us walked together and spoke German.

After we had walked awhile, there was an enchanting home with a wooden fence near the main house, hidden in the woods. It looked like something from fairy tales I had read as a young child.

"What is this?" I asked him.

"I brought you here, Michael, so that when you find Susanne and are telling her about how much you know of Hamburg, you can say to her, "And I also visited Muhlenteich." She will think you are a charming prince." He smiled. "Provided that she does not already think that. This is the winter home of the Alster Swans. They are Royal White Mute swans, the ones which are in the fairy tales. For example, in the opera Lohengrin, the Swan Knight was a knight of the holy grail and the son of King Arthur's Sir Parsifal. He was led by such a swan to the rescue of a German princess. In King Arthur's court the swan was the symbol of purity. Prospective brides offered food to this swan and if it wouldn't eat, it was a sign that the marriage was not pure and should not go forward. To the people of Hamburg, the swan is important."

We stopped for lunch at a sunny outside café where after tea Mr. Seiler took a nap in the sun.

When he awoke he said, "Now we shall find Horst."

"Let's go to Stadpark first," I said, "And see his sculptures."

"An excellent idea," he said.

Stadpark was an enormous open area northeast of the Upper Alster in Winterhude. Devastated during the war and not far above Mr. Seiler's old home in Uhlenhorst, it had special significance for him.

He said it was there that he had spent time with his family on Sundays, picnicking with other families.

The park was so big that there were lots of diverse things, including a huge planetarium, businesses, forests, playing fields, and in the southeast part of it was a lake half the size of the Binnen-Alster. It was here that we found a museum of modern art produced by Hamburg artists. One of Horst's sculptures was inside the museum and there was a map directing us to two others outside near the lake.

The piece inside was a globe on top of a pedestal which revolved like the earth. Everywhere on its surface were tiny scenes in relief depicting significant events at various spots throughout the earth. On closer inspection I could see that the globe was the head of a deity and its painful expressions were the scenes.

At the north side of the lake we found two other abstract sculptures, placed at the edge of trees. One of them, in fact, looked like a tree in shape and color. The other was round and feminine, sensuous. Without knowing how to judge art, I thought they were worthy pieces.

Mr. Seiler was moved by them, I could tell. He must have been proud to have his son represented for all the city to see.

"Even as a very young boy he had an understanding of how matter could be manipulated for a purpose," Mr Seiler said. "I thought he would be an inventor, but of course this is also invention."

We had the name of Horst's woman-friend and where she taught school, and we drove there. Her name was Angela Bulgrin. We inquired at the office and they told us she was teaching a class, so we waited in the foyer for the class to end.

Within fifteen minutes the empty hallways were glutted with students moving quickly in every direction, talking and laughing. I was watching her doorway and caught a glimpse of a woman I thought must be her moving in the opposite direction, slipping deftly through spaces between students. I told the others to wait and hurried after her.

I caught up to her and grabbed her by the elbow just before she reached another doorway to an unmarked room. She stopped abruptly and turned. She had long reddish hair and a receptive face which made her seem younger than I'd expected her to be.

"Yes, what do you want?"

"My name is Michael Langhen. I'm from America. I'm looking for Horst Seiler."

"Why?" she asked suspiciously.

"I have his father with me from America, who wishes to find him. Kurt Seiler."

Suddenly the expression was stunned from her face, which lost tune with me for an instant. Then she touched the back of my hand and said, "Wait here. I'll be right out."

She went inside the door and was there a few minutes. I leaned awkwardly against the wall and watched the hallway, dense with people, become vacant again gradually, as if the bodies were being vacuumed one at a time into the doorways along the corridor. By the time she returned there were only a few people remaining and I could see Karl and Kurt at the end looking for me.

"Where is he?" she asked. She looked nervous, the way someone looks whose anxiety at performing an unpleasant task is compounded by her sense of responsibility.

We walked quickly to the two men who walked toward us as they saw us coming.

"I'm not exactly sure where Horst is now," she said to Kurt before being introduced. "He's been working on a project north of here along the Alster."

"Are you his girlfriend?"

She was pretty when she smiled, her face revealing attributes I would not have imagined could have come from the plain and serious face she'd shown before.

"You might say that," she said.

"Well, I'm his father. Did you know he had a father?"

"I assumed he did, since even he must have been born of man." They both laughed. They spoke in English and German.

"He's talked of you. But actually, he assumed you were dead."

"No, I'm not. Just a bit slow." They laughed again.

Angela informed us she had another class to teach but suggested we meet in an hour at a café not far away.

We drove around a bit and then found the café. After a while Angela arrived. She sat down at the table and talked quickly about the little problems of the day at school and the students, as if we were old friends involved in the chain of her daily life instead of strangers she'd just met. Her small talk was designed, I felt, to feather into a more serious discussion of Horst.

Mr. Seiler let her talk until she had nothing left to say, and then he said, "So tell me about Horst."

Abruptness was not her way. "You remind me of him."

"Oh? Tell me how."

"You look like him. And you talk like him. And you don't waste time on small things, do you?"

"Sometimes I do, but I rather prefer to get to the point."

"So does Horst."

He smiled and leaned forward. "Maybe I got it from him."

"He told me you left after the war."

"He didn't want to come with me."

"No, he is a German first."

Mr. Seiler sighed and changed his manner. "Angela, let us be candid with one another, all right?"

"Certainly," she said.

"Horst is my son. I know him. I don't expect him to be thrilled to see me. I'm 83 years old. I have come to Hamburg because my life is near its end, and it is time to make amends with those things from my past which I have not forgiven and which have not forgiven me. I don't know what he has told you about me, but let's start afresh, you and me, instead of relying upon secondhand information. I would like to take you to dinner, and I would like you to tell me who my son is now and what I should expect upon seeing him again. And then I would like to look for him. I would be happy to have you come with us if you will."

She seemed thrilled to be invited.

Angela had taken the bus to the café, and so she rode with us back to her house.

She changed her clothes and then walked us to the door. She lit a cigarette on the way to the car and took a few quick puffs then stubbed it out on a stepping stone and put the butt in her pocket. I sat in the back of the car with her. She had put on a bit of perfume in her bedroom, and it smelled nice. She was full of energy and enthusiasm. As she talked, I could see that she was powerful and perceptive as well, which her childlike femininity had masked at first.

Mr. Seiler asked about the work Horst was doing.

"He's building a huge fireplace in the home of a wealthy man and woman. A whole wall really. And he is also sculpting the man's wife in the stone wall of which the fireplace is a part. It's very tedious work. He has been working there for months. In fact, he is now living in the man's guest house during the week and returning to Hamburg on

Saturday or Sunday. These people *adore* him! As you might remember, one does not simply contract for Horst the stone mason or Horst the sculptor. You also must take Horst the raging politician and Horst the barroom oracle. These people love that about him. He tells them they are bourgeois pigs. It helps them with their guilt."

"Why do they feel guilty?"

"Oh, they're disgustingly wealthy. They don't have the slightest idea what the world is really like. They have servants and butlers and maids. The children are completely spoiled. They've earned none of their money, it's all been handed to them from their family. Horst tells them they wouldn't know how to 'wipe their asses without someone showing them.'"

"Why does he work for them if he doesn't respect them?" Mr. Seiler asked.

"I don't know why Horst does what he does. Some people he won't even talk to and others he can tolerate like family. I don't know what motivates him. In some strange way, he likes these people. It is insulting the way he treats them but they don't care. They just want him around. They need his strength and his certainty. I don't think any of them understands what's going on."

"Is it for the money?"

"In a way. But money to him is just an inconvenience."

"Angela, how long have you been with Horst?" Mr. Seiler asked.

She laughed. "Forever! No, I think about seventeen years. It's hard to say. We have not been together all of that time. He leaves and comes back. But somehow he's always here with me because I know he'll come back. Your son, Kurt, is not a typical man."

"What does he do when he leaves?"

"He just disappears sometimes and is gone for weeks. Eventually I find him back at his house, reading."

"Are there other women?"

"Usually. Horst has his women, that's for sure. We don't have a relationship of man and woman anymore."

"What is he, your brother?"

"I don't know what he is. My brother, my father, my mother, my friend, a warm body on a cold night. It's not typical, Kurt. He's not typical and I'm no longer typical either."

"Do you have other men you see?"

"Of course."

"Does he get jealous?"

"Well, the closest he comes to that is when he doesn't like one of them, but that has nothing to do with me. Often he ends up being friends with them. In either case he hangs around all the time and always causes some kind of disruption, either a fight or else he steals them from me. I think he secretly wants to have me to himself but also to have his other life."

Mr. Seiler shook his head and muttered something.

"Kurt, you have to understand something. We were both abandoned by our families. His mother died in the war along with his brother, and you left Germany with his grandmother and never saw him again. My parents divorced when I was very young and my mother left and I have only seen her once in my life, at which time she indicated her disapproval of me and left forever. My father lived with an assortment of women. We are wounded creatures, Horst and I, whose shelter comes from strange places. I understand this about him in a way which most people don't."

"Horst was that way before I left Germany."

"Well, maybe he felt abandoned before the war. He's confused, Kurt, by who you are to him. He sees you as a powerful man with strong values, but he also sees you as someone who dropped out of his life forever, and he can't reconcile these things. He'll be shocked to see you. He won't know how to react, but let me tell you something now. You must allow him to react the way that he'll need to react and not interfere with it or be hurt by it, because it will be hard to reach Horst even with the greatest sensitivity. If you respond with anger or defensiveness, you'll lose him behind a wall of strength which you will never penetrate. You've come here to Hamburg partly to re-establish a relationship with your son. But he hasn't been forewarned of it, which is not entirely fair, so it will have to be done on his terms more than on yours. He is a fascinating man, Kurt. No one understands him fully. He won't let them. And he probably doesn't understand himself. He has adapted to the situations in his life with a power and a strength probably equal to yours but different, because the circumstances of your lives were different."

The car was silent. The charge of the air had become neutral again as the emotional electrons reluctantly found their new accord. "I understand. I'll do as you say," Mr. Seiler said.

She put her hand on his shoulder. The hand was calloused and rough and the knuckles big. "I know you'll do the right thing. I can see you are a good man, Kurt. It's wonderful that you are here. He needs this as much as you do. He needs you. He's not a young man anymore. He doesn't have much more time to try to straighten it out."

"Nor do I," Mr. Seiler added.

"Ah!" she said grabbing his arm and lightening the somber mood, "You look young!"

Mr. Seiler smiled.

"Listen, here is the plan," she said. "Horst will go to an inn near where he works around 18:00. He always eats there after having a few drinks. In those ways Horst is predictable.

"We can eat there too, but first I have to stop at a friend's house near there to see her about some problems she is having. I'll drop you off at the inn and you have something to drink and wait for me. I'll be just a short time. Horst won't be there until 1800. If he happens to be there, he won't recognize you."

It seemed like the end of a long journey home for Mr Seiler, as if a symphony had achieved its voice and was ready to reach its conclusion to which all of the previous movements had pointed.

Omens were once again visible in the duskskies over Hamburg, proclaiming again resolutely that things would change. The last moments between now and then, it seemed, could be gathered and cherished only with prodigious concentration, and even at that, only a transitory apparent peace could be attained.

Angela let us off at the inn. The bar was dark. We sat at a table just inside the door. Several men were at the bar arguing loudly about something. When the man with his back to us turned to the side, I could see it was Horst. I looked at Mr. Seiler.

I watched him watch his son. With a surprising feeling of identification with Horst that until that moment I'd not known was present within me, I felt strangely nervous for him, like a father whose child was about to perform publicly. More than anything I wanted him to do his best, to access the finest features of himself in a display which would move the audience to its feet.

In just the few minutes of listening to Horst's brilliant voice, its deep resonance and passion and edgy humor, I saw, as Angela had suggested, a glimpse of the good things that were inside of him, and I prayed that he could bring them forth.

Mr. Seiler's face looked sad and I wished that I could be inside of his consciousness, sorting out his thoughts for him and shunting them into safe directions of detachment and unemotional understanding. I felt like the protector of both men, a tiny David laughably powerless against this Goliath situation.

I noticed outside the window an edge of twilight, and I took it to be an auspicious garb meant to wrap the last moments of illumination in a cushion of transition and to chaperone them safely into the darkness that was sure to follow.

Mr. Seiler arose from the table and walked slowly toward his son whose back was facing us. At the same time Angela opened the huge wooden door at the entrance to the inn, the two of them arriving together at the instant of reunion. As Mr. Seiler put his hand on Horst's shoulder while he was talking, unmindful of the circumstance behind him, Horst turned to acknowledge his father's touch, but the first thing he saw was Angela walking into the bar toward them.

"So you've met, eh?" she said.

"Who?"

"You've met your father."

"My what?" he said to Angela and then looked at his father for the first time in decades.

Conflicting crosscurrents of understanding made it impossible for either of them to speak. I wanted to run forward and explain it all clearly to both of them before they had a chance to make a mistake, but it wasn't my moment and my explanation would doubtlessly have fallen short of the eloquence required for understanding to be achieved between them. There was no way to assuage in a single utterance the feelings needing to be expressed. I felt helpless to aid either this remarkable man who had taken me in as a guttersnipe on the streets of his life and expanded my horizons forever, or his remarkable son of whom I was instantly in awe.

"I am Kurt Seiler. Your father."

Horst's face was spectacular in power and magnitude and his eyes incomprehensible in revealing nothing, like a heartless gambler.

He stood staring at his father long past the boundaries of propriety. Then he said, "Do you have an ID?"

The men at the bar laughed.

Mr. Seiler reached into his pocket and pulled out his wallet and held it up for Horst to see. Horst didn't look at it but stared longer at his father. "Are you in Hamburg on a tour or do you have relatives here?"

"I have relatives here."

Horst motioned to an empty chair at the bar. "Sit down."

Mr. Seiler turned to our table and said, "Why don't you come sit with us?"

Horst picked up his drink and left the two men sitting alone at the bar and followed Kurt to our table.

"This is Michael Langhen and Karl, our driver." I stood up and shook his hand. His handshake was firm and, I dare say, friendly, which relieved me a little.

"You hired a driver to come to the inn?" he asked. "That's probably a first."

"They came by the school this afternoon, Horst," Angela said. "We had a nice visit."

"And who are you?" he said to me.

"I'm a friend of Mr. Seiler's."

"Do all of his friends call him 'Mister Seiler'?"

He turned to Kurt and said, "I thought maybe he was your grandson."

"I don't have a grandson, do I, Horst?"

I was beginning to worry. I could hear the bombers roaring again in the skies and the bombs whistling on their way to the ground. My instinct was to run for shelter.

"How would you know if you do or don't?"

"I wouldn't know, Horst. Tell me if I do."

"Don't worry, you don't. I wouldn't subject a kid to that again."

"There would be no children if everyone thought that way." Horst didn't reply.

"So tell me, Mr. Seiler, what has brought you back to Hamburg after so long?"

Already Mr. Seiler seemed cautious of answering his mistrustful son. "Well, it was actually Michael's idea. He thought of it first and as time went by it seemed like a good thing to do."

Horst turned to me. "And why did you want to come here?"

I was intimidated by him. "Because my girlfriend is here." In his presence I felt insignificant and petty. The words I spoke seemed pallid and ineffective, embarrassingly feeble.

"In Hamburg? What is she doing here?"

"She was going to school in the States but came back here."

"My God, and you have come all the way here to see her? Let me tell you something about Hamburg girls: You are better off finding one in the States. Haven't you found her yet?"

"Not yet."

"How long have you been here?"

"Almost a week."

"And you haven't found her yet?"

"No."

He laughed. "A terminal case of young love."

I didn't know what to say. He was so cynical that it took away our voices. Finally Mr. Seiler asked him about his work, and they exchanged a few sentences. Then Kurt bravely said, "It is good to find you, Horst."

"It is?" Horst asked cynically and incredulously.

"Yes, it is."

"Why is it good to find me? Does it make you feel less guilty?"

"I don't feel guilty, Horst. About what? Leaving Hamburg? Was I not entitled to leave Hamburg? A city destroyed. I left Hamburg because I couldn't stay here. I tried to get you to go, but you wouldn't. I wrote you many times from America, but you didn't answer."

"Hmm. You abandoned your country and your city when they needed you most. You abandoned your friends. You abandoned me. Don't you think there were many who felt the way you did, but who nonetheless stayed here to help rebuild their city?"

"Yes, I suppose there were. But I could not have survived looking at the destruction here. Katerina and the baby dead. Your brother dead. Thousands of people tortured and burned alive in front of me. I couldn't go on here. My reaction to it was not the same as yours. Maybe you were stronger than I and were not so affected by it. Listen to what I am telling you: I could not have continued here. It is a fact. I did it for survival, just as you do what you must do for survival."

Horst went to the bar to get another drink and stayed talking to the men at the bar awhile. Angela tried to make small talk, but everyone was too uncomfortable for that. Then Horst came back.

"Let me tell you something, Mr. Seiler. I forgot you long ago. I made a life here without you. Not one that you would have approved, of course, but my life."

"I approve of your life. I have seen some of your artwork and it is quite good. From what I have heard you are a well-respected artisan."

"You don't know my life. You've not been here to see it happen. The pieces of art you saw are just tiny fragments of it. I am fifty-eight years old. More has happened to me than that. I am the same person you didn't like before. Nothing has changed except the details."

Mr. Seiler's face looked sad and hopeless and weary.

"How can you imply that I didn't like you. You are my son. Indeed I am glad to see you. I'll be here another week, Horst. I hope that we can talk much more. Do you think that you could have dinner with me tomorrow?"

"Impossible. I have to finish the project and I'm short of help. This will be a busy week. You can't just appear in someone's life after thirty years of absence and expect them to drop everything to accommodate you."

"Horst, I've come to Hamburg to see you. I've come here to ask your forgiveness. I have come to receive your blessing."

"Well then, you've come to the wrong place, Mr. Seiler. I'm not in a forgiving mood and I have no blessings to give you."

Angela grabbed his arm and looked at him gravely. "Horst, this is your father. You need to talk to him." He pulled away from her.

"I don't need anything of the sort. He's waited until he is about to die and then, like a convert, he's come for forgiveness. He should have looked for me earlier in my life when I was more forgiving." He turned to me and my blood ran cold. "He shows up with this child in search of his girlfriend, hoping for a pardon from me along the way. I'm not interested." And with that he returned to the bar and sat a few moments with the two men before disappearing through the other door into the back of the bar.

I couldn't have imagined a worse reunion. Mr. Seiler and I were crushed and speechless. Angela mercifully remained positive and assured us that we did just fine and that Horst would think it over and come back to us.

"I'm not so sure. He's very bitter. I need time to think about this myself. Michael, let's take Angela back to her house and you and I will go back to the hotel, all right?"

We were all quiet driving back to Angela's house. Before she got out of the car she made a plea for clemency.

"Kurt, that was not your son you saw. Believe me, will you please? He is compassionate and caring and heroic in his heart. Those qualities are a major part of him, and you'll find them if you're patient with him and let them come out. Because he's not like others and chooses a life entirely his own, he's had to fight all of his life to explain and defend who he is, so his first reaction is to be antagonistic. But he has nobility and strength unlike anyone I have known. Please don't give up on him yet. Another thing, Kurt. He is under a crushing deadline to finish this project he's working on. Tension is developing day by day between him and the money providers and the owners. His two assistants are gone. One is sick and the other has disappeared, so he has to work alone, which is exhausting him every day."

"I want to believe that what you say is true, Angela. But for now I need some time to think. Michael has to find his friend. We've been here a week and he has no good clues. Tomorrow we must begin to seriously look for her. I'm afraid it will take some time. But I'll do my best to make contact with my son again as soon as possible. Maybe he needs some time to think as well."

———

I heard Mr. Seiler rolling and moaning in his sleep that night.

In the morning I awoke before sunrise and went downstairs to call Angela. I asked her if she could take me to the place where Horst was working.

"He won't like that. He hates to be disturbed when he's working."

"I don't want to disturb him. I want to help him with the job."

"Oh, Michael! That won't work. First of all, I don't think he will accept help from you at this point. But also, he can be terrible to work for, he is such a perfectionist. That's why most people don't stay with him."

"I don't care. I can work hard. I can help him."

"Michael, you don't want to spend all of your time in Hamburg working with Horst."

"Please, Angela. Take me there."

She agreed. She told me how to take a bus to where she would meet me. Then I could take her to school and drive her car to the project. "If I take you there, he will think I put you up to it," she said.

I had some older clothes in my room. I left a note for Kurt telling him where I was and that I would call him. I asked him to meet me and Angela later and asked Angela to call him during the day.

The morning was cool and misty, steam rising above the earth near the valley of the river. I followed Angela's directions and saw an old red truck she said would be in the driveway of a beautiful home that was alone above the stream. It was quite early, but already Horst was mixing cement in an old hand mixer behind his truck. He looked up for just a second as I arrived.

I was scared, but what could he do? Tell me to leave?

I got out of Angela's car and walked toward him and I heard Brahms's Andante coming from an ancient cement mixer! When he looked up again, he realized it wasn't Angela and was startled.

Before he could say a word I said, "I have come to help you."

"Help me what?" His face was creased and tired-looking. He looked older than the night before.

"Help you work. You said you needed help."

"No, I didn't. I said I need to finish the project and that my assistants were gone. I didn't say I needed your help."

"Well, you do."

He laughed a mean laugh and said, "I need someone who can work, not a child."

"I can work, you'll see."

"Where have you worked before?"

"I worked in your father's bookstore. I ran it for him."

"A bookstore? Ha! Kurt had a bookstore? Do you think putting books on shelves is like doing masonry? You couldn't last an hour at this work."

"Yes, I can. I promise I can."

"Go home, Michael. I have to work." He began turning the mixer again. At least he'd called me by my first name.

I stood watching him, determined to be used. By his very silence I felt tacitly approved. I knew that I would help him and that by the end of the day he would respect me. I could feel an abundant energy soar within my body, propelled by the opportunity which this could represent. I was like a hunting dog by the side of its master, a thoroughbred waiting for the gate to open.

"Tell me what to do," I urged him.

He was thinking. He knew as well as I that to use me had far-reaching implications. It meant, most likely, an agreement to re-engage his past with his father and perhaps even to unearth things inside of himself buried deeply.

"You won't be sorry," I said.

"Okay," he said still turning the mixer and not even looking up. "Here is your first masonry lesson. The space between the stones is called the 'joint'. The best masonry has the thinnest joints - stones close together. The masons in your country have joints as wide as the stones themselves. That's the worst extreme. The Incas in South America made joints so tight that they did not even need mortar to tie them together. That's what we want to approach. This is mortar," he said pulling out the gray stewy mud from the cement mixer's mouth. "More about mortar later. See that pile of stones over there? I want you to separate it into three piles: small, medium, and large stones. Understand?"

"Yes," I said and went to start making three piles of the one huge mound of stones, while Horst continued to pump the cement mixer.

"Also, wash the stones off well with water."

He was talking to me and letting me work with him. It was an unbelievable concession, like a wild horse accepting a bridle. I had to prove myself to him or all would be lost. My first job was to separate the stones into three piles.

"Come here, Michael," he yelled as he walked to the house. "Let me show you what I want."

We walked into the garage of the house and up some stairs and through a door into a cathedral-like room with a wooden ceiling two stories tall. One wall was glass which faced the stream in the back. The other, unfinished, was being built of stone. Next to the firebox at the height of the mantle was a partially finished sculpture of a woman carved from the rock. It was just her unfinished face and shoulders looking into the room.

"Look at these joints," he said touching the wall next to the sculpture. "That's how the rocks should look. Or better."

"This is amazing," I said.

"Huh!" he scoffed. "The best stonemasons in Germany would laugh at that. They make walls of stone with cracks the width of a pencil. Okay, you go to work now. I'm going to stay inside and work on this woman."

First I separated the huge pile into three smaller piles, but I didn't just throw each stone on its appropriate pile. Even though Horst had only asked me to make three piles, I began to assemble them into three pictures right from the start. I realized that the result would be a wall of stones yielding not one picture but three: little stones, medium stones, and large stones. The true job, I surmised, was to artistically design the wall using all three sizes of stones in all places. I made a bold decision. Instead of making three piles from which Horst would have to create a composite, I made one composite of all the stones. I designed the entire wall there in the driveway, the way one usually did it on the work itself, one stone at a time. I felt he was a man who could accept that, if I did it artfully. And it was fast. If he disapproved, nothing would have been accomplished and I would have wasted the morning.

I went back inside, apparently to ask him a question but really I needed to assess how wide and tall the space was to be finished, which I did by pacing it off as I walked back out the door after he answered me. I made the wall in the driveway a little smaller than that, to allow for mortar.

I worked feverishly, knowing that I would have only one chance. He would either like it or would reject it outright.

Horst was obsessively focused upon what he was doing and so left me alone for a long time. I discovered later that he routinely lost the sense of time when deeply involved in something. That's how I was too.

Much later, as I was standing in the sun with my shirt off looking at the almost-complete wall, occasionally rearranging a stone here or there in order to more nearly approximate a seamless depiction, Horst came from the house. He stopped in his tracks, still too far away to see exactly what I had done, frowning deeply with the sun in his eyes.

"What's that?" he asked disparagingly.

I didn't answer.

He walked toward me slowly, pondering what he was beginning to see more clearly. "What have you done here?"

"I built the wall."

He walked around and around it, occasionally replacing a stone with one still in the pile at the side or turning one in place to expose a better facet.

"Amazing! I've never seen anyone do this. How will we get it inside?"

I was happy that he approved of it enough to contemplate its movement that I didn't even think about his question. My heart was pounding. I felt a tremendous relief and realized then that I had been focusing intently upon this job since leaving him the night before and that somehow in some divine place inside of me I had pre-solved this puzzle before knowing precisely what it was.

My head ached from concentrating so totally for so long.

"Do you have a suggestion?" he asked. His voice was cynical but it was playful too and there was a smile on his face which seemed to appreciate the absurdity of what I had done.

"I've almost finished the bust. I need a little longer. You figure out how to get this inside." And he walked back to the house.

Horst came back out to the driveway and handed me some money and said, "Go get us something to eat. And a beer. Take the truck. The inn is open now."

His truck was a relic of patchwork, with missing handles and replacement levers and gadgets. It looked like his house, stuff all over the seats and floors. Tools and bills, letters and books were piled everywhere, with dust covering it all. It looked as if it had never been washed or cleaned. One couldn't avoid becoming dust-covered by driving or merely riding in it.

I moved a few items on the seat in order to have room to sit more comfortably, and I saw a picture of a man with his arm around a teenage boy, standing together near a beautiful home. They looked alike. It was springtime and the sun was shining in their faces which were smiling happily. Holding it closer to my eyes, I could see that it was Horst and Kurt. Horst was without a beard and Kurt was young, in his forties perhaps. For me who had never known either of them except at one age, it was a new revelation.

The man at the inn could not understand my request. I guessed from his accent that he was from another Eastern European country. So many people in Hamburg had spoken English that I had almost forgotten I was in a foreign country. Finally I just said in German, "Food for Horst Seiler," and pointed towards the house, and he nodded with understanding. He pointed at me too and I nodded back that I wanted food too. He said something that I couldn't understand and I said in German, "Lots of food."

We ate in the driveway next to the stone puzzle I'd put together. Horst studied it carefully while we ate.

"When I finish the woman, we'll start the wall. Can you bring this in to me one stone at a time, just like you have it here?"

"I think so."

"You have a good memory, no?"

"Yes, I do."

"Don't forget how these stones go together, because sometimes they will fit several ways and if we get them wrong at the start we'll be way off at the bottom and we'll have to find correction stones. But if we can do it just like you have it here, it might work. I've never done it this way, but it might work. Tell me about your girlfriend."

I couldn't seem to get started telling him anything important, because he'd been so cynical the night before. He continued with his outspoken questions until I finally opened up a little about her. Although he was not sensitive, I needed to speak to someone about her.

"Are you in love?"

"I don't know what I am."

"You must be in love then. Love is confusion."

"Really?"

"Of course. Two people from different sexes, which is almost the same as two different species, are fatally pulled together by biological forces they can't control, manipulated by the Deus Ex Machina to endlessly propagate His invention. And they are supposed to live happily together ever after. So they're confused, naturally. Once they regain control of themselves, after a few kids, they want themselves back but it's too late by then."

"That's pretty cynical."

"That's what reality is."

"Have you ever been in love?"

"Of course, many times."

"I mean have you ever felt like someone had the answers to you and you needed that person in order to be complete?"

"For a short while. Until I recovered my senses."

"That's how I feel with Susanne."

"That's because she left you. It's human nature to want someone who doesn't want you. After you find her and you discover she's just flesh and blood like you, you'll change. Especially if she starts wanting you back, because then the mystery and challenge of rejection will be gone. Is she your first love?"

"Yes."

He raised his eyebrows and grunted. "Michael, I hate to be the one to tell you this but everyone feels the way you do the first time they fall in love. Accept that she has gone. Your life will be easier. Find another girl. Then you'll forget her. By the time you get to be my age, you won't get so hurt by rejection, believe me."

"Why?"

"Because you'll be worn out from being consistently disappointed in your expectations."

"I think you're wrong about this."

"About love? No, I'm right. You'll see."

"About love and about Susanne. She didn't leave me voluntarily. I know. I wouldn't be here otherwise."

He looked at me pityingly, but didn't reply.

"What about Angela?"

"What about her?"

"She loves you."

"She loves me like a brother."

"I can see that she loves you different from that."

"Sure, but that's not what you're experiencing. I know what you're experiencing. I've felt it many times."

"I think Angela still experiences that with you. It is you who doesn't feel it."

"Perhaps."

"Do you fight it?"

"What?"

"Love."

"Probably. I don't trust it."

"Maybe if a person didn't fight it but believed in it and had faith in its power, then he would discover another side of it."

"You're naive, Michael. Let's go back to work."

And with that he stood up and walked toward the house. His walk was stiff, as if he was in pain at the legs or in the back. His body was getting too old for stone work, I thought. I liked him. He was like his father in a way that was not obvious at first.

I followed him into the cathedral room. There it was: the woman on the wall. He had almost completed her. I could see her face clearly now. Her pained, reaching eyes and hair sweeping her high cheekbones. The collar on her shirt was turned up. All was chiseled and shaped from stone. What a beautiful dedication to one's wife, I thought.

"That's beautiful, Horst."

"It came out well. This is the first time I've worked on it for two weeks. I needed some time."

"He must really love her to commission something like this," I said.

"No, I'm afraid not. He's trying to buy her affection, trying to convince himself that he still wants it, I should say. They've been talking about divorce for months, and they think this idolatrous wall will keep them from it, the way shallow people think all solutions can be constructed of matter. I call it the 'wailing wall.'"

"Is she as handsome as you've made her here?"

"'Handsome.' I like that word. Yes, she is very handsome. It would be easier for him to understand his feelings for her if she weren't so handsome. But, then, he should not have been able to capture such a handsome woman. She was charmed by his money, which now is no good to her because he comes with it. He's a nice guy. Weak, though. She treats him without respect. They've grown together like a weed with a flower, so that now both of them share one earth, one source of nourishment. That's what you have to be careful of: the qualities in others which we find attractive are attractive usually because they are not in us. But then we destroy and alter that person in order to make them like ourselves. Once they're like ourselves, we can't stand them anymore and want the person back that was there before we forced them to change into us. But it's too late by then: they have become us! So then we're reminded doubly of our faults!" He laughed.

"Are you saying we should become perfect before we involve ourselves with others?"

"No. I'm just observing that we change and corrupt each other. Two saints living together would probably do the same. That's why you never hear of Mrs. St. Augustine."

"Don't you believe there are couples who are good together?" I asked him.

"Only if one has yielded power to the other. It always ends up being a struggle for power. I really don't see how two good people end up being better by being together in marriage. Of course in the beginning they will learn from each other, but after the learning is over, which is in a short period usually, what remains is a complex of habits, usually annoying and bad ones. Marriage is a matter of adjusting to each other's habits, the bad ones especially."

I had never listened to anyone so cynical and negative. On one hand it was fascinating but on the other I saw how it could be paralyzing. He continued to work on the face of the woman, and I felt certain that he had made her more beautiful than she was. How could he do this and not be romantic and idealistic? I wondered.

"Start bringing the wall in," he instructed me. He turned back to his sculpture.

While he worked on the woman I began cleaning up the room which looked like his truck. I took all the things outside which I knew he would not use again. I picked up his tools which were everywhere and arranged them by use underneath the window after cleaning them off outside. I picked up all the debris and rubbish, chips of stone, pop bottles and beer cans, crumpled up paper and old newspapers, and threw them in an empty box. Then I carefully swept the wooden floor so that it wouldn't be scratched and I re-covered it with the tarpaulin he had put down but which had pulled away from its original position. I tuned his radio which was filled with static so that it once again played classical music nicely. Then I began bringing in the wall, stone by stone.

Finally he looked up and saw all that I had done. I could tell he was pleased. "You're a good guy, Michael."

"You're father's a good guy too, Horst."

"Maybe."

"He is."

"You don't know everything about my father."

"You don't either."

The sun was moving underneath the horizon flirtatiously, the way it does in the late spring, not falling off the earth altogether and taking with it all of its light at once as it does in the winter, but spreading out warmth and glow long past the disappearance of its orb, stretching its allure like golden strings of atmospheric taffy.

We worked on and on into that good night, hardly saying another word except short instructions to each other. He wasn't difficult to work with at all. On the contrary, working beside him was a joy. He was a man who expected a helper to proudly accomplish what needed to be accomplished and to give all of himself to the effort. That was all. After he saw that I could use my head and was willing to work hard, he gave me whatever authority I was willing to take. He was a great teacher, like his father.

The way he moved was like a cat setting up the conditions for his attack. It was the recognition that the time was at hand only while the hourglass of the muse was running. That imperative restored his youthful energy like an elixir.

I was the facilitator, the enabler, the catalyst if you will. My job was to see that not an inspired moment was wasted. And I was witness to his confession in stone. To the contrition and the sensitivity and even the pathos I could see in his hands and face as he put the stones together and shaped them expertly to the theme.

———

"You're almost finished," Mr. Seiler said. He was standing with Angela in the doorway behind us. "It is quite remarkable what you've done here."

I could see the nighttime behind them through the wall of towering windows, and above the trees through which the glittering stream ran onward was a quarter-moon shining at the center of a thousand flecks of stardust.

"What time is it?" Horst asked.

"Almost midnight," Angela whispered. "We came here earlier and watched you through the window but we didn't want to bother you. You're a good team."

"He's great!" Horst said, slapping his hand firmly onto my shoulder and holding it there. "You're lucky to have him, Kurt."

"I know I am. Think of what a doctor he will be."

His voice towards his father sounded gentle and endearing. His father's voice in reply sounded the same. They were talking again, father Seiler and his son Horst.

Stentorian cannons in the distance thunderously ceased to roar. Slender bells of truce timidly began to sound. Battle-weary veterans sauntered slowly on a mossgrown path bound homeward. At last the War was over now, and peace waited quietly near at hand.

CHAPTER 18

O n the fifth day God made the birds of the rain forest. He made the musical brown-headed parrots, the scarlet-thighed blue dacnis to drink at the nectaries of the Inga tree, the nightingale wren to sing a sound of jazz in the purple evening. The crested guans, the white hawks, the chestnut-headed oropendolas, the woodcreeper with its mournful morning sound, the black skimmers and cool white terns, the Orinoco geese and the lonesome cocoi heron, kingfishers and horned scammers. They were all colors, and sometimes all colors at once. He made more than 1500 species of birds alone to live in the Amazon. How could He have imagined so many birds with so many odd characteristics? Every one of them sang at our first early morning, as we lay sleeping.

He also made frogs. The poison arrow frogs, like tiny wrestlers, the smoky jungle frog with its teeny sucker toes, the emerald tree frogs, reticulated glass frogs, lemur frogs with huge alien eyes. Over 300 species of frogs in the rain forest.

Only part of them sang and croaked in that early morning. The rest waited until night.

The sounds of the Amazon birds and frogs of a morning can be grasped by imagining all of the commuters at a huge train station in a big city early in the morning singing at the top of their lungs whatever song comes into their heads to express how happy they are to be alive.

All of the birds, surely by the first photon of new morning and some in early anticipation of that, began screaming and shouting, belly laughing and howling, clamoring and squalling, shrieking and roaring and jabbering and ranting and raving. And it seemed to me that they were saying: "Look, another beautiful sunrise of another wonderful day. We are lucky to be alive here in the Amazon rain forest where we are the kings."

All of the others slept through this euphony of birds and frogs except me. I couldn't move, but could only listen, because Simon had his arms around me. As I lay sandwiched between Christiane and her son, I tried to cull out leaders from the voices, but there were none. They were all in fierce competition for stage center. It was hilarious. And beautiful in an almost brutal way.

The village seemed different to me than I'd expected. It was peopleless. There were no reminders of civilization. Amidst the mysteriousness of the place, there was a feeling of predictability and trustworthiness, even inevitability and almost a sameness within the vast diversity, as if options were limited with a machine-like regularity occurring within a boundlessness. By being limited in this confounding way it seemed to make one's choices simple and necessary.

The forest was deeply impenetrable in one sense and in another sense it was completely open. It was odd that I could sense this after just one day, and Simon could too; odd that we both had had this initial feeling, because later we learned that to many natives the river and the jungle are frightening places, that the shrill whistles at dusk are the sounds of recent dead who roam the earth. Some even believe that there is a huge city below the surface of the river where strange creatures live, an upside-down city which is a reverse image of that found on earth, with creatures whose heads are on backwards. They think that this reverse city under water is paradise, preferable to life above it.

An assistant brought us fruit for breakfast. Peculiar-looking fruit. Some like kiwi fruit and some not tasty like fruit at all but oily and filling. We learned that we needed to embark upon a strict diet for several days before our healing experience. That impressed me.

We spent the morning touring the area with one of the curandero's assistants who explained native plants to us and showed us beautiful orchids which surrounded the area where the ayahuasca plants grew. I was impressed that our leader grew his own ayahuasca and made his own blend of medicine rather than relying upon resources bought from others. Later we would come back as a group and sit among the huge ayahuasca leaves to gain power and vision prior to ingesting it. For now we were getting used to the area and feeling comfortable with it and with ourselves. The three others in our group were native Peruvians, one a professional man and the other two women were related to him.

On the second day we went as a group to a "sweat lodge," a natural sauna where we spent several sessions sweating out impurities and ridding ourselves of toxins.

After the second day, the borders between the days disappeared and gradually became one long line of time with subtle gradations. That change brought with it a closer merging of ourselves with the way of life of the jungle which marks time more arbitrarily, as territories of time, not lucid points.

I was fascinated with the presentation of the healing ritual. It was gradual and slow and took days. American medicine, so impersonal and mechanical, rushes into healing with no ceremony at all, no way for the patient to become comfortable in his surroundings or feel the ritualistic connection to the process of healing. How could one become comfortable in a sterile room with tubes and catheters and bottles hanging from steel racks and massive computerized machinery everywhere? The soul is not attended to in that environment the way that our souls were being attended to here.

After the sweating sessions, we revisited the ayahuasca gardens where we sat quietly as a group among the hallucinogen. After sitting there awhile quietly, I began to sense a power coming from these plants. I thought at first it was just that I was fulfilling the expectation that I thought incumbent upon me, but then I began to feel otherwise. We were instructed to sit erectly and breathe rhythmically, counting to ourselves our inhalations and our exhalations in an effort to focus our minds only on that, and to keep our eyes closed.

After a few minutes I was at peace. It was hot, and sweat had formed on my forehead and ran down into my eyelids, and I could feel flies landing around my head, something that would ordinarily have caused me annoyance. However, it didn't bother me. In fact, I enjoyed feeling the bugs crawl through the sweat and wondered if it was giving them nourishment of some kind.

I felt my body lift out of the chair, as if I were rising above it somehow. It was a pleasing feeling which caused me to open my eyes for an instant. I saw a dazzling light from the center of the field of ayahuasca.

I talked to Simon and Christiane later and they had had similar feelings. That experience, for us all, served to announce an awakening of our consciousness.

———

I realized that all over the earth there are healers healing the sick and the wounded. Some of them have access to dazzling modern computerized equipment and some have nothing but a clipboard and the limits of their own personal power. Whoever brings about a healing, using whatever method, is a hero performing the most noble service there is: to deliver others from their suffering.

Francisco Alvaro stood before us. I could discern at once, in listening to the neat articulation of his words and the rhythmic, almost entrancing modulation of his voice, that he possessed the golden quality.

"I am your doctor. You should know some things about me. I was born and raised here in the Amazon. I was educated and taught English by Christian missionaries. My father before me was a shaman and so was his father. They used traditional shamanic methods for healing. I received a medical degree from an American University and practiced there for a short time before returning to the Amazon to practice shamanism. I'm a follower of different types of medicine, and I don't discredit any of them. They all accomplish healing. Some people can only be cured by modern medicine and some can only be cured by shamanism. Sometimes it is necessary to combine them both in a ratio which is appropriate for the individual.

"Our session will involve the healing agent, ayahuasca. Ayahuasca is the medium through which you can have symbolic and actual visions of your problems. In my opinion all sickness is related to the mind and the spirit. Ayahuasca is a spiritual teacher. The word ayahuasca means 'vine of the soul.' It is an instructor of life's purpose. One may heal one's past with ayahuasca, discharge oneself of guilt, and even retrieve one's soul or one's heart, which has become lost or abducted. Illness of the spirit and the mind manifests itself as physical illness and ayahuasca can help you understand its origin. Ayahuasca is a bridge between the world you think is real and the world which is supernatural and can only be accessed with sacred plants. It will allow you to recover the enchanted view of the world which you once had. You did once have an enchanted view, remember?" He smiled. "It can also show you your future, not just tomorrow or next year or even next decade, but thousands of years away.

"Outsiders use the word 'hallucination' to describe the experience of ayahuasca, but that is a poor word which implies that what one sees with ayahuasca is not real, that it is illusory and perhaps just a haphazard neural association no more meaningful than a kaleidoscope.

"They are wrong. It is real, the most real thing you will ever see, and you will know that with certainty when the visions occur to you. In the same way that there are radio waves and light waves, so there are invisible beings in space who can transport themselves telepathically, as you will be able to do also. You will see them and they will talk to you. Some will be obvious, some will be symbolic, depending partly upon how you choose to process your experiences. Be open-minded about this. Do not approach this experience with rationalizations or explanations or words which diminish its importance. Let it happen to you. You will be changed and you will be healed.

"Ayahuasca is an experience of death. And then rebirth. What dies will be the things that cling to you like barnacles on a ship or which you think you need for security but which prevent you from seeing clearly and peripherally and moving deliberately. What will be born is a new vision, more complete, more fulfilling, more peaceful and true, not possessive or selfish. Be prepared to die. Be prepared to live anew more fully alive."

I couldn't take my eyes off Francisco Alvaro. He looked like a spectacular firebird of the Amazon, a long legged waterfowl that moves stealthily with utmost deliberation but carries itself softly forward, delicately placing one sure foot in front of the next, seeing through the top of the dark water to the world below the surface.

Christiane decided to take ayahuasca with me. I was pleased with her decision, but also I was concerned that we would both be so preoccupied with our own experiences that it would be hard to be available to each other. Since we had been so closely associated with one another for months, it had been hard for me to see just how integral she had become to my own self-understanding until the thought of her absence, especially her emotional absence, occurred to me. I didn't want to become estranged from her in any way at this crucial moment

In the rainforest one sees clearly, in the starkest ways imaginable, that there is no true independence in life. Everything is dependent for survival upon not just other things but entire systems of other things. After seeing some of the strangest symbiotic relationships formed for survival – from microbes that feed in the stomachs of grazing animals and help them digest their food, to small "cleaner fish" that wait in tropical waters for bigger fish so that they can eat the harmful fungi from their mouths, to ants living on the secretions of aphids whom they protect like livestock, to two entirely different species of insects living as master and slave – it is easier to forgive the oddness of the dependencies in which people find themselves involved with one another.

The ayahuasca brew boiled for fifteen hours, not only to extract all of the ingredients from the sacred plant but also to blend them with the other added ingredients which were specially designed by Francisco Alvaro himself.

In the afternoon we met as a group in the large hut where the curandero's assistant instructed us in various precautions. He told us that we would inevitably vomit from drinking the concoction and that we must not be ashamed of this. He told us that we must remain as a group and that we would probably feel a desire to be together anyway. "There are some dangerous animals in the forest," he said. "The jaguar's eyes are always upon its prey, so don't wander off."

From the readings I had done about the Amazon, I knew that perhaps no animal was dreaded more than El Tigre, the Jaguar. Its presence is perpetually feared by the natives of the jungle, since stories of its prowess and cunning are legendary. Weighing up to 350 pounds, it is capable of killing any vertebrate it encounters except the tapir. Its presence is ecologically fearsome in addition because it represents the end point of thousands of other lives, from plant to insect to small mammal to bird to fish to reptile and finally to this awesome creature which prowls the forest and ranges both night and day, using the element of surprise as its primary tool to kill its prey, in addition to its frightening strength. It has no fear of humans and has attacked them frequently. Many times people on ayahuasca have claimed to have become one with the black jaguar and to hear, see, smell, and feel instinctively, the way it does, and to prowl with it in the forest using all of its senses.

Fortunately, the curandero's assistant did not tell us all of those things. I had found them out on my own. I also knew that there were not many jaguars left and that myth was behind many of these sightings.

Francisco Alvaro arrived after his assistant was through. He then asked us to follow him.

Dusk was coming slowly and the feel of the forest was right. But I had suppressed a fear that morning which arose again. A headache and a sickness seemed to be starting. I couldn't be certain yet; it was still possible that, instead, it was the occasional false alarm.

The pain always started in the left side of my head. Once it began it migrated to the right side and by then my vision contained a cloudy dark aura at the center of my sight which made it hard to see.

Along with the movement from left to right, erosion of my sensibilities occurred and perception became flat and lifeless. I had learned that when certain appeals left me, like beauty and tonality and taste and the excitement of life in general, I was entering the second stage – that the hurricane was near to land.

As we walked farther and farther into the forest, close to the river, and as the rest of them talked excitedly about the glorious sunset in the west, I felt nothing but dullness. We walked on and on until I had no idea where we were. I followed the rest of them like an obedient chattel, barely able to see them.

I was suddenly afraid. I took Christiane aside.

"I'm getting sick."

"Oh no, Michael! We must tell Francisco Alvaro."

"Not yet. It'll come slowly. I'll be able to function for several more hours. That will give the rest of you time to become committed to the ceremony, and then I'll tell him privately that I cannot go through with it."

It was unimaginable that I could take ayahuasca while experiencing the illness. By ten in the evening I would be nearly unconscious or delirious.

Christiane tried to look upbeat but we both felt defeated. Months of planning and anticipation had gone into arriving at this moment. The belief of both of us that our winding path had been preordained, involving psychic predictions, fulfilled visions, healing stories, sacred happenings, even the touch of the condor, was about to unravel because of the very thing which provoked this odyssey in the first place. I wanted to believe that sickness was naturally the ultimate stage of the journey. How could it be more suitably expressed than to become sick prior to being healed?

"I'm going to go through with the ceremony," I told Christiane.

"Michael, you can't! I saw you before when you were sick. You can't even talk or move. I won't let you."

"I believe in this man, Christiane. I've been brought to him, we both believe that. So this is part of my destiny. If his medicine can heal the source of my illness, it can surely also heal an incident of it."

She took my forearm in her hand and looked at me intently. "If we decide to do this, Michael, I insist that you tell him first of all and see what he says. If you don't tell him, then I will."

I looked at her with a feeling of lifeless muffled dullness. "Okay," I relented easily. "I'll tell him at the appropriate time."

"I want you to know, Michael, that I can stop this at any time. I am not committed to this unless the conditions are right for us all, and for my sake you do not have to do this, and you should only consider it if you are positively sure that it is going to be all right. Even if Francisco Alvaro tells you to go ahead, I want us still to talk about it once more and decide if we should do it. Do you understand? Do you promise?"

"Yes, I do," I said. But I knew then that I would eat the sacred plant ayahuasca and follow its journey to the end. The only thing that would stop me now would be for Francisco Alvaro to forbid it.

I wondered what collage of frightful characters would represent my sick soul on ayahuasca.

Christiane took my hand and pulled me behind her like a small child whose legs were too small to keep up. When I told her I was losing my vision, she was aghast.

The locus of pain moved slowly from the left to the right, and then it was agony. Always at that time I had reflected upon how sensible it is to take one's own life under hopelessly adverse circumstances, when living affirms nothing but the fear of dying.

I could hardly go on because the pain was so agonizing. I recognized that I had hidden my anxiety about the healing experience I was about to undergo, the way I had always hidden anxiety, and now it was becoming somatically manifest. I was scared and pained at once, not knowing which one to concentrate upon. I had to stop and hold my head. I felt like an adolescent enduring a contest for a vacant proud reason.

The others went on without noticing that we'd stopped. Simon was with them. Christiane comforted me and rubbed my temples and made me lie down. It consoled me in a deep metaphysical way that carried with it the simultaneous awareness that Christiane and Simon could now give me surcease from agony, which before I had borne alone, and also that I no longer considered myself apart from them.

I heard Franciso Alvaro talking to Christiane back and forth and back and forth, like an amusing tennis game played in the gentle Spanish tongue. The next thing I knew they had picked me up from the ground and were carrying me between them to the spot where the rest of the group was sitting in a circle. A fire was just beginning to burn in the center of it. The sun was down and the cushion of the night's blank presence felt good against the blistering pain of my head. The doctor let me lie with my head upon Christiane's lap while she stroked my temples tenderly, as she'd done before in Lima. Simon joined her on the other side, and the whole group offered me their good wishes. Someone rubbed my feet.

The chills came upon me as they usually did and people covered me with coats and moved me closer to the fire. The chirping sounds of wooden reed flutes began. And then the most beautiful sound, like a wiry harp of fairies, began to harmonize behind them. It played for what seemed like hours while others chanted icaros tunes in the background. Finally someone else handed out the brews of ayahuasca to all of those taking it. I was in the hands of fate now.

The music and the light of the fire transported us to a nether world of tobacco smoke lightly exhaled across the forest's opening. I could see only an orange glow and hear the lovely harp rising metallically, high above the group, soaring like an aluminum nightbird. Then I felt something at my nose. I raised my head to see but all I saw was an aura, like a man in the wrong zone of trifocals.

"What's happening?" I asked Christiane.

She didn't answer. Francisco Alvaro whispered in my ear. "This is vine of wyanatude mixed with ayahuasca. It will take your pain away. Lie down and accept this sacred blessing, my friend."

I lay down and in so doing noticed a hollow wooden reed four or five feet long. At the end of it was the assistant filling the tube with something. Francisco Alvaro put the near end of the reed tube deep into my nostril and nodded at the assistant who blew explosively with all of his might from the other end. The cartridge of ayahuasca and wyanatude hit my nasal cavity like a bullet and knocked my head back to the ground. Quickly they did it again to the other nostril. The pain from it was excruciating. But, miraculously, my vision began to return and the aura at the center of my sight began to fade, and then my head-ache disappeared.

"It's gone!" was all I could think or say. It was the first time it had ever stopped before the end of its interminable path of destruction. I felt as if I'd been snatched from a burning building or lifted from an angry sea.

Then I entered the world of ayahuasca.

I was delivered first from unthinkable pain and then, at that raptur-ous moment, taken onward to a world literally beyond one's imagina-tion, beyond what one could even dream.

CHAPTER 19

Horst and I finished the wall the following day. Not completely, but close enough to stop working. I had the feeling that with Horst nothing was ever finished entirely.

Both of the owners of the home returned that day at different times to inspect it and were elated at its progress. This was enough to induce Horst to "take a few days off."

"Let's go get Angela and Kurt," Horst said, "and eat and go on a tour of Hamburg. He wants to see some things."

I suggested that we clean up his tools. "They're fine," he said. "Why move them away from where we'll need them again?"

We took his dilapidated truck and followed the stream back to the inn where he stopped for a beer. Instead of continuing to follow the stream Horst turned in the other direction at the bottom of the road at an intersection. I asked where he was going.

"To get Angela."

"Where is she?"

"She's at the temple."

"At the temple?"

"At the temple, the synagogue, whatever it's called. She's Jewish. She does volunteer work there."

We took Angela's car and left his truck sitting strangely alone in the parking lot outside of the synagogue, like a migrant's vehicle. We drove to Angela's house where they both cleaned up.

Horst emerged from the bedroom after a shower and was handsome and gallant-looking and smelled of cologne. Angela joined us soon after in the living room, looking vivacious.

Alone after two days of hard work and after more than a week of being in Hamburg, I could finally allow myself a moment to reflect upon finding Susanne. A momentary worry came to me that what I needed to find in her was no longer available and that she would be someone else entirely.

I showered and dressed and walked to the Alsterpavillion where I found the other three. Horst's presence was huge. His hands occupied a great portion of airspace at the center of the table as he gestured emphatically about each of his points of argument. I didn't feel like straining to understand the German they were speaking, much of which seemed to be slang, so instead I tried to organize the next day in my thoughts.

At an appropriate calm moment I said, "I need to find Susanne now. Our time here is running out and I'll feel terrible if I go home without seeing her."

"We know that, Michael," Angela said, "we were talking about that before you came. We decided in the morning that we will return to the Palmaille and begin our search there. Then we'll go back to the doctor's office. It sounds as if the man you talked to knows something. That will be a good lead. If neither of those things works out we will try to find public records of the doctor's death and see who handled the estate. Those offices will be closed until Monday. Michael, do you have a picture of Susanne? That would help."

I had one in my wallet which I showed to them. It was a picture we had taken in a booth in a department store. It was staged. She looked happy and a bit naughty. They passed it around and I felt glad that the secret of her was being shared and somehow taken from its lonely spot inside of me.

"She is very attractive," Angela said.

"'Handsome' is the word that Michael uses," Horst said. "He likes handsome women. Strong and handsome. You've come to the right place. Hamburg is full of handsome and strong women." He took the picture from Angela and studied it a long time. He was captivated with her looks, which pleased me.

When we arrived at the hotel, Horst and his father strolled into the Conditorei and had a sweet dessert of chocolate and ice cream and Angela and I went up to our room and talked. Angela looked so tired that I invited her to lie on Mr. Seiler's bed and covered her with a blanket. She fell fast asleep. I turned the light off and went into my room.

In the late morning they picked me up and we began our search in the Palmaille. We stopped on the road below Susanne's house, where we'd stopped before, and Mr. Seiler pointed at it. There was no way to get to the house except to trespass, and no one but Horst was willing to do that. He left the car and climbed over the tall wrought iron fence, walked up to her house, and never looked back. After a few minutes, I went after him.

The house was deeply shaded and dark and seemed abandoned. I walked around it and Horst was sitting talking to a man who was dressed in work clothes. As usual, Horst's voice was loud, as if he were arguing. They were discussing the political climate of Hamburg. Then they laughed and Horst grabbed his upper arm and held onto it and turned to present him to me.

"Here is your answer," he said. "Tell him," he instructed the man.

"Susanne left here before the doctor died. No one's sure where she went."

"But there are rumors," Horst added. "She met a man at the Reeperbahn and became pregnant by him. Her father told her she could not keep the child. Some say she ran off with the man and others say she lost the child at birth and went mad and is hospitalized somewhere."

I felt brutalized by his words. Maybe it was *my* child. How could someone put her in an institution?

Horst seemed elated that we had solved the problem. "Forget her, Michael," he said. "Find someone else."

I asked the man if he knew her. He didn't. He'd only seen her twice. I asked him who was there in Hamburg that we could talk to about her, and he knew no one. He said her sister hadn't lived there for a long time and he didn't know where she was. He didn't believe there were any living relatives in Hamburg and that the estate was tied up in the courts. I asked him who handled the estate but he didn't know. Then I asked him if we could go inside and look for information that would help us find her, and he said it was out of the question. I looked at Horst for help.

"Give her up, Michael," he said.

"I have to find her! I have to know what's going on here. Not just rumors from the gardener who doesn't even know her. You don't understand, Horst. You're different from me. I need your help, not your cynicism." My boldness surprised me.

Horst put his arm around me and said, "We'll find her, Michael." He looked at the man again and said, "Can you let us inside?"

"Absolutely not!" he said. "There is nothing there. Please go before I get in trouble."

The image of Susanne locked up in an institution made me feel sick. I didn't want to report it to Angela and Mr. Seiler, nor even record it in my own mind. The day was disintegrating.

I took Horst's arm and turned him until we were face to face. "She is a good person, an exceptional person, Horst. She saved my life once, and whatever may have happened to her, to me she will always be that person. I also have to find her because it is possible that her child is mine. Would you help me find her? I love your father and I don't want him to be part of what may turn out to be something that is ugly. This is his reunion. It should only be joyous for him."

He nodded instead of answering, then said "Yes, I'll help you. But we need Angela too. She has a way with things like this."

Next we went to the former office of Dr. Ludendorff. We followed the street along the river where I had run before. It looked different from a car, though, and I had trouble finding the storefront.

The day was still warm. Tall historical buildings on the winding waterfront drew our attention. Horst needed to explain the history of them all.

We eventually arrived at the office which now belonged to the man I'd confronted before. The door was unlocked again and the bells hanging on it announced our entrance. Again no one came to the front. Horst meanwhile inspected everything, like a detective.

"Where are these people?" he said. He pounded on the desk, and a woman came to the front. He turned to me and said, "Who are you looking for?"

"Susanne Ludendorff," I said. He repeated her name to the woman who looked at us suspiciously.

"I don't know where she is." She started to walk away and Horst grabbed her arm like a rag doll. "Yes, you do," he said. "Who knows if you don't? Where is the doctor?" He looked at me and said, "Who did you talk to here yesterday?"

"I don't know his name but he knew her and her father."

"Listen, Fraulein. We'll stay until you produce someone who knows what's going on here. Do you understand?"

The curtain separating the front from the back opened, and the man emerged to whom I'd spoken previously.

"What do you want now?" he said.

"We want to know where Susanne Ludendorff is."

"I'll call the police if you don't leave now."

Horst laughed and sat down on a chair.

All of us remained silent. Finally I said, "We don't want to cause trouble. I'm only trying to find my friend Susanne."

"I cannot help you," he said and walked toward the back again.

"Do you know her?"

"Yes."

"Do you know where she is?"

"Young man, you would be well advised to leave before there is trouble. Do you understand?"

Before I had a chance to answer, Horst was on his feet again. "There is already trouble. Tell us where she is!" He grabbed the man hard on both shoulders as if he were pushing him down to the ground."

"I don't know where she is, I told you."

"What do you know?"

By this time the man was practically on his knees overloaded with Horst's pressure upon him. The woman was cowering away from them. The situation looked graver than it was, and I hoped that no one on the street would notice us. I felt sorry for the man and woman but I did nothing to intervene, knowing that if they couldn't provide answers we might never find more clues in time before I left.

"We are not going to hurt you," Angela said. "We just want some answers. What do you know about her?"

"She ran away from Dr. Ludendorff's home when he found out she was pregnant and insisted she could not have the child," the woman said.

"Where did she go?"

"All I know is rumors, nothing for sure."

"What rumors?"

She sighed. "I'm not sure. Some say she went to the Reeperbahn."

"The Reeperbahn? Why?"

"I heard she had a friend there who took her in."

Angela came forward and helped the man and woman to a chair. She kneeled between them. "Please understand that Michael here has come from the USA to see this girl. We are very appreciative of your help."

"She was a beautiful girl," the woman sobbed. "A skilled pianist. She had great possibilities ahead for her. Her father was quite traditional. He lived alone in the house and had no friends. When she came to live with him, he controlled her life completely, insisting that she only go out at certain times and only do certain things and see certain people. She became pregnant not long after returning to Hamburg, although no one ever saw the boy who made her pregnant. She would not name him either. Her father was so upset that he wouldn't speak to her. As her pregnancy progressed and she needed comfort and assistance, he became more withdrawn. Both of their lives disintegrated. They lived like two hermits on the hilltop of Palmaille. She disappeared one day, just before Dr. Ludendorff had a severe heart attack. We tried to find her but couldn't. Just before he died she came forward. She tried to make contact with him, but he was in a coma. She sat for days in the hospital room, whispering to him as if she were telling him stories at the end to make his passage easier. She didn't attend his funeral, and we've not seen her since. We have heard that she is in an institution. That her brother put her there."

"I didn't know she had a brother," I said.

"He is a half-brother. Her mother was married before to a ship captain. The brother is a seaman."

"How could he have the authority to do that to her?" I asked.

"Susanne has always been imaginary and frail. Her mind does not function like others. She is dreamy and otherworldly. You can tell it when you listen to her play the piano or sing or tell a story. Several times in her life she has had breakdowns. This world is too hard for her, she cannot cope with it. After her father's death, she had another one and it is said that her brother had her put away."

"Do you know where she is?" Angela asked.

"Not for sure. We've heard it is the state-run center near Borgfelde. The one for soldiers and sailors."

Horst moaned. "The old Neuengamme at Fuhlsbuttel? It's the end of the world. A huge brick prison on top of a treeless hill. The worst cases are there. They walk around like the living dead, with blank stares and fear in their eyes. Half the city of Hamburg was there after the war."

"Do they allow visitors?" I asked him.

"I don't know."

"What about the child? Did she have the child?"

"I'm not sure of any of this, you understand, but I heard that it died at birth. That along with her father's death caused her collapse."

"Where was she staying at the time?"

"I suppose with her friend in the Reeperbahn, I don't really know."

"Do you know where the friend lived in the Reeperbahn?" I asked.

"No, I have no idea," the man said.

The room became silent. There was nothing left to say. Horst walked out of the office without saying a word. Both Angela and I thanked them for sharing what they knew with us. They seemed shaken.

Horst was across the street leaning against a stone balustrade that looked out across the water, smoking a cigarette. Angela put her hand on his arm as she approached. "What's wrong, Horst?"

"Nothing," he answered curtly. "Let's go."

"Go where?" Angela asked.

"To find Susanne."

"To the institution?"

"Yes, of course. We can't go to the Reeperbahn in the day and we can't get into the mental hospital at night. Let's go where we can. Michael only has a few days." He was serious and disturbed.

"What's wrong, Horst?" I asked him.

"I said nothing is wrong."

He turned to walk away and we followed. After a few steps he turned and looked at me with an angry face. "Why do you want to see her like this? She's gone crazy. Is that what you want to see? Her father abandoned her when she needed him, the way fathers do, and she went crazy. Isn't that enough to know? Do you have to look at her?"

"Maybe I can help her."

"Help her what? Escape? And then what? You are then obliged to take care of a crazy woman. Is that what you want? What responsibility is she of yours?"

"She's not crazy."

He laughed cynically. "Michael, no one gets better there, they get worse. It's the last stop before the end of the world. If she was not crazy before, she is crazy now."

I didn't know what to say. I was angry. "You don't need to go. I'll go alone."

"Don't be an idiot, Michael. You wouldn't even be able to tell them what you want. They would laugh at you. These are hard people, prison guards."

"How do you know so much about it?" Angela asked.

"Because I was there!"

"When were you there?" she asked.

"After the bombing, in 1943."

"I didn't know that."

"Of course not, I never told anyone. No one knows except the thugs who tortured me and the mad victims of the war who are all dead now."

"I'm sorry, Horst."

"Sorry? What is there to be sorry for?

It was not a long distance to Borgefelde, but all distances could be long when traveling with Horst. We first stopped by his house because he had to find a tool for a job he was going to start. He couldn't find the tool so he went to a friend's house to borrow it.

Angela and I waited in the car, and finally she said, "I think he's afraid to go to Borgefelde. He's always late and does things his way, but this is ridiculous even for him. He's avoiding it as long as possible. Maybe he hopes they'll be closed by the time we get there. I had no idea he was hospitalized there, but it makes sense to me now. He has seen a therapist a few times, and once he even put himself in a hospital for a month. He told me it was exhaustion but that was probably only part of it. He lived through some terrible things in the war. I don't think he even remembers them all. I think that that part of his life just runs automatically without a memory. He rants and raves about who did what and whose fault it was, but he never talks about specific things."

"I shouldn't let him go to Borgefelde, should I?"

"Probably not. But it's too late now. The question is: when will we get there?"

I felt sad and perplexed. It seemed that the deeper I went into solving the riddle of Susanne, the more riddles I uncovered.

We did finally arrive at Borgefelde, and as Angela astutely predicted, it was not possible to visit patients at that late time. However, it would not have been possible anyway, because they only allowed relatives to visit.

Susanne was there, they told us.

Horst told the administrator that I was her brother and would want to see her at the next opportunity. They said it would be required that I have identification with a picture showing who I am. "He has it right here," Horst said. "But he lives in America, so all he has is identification from there. Is that all right?"

"Yes, but his name must be the same as hers, Ludendorff."

"Would you like to see it right now?" Horst bluffed indignantly.

"That's not necessary. Whenever you return will be sufficient. But only he can go in to visit, and someone from the hospital will have to accompany him."

"Will you be here?" he asked the woman, and she gave him the hours that she worked.

"We want to see you, since you understand what is required and we won't have to explain our purpose again."

"Whatever you want," she said, "but anyone will require the same things of you."

"Michael's sister has only been here a short time," Angela said, "and Michael hasn't seen her for years, so it will be a reunion for them both."

The woman raised her eyebrows. "I don't really see how a nice re-union is possible in this place."

"Do you think we could take her for a walk?" Angela asked.

"No," she said sternly.

"Can I go into her room with Michael?"

"Are you related to her?"

"Not directly, no."

"You must be directly related to the patient and have identification to prove it," she said stiffly.

We thanked her and told her we'd see her tomorrow.

"She'll let us in," Horst said as we were walking to the car.

"What about the ID?"

"I'll make you one tonight. Don't worry."

Horst didn't wake up until early afternoon and predictably he was with-drawn and grouchy. Neither of us engaged him but just waited for him to talk to us. He showed me the ID he'd made for me. It was perfect.

We ate breakfast and Horst smoked cigarettes. At 3:30 we left for the institution. Horst pushed the deadline to the edge. They closed at 5:30. We arrived at 4:45. As it turned out, the woman at the office had not arrived until 4:30.

We walked up to her desk. She looked at us blankly. Horst asked me for my ID and handed it to her. "He wants to see his sister, remember? Susanne Ludendorff." He stared at her with complete confidence, not revealing even a hint of our deception. She inspected the document carefully.

"Is something wrong?" he asked. "We only have an hour left, you know?"

She looked back at him and I could tell that she was going to deny our request. I felt heartsick, because I knew that if I could not make it into the building at that time, other officials would become involved and our fraud would be discovered. Any chance of seeing Susanne again would be gone. My heart pounded and my hands became sweaty. It was all I could do to keep my face from twitching out of control. The woman looked up at Horst and engaged her eyes with his, ready, it appeared, to veto our plans.

I turned and looked at Horst and suddenly it seemed as if he had grown in size to a giant predator towering over her, his dark eyes riveting through her and his entire body braced like a rapacious animal about to strike. I could see a terrible grim aura of charisma surrounding him and redirecting towards her all of the energy flowing between them. Gradually she shrank in size and averted her eyes like a lesser dog in the presence of the alpha dog.

"An attendant has to go with him, you understand?"

"I understand," he said.

They accompanied me to a double steel door where I waited for an attendant to lead me into the abyss of the asylum where she was. The door opened and before me was a dark unending hallway with strange noises, screams, and cries in the distance. Angela took my hand to comfort me, and then to my distress she had to let go of it. The last familiar thing I remember was turning and seeing her and Horst silhouetted in the doorway starting to close. They looked like my mother and father waving goodbye to me forever.

CHAPTER 20

The fairy tunes of icaros sounded inside of me and around me in space-time beyond previous experience. Events in timelessness overlapped and simultaneously expanded boundlessly.

On the walls of the long hallway jungle were doors. A slouching figure led me towards a place that seemed an endpoint of our trip. Then he changed identities and became someone else and then an animal and then who he was at first, changing identities as quickly as my thoughts changed. This being and beast was at my control. When I simply followed him and let him walk ahead of me as the leader, the path was almost pleasant, endearing, and certain to end at its destination. But when I reflected upon who he was or where he was taking me, he became a frightening presence carrying me against my will into a place I didn't want to go. Both of them were me.

The hallway changed to a dense colorful forest with a thousand blooming flowers growing before my eyes to unbelievable heights, heights which, I could see to my dismay, would penetrate the towering canopy of vegetation above me if they continued to grow. With that pointless worry all at once they receded and shrank down to tiny tendrils disappearing into the ground, stealing the color from the world and leaving it dark and gray, foreboding. Once again in front of me was the changeable leader moving inexorably down the long dark hallway, but this time inside of the doorways emptying into the hallway were shrieking shrinking bony men and hopeless old women clothed in degrading gowns denoting the subservience of sickness. Some whimpered and cried, others screamed in terror.

Then I was in the forest again where the flowers grew to dizzying heights. By controlling my thoughts so that I saw only with my eyes, the flowers continued growing and the wiry icaros angelic tunes flourished, accompanied by the harp's melodically growing flowersongs. When I restricted freedom with my thoughts by doubting, disbelieving or reflecting, the flowers shrank, the music stopped, and I was again walking down the dark hallway, more grim than the time before. I wanted to give up all control and let the flowers grow on through the ceiling of the heavens and allow the icaros to chant forever behind the celestial harp, but I couldn't sustain my discipline. Always I wanted to re-grasp, at least for an instant, enough command to make myself feel that all was not out of my control. But by controlling it, all I really controlled was the collapse of my own joy.

I heard a strange language. A leader was giving instructions to a group I suddenly realized I was a part of. It was Francisco Alvaro. And Christiane. And the couple named Miles. And little dear Simon. I was comforted at seeing them, and as I walked in their direction, the strange language became understandable in a totally different way than I had ever understood language. Only its meaning was transmitted to me, without a connection between words and understanding. I had no idea what the words meant but I apprehended their meaning. I needed an explanation, but when I opened my mouth to speak, what came out instead of words were long strings of tiny white worms like maggots pouring forth as vomit, in one continuous flow from my mouth to the ground. I was aghast! No one seemed to care. Or even notice. I moved next to Christiane. I could smell her scent and feel the satin texture of her skin. Her deep black eyes were tender and gentle as usual. I tried to speak to her but couldn't, as if there was a lock upon the doorway out of which my words ordinarily came. She spoke to me. The same thing happened. The words themselves meant nothing to me. There was no medium of words, just simple understanding, direct communication. I questioned it, and when I did she became an old woman, wrinkled and weak. I could see the Christiane I knew in the old woman's eyes but she was not desirable anymore. She frightened me. I turned to run and she pleaded after me in her same sweet voice, "Michael, where are you going?" I turned back and saw the old woman disappear into the young and beautiful Christiane again. I walked toward her and was compelled by the need to receive her comfort. She put her arms around me and I felt myself begin to burn in a benign flame of desire. It felt like radiant heat warming me all over. Then she touched her lips to mine and I could detect upon them a taste of comfort and a smell of assurance with a feeling of a fruit's opulence. My senses were merging into a blur of synaesthesia, affecting marriages of one sense to the other. I let myself be taken into this foreign world of pleasurable sensations until I was beside myself with the deepest most gratifying feelings, not unlike experiencing the flowers which had seemed to grow forever, empowered by my own spontaneity.

I felt a volcanic tumescence in my entire lower body which radiated out even to my fingertips and pulsated with what I envisioned would be an eruption originating somewhere in my thorax. I became frightened. Christiane's face changed back into an old woman's and her fingers became spines rasping my back. The forest became the hallway again and now there were screams from the rooms on either side, growing louder as I seemed to be nearing the place I was intended to reach.

I ran in terror, afraid to face the demons that were coming forth from within me. I heard voices call for me, but I needed to be alone at whatever cost.

The forest was moist and dark and everything about it was alive. The liana vines were huge snakes coiled to strike at me. Despite the darkness of the nighttime canopy, there was illumination from somewhere which allowed me to see my way. I went deeper and deeper into a fantastic scenery of unimaginable visions. It seemed that each step enlivened a myriad of fantasy creatures.

I was lost, I realized. Lost in a place that no one had ever pioneered. I wanted to go back, for I saw from my ever-burgeoning fear that I had made a huge mistake leaving the rest of them. Desperately I searched for the way back to them, becoming hopelessly confused and frightened. I stopped and yelled out for Christiane and then Simon. The sound of my words transfixed me in their rhythm and resonance like drums playing in an enclosed theatre. I felt as if I could climb upon any one of them, a single word, and it would fly me on waves of sound to the thing it signified.

There was no answer. I sat down on the boggy earth, my feet soaking wet. Suddenly I noticed that huge leeches had attached themselves to my ankles and I could literally see the blood flowing from my body to theirs. I frantically pulled them off and ran for solid ground, but there was none nearby.

At last I found a place free of muck and marsh, and I stood there to gather my thoughts which were scattered everywhere. I remembered my lesson and tried not to panic, but not only was I lost in the outside world, I was lost inside of myself as well. I had no reference points or boundaries to understand what was happening to me.

As if it were a living painting with hidden faces, the forest revealed many eyes to me as I stopped looking inside of myself and directed my vision outward. There is no way to assess how much time passed with me just staring at the incredible scenes all around me. Vines as snakes. Flies as airplanes. Sounds as entities. All of my senses were mixed into a potpourri of apprehensions indistinguishable from each other in a startling theme of interdependence of one upon the other. This theme took over my thoughts and I realized that no matter how hard we try, we are not independent, we are not free from each other, we are all involved in the great ecology of being. The rainforest is the starkest expression of that truth. Each of us is a parasite upon the other and each of us is a host, each of us needing the others for survival. Alone in the Amazon rain forest on ayahuasca for the first time was not the most comforting place to have that realization.

Then I heard a sound that scared me. It was different than the rest. It was a big sound. Stealthy and foreboding. The forest quieted. It was footsteps, I was sure, and they were moving toward me. The sounds of the footsteps were momentous and huge like an elephant stepping in soft grass. I knew I was its prey. But instead of panicking and running, I had a strange desire to face the foe. I was afraid, but I was more curious.

I listened to its footsteps moving closer and closer. And then they stopped. Somewhere in the night it was staring at me. It was a cat, I knew, the fiercest animal in the forest, the end of the food chain, for which a thousand other creatures had lived and died and produced food and nourishment, so that it could live its regal existence. It was the dreaded jaguar, cunning and beautiful, powerful and detached. The black jaguar.

I looked ahead of myself and there in the distance were two large green shining orbs. Light sparkled around them like specks of dust igniting. Moving toward me. I knew it was my end, that I was finished. A sadness came over me and I began to weep. Tears poured down my face in rivulets which washed away fears from my lifetime, so that I could actually see them personified in the stream of tears floating off with their contamination, like tiny little beings rolling down my face and finally falling to their death. Ironically, I was happy to be finally released of these impediments. I cried and cried until there was nothing left to float away, and then I was prepared to die. The cat would crush my skull in an instant. He came closer and closer. I could see now that he was black. The rare black jaguar. He stopped, not twenty yards from me. He was awesome, staring at me in an odd, curious way, as if he needed to understand something about me before killing me.

The themes of my life played surprisingly slowly in my thoughts and revealed me to myself with a remarkable singularity which I had never seen before. It was a great and liberating insight which most people never achieve, to see the line of events which were my life and meaning. To remember all at once, serially but abstractly, only the most crucial moments of synapse between each direction that my life had gone. It was a picture, a terse and accurate depiction of my essence.

I had lived over forty years with no awareness of the whole picture of who I was and why. Instead, like most of us, I'd busied myself with undertakings, never considering how they were a part of my plan or even that I had a plan.

The jaguar's eyes moved closer. I instinctively rolled into a ball and lay with my hands covering my head. My forehead was in the soggy ground which smelled like a billion years of life and death together.

Strange tiny creatures, real and hallucinogenic, crawled toward my face the moment it neared the ground.

The earth rumbled with footsteps drawing closer and I could feel that the moment of my death was upon me. Nearer and nearer he came and the entire spectrum of my anticipation was filled with wondering when he would devour me.

He was upon me. I could literally feel his hot breath against my neck. Then I felt him touch me with his paw, the way that cats do before they kill. My body trembled in fear and I tried to pull inside of myself and minimize my exposure to his fearsome blows.

And then upon my cheek was a feeling like sandpaper being rubbed slowly, coarsely, but not painfully. Again and again I felt it, until finally I had the courage to turn my eyes toward him. His face was only inches from mine. His mouth opened and he revealed his jagged fangs. And then he licked me.

Still afraid, I slowly unraveled myself from the ball I'd become to get a better look. I got to my knees and opened my eyes timidly, still holding my forearms about my ears.

It was not the dreaded black jaguar. It was Shaman, my dog from home who'd disappeared the night before I'd left for South America. I put my arms around him while he kept licking from my face the creatures that had attached themselves. And then he grabbed my shirt with his teeth and pulled at me, indicating he wanted me to follow him. I did, into the thick dark forest.

He led me slowly and stealthily with dexterity and purpose through the thick obscure forest, turning occasionally to make sure I was still close behind him. We eventually reached a river too wide to cross. He stood there with me at his side as if waiting for the river to part and to allow us to walk across on its bed. We waited and waited, staring at the fast moving river that looked blue in the moonlight. And then I saw a head bobbing along on top of the water. I couldn't make out what it was until it came closer to us, but finally I saw its face. It climbed onto the rocks that the river had washed into a shoal that extended perhaps thirty yards out from the shoreline where we were standing. The everpresent forest motion around us de-accelerated, everything slowed down, even my own heartbeat and the race of my thoughts.

Shaman and I stood like stalwart soldiers for hours, years, lifetimes, watching the languorous sloth crawl toward us over the rocks on the shoal. It was so peaceful and serene that I hoped he would move even slower than his almost imperceptible pace so that the measure of my own metabolism would continue to be tuned to him, and my thoughts, instead of racing madly forward and backward, would continue to roll off the press of my mind in slow understandable revolutions, and the blood from my heart would move around my body only fast enough to provide nourishment; and I would continue to feel as if I had attained a state of being which had no extra parts, no unused portions, no squandered ingredients.

The dangerous river narrowed and we forded it by branches of trees which almost touched across it. Looking at the ground below me, I saw that Shaman had disappeared and in his place was Simon. I climbed down.

"Michael, where have you been?"

"I've been lost, Simon. I thought I would die."

"When you ran off, Michael, I followed you but you disappeared. I've been looking for you a long time. But guess what, Michael? Do you know what else I found?" I was holding him so tightly that my fingers hurt me, and I let go. "Tell me, Simon, what else did you see?"

"I saw the waterfall, Michael."

"The waterfall?"

"You know, the one that goes to the Land of Fathers."

I was so full of astonishing experiences that I didn't understand what he was talking about at first. "How do you know that was it, Simon?"

"Because. The entrance was just as you described in the story. I noticed a condor sitting high on a wall of stone above the waterfall, staring back at me, the same condor that touched our fingers in Macchu Picchu. And the condor said, 'Find Michael and Susanne and I will fly you to the Land of Fathers.' But how can we find Susanne?"

I wondered if she was at the end of the long hallway I had been going down earlier, led by the strange being, which had alternated with the flowering forest. I told Simon. I didn't know how to get back to her, I said. Then he said this to me: "Remember, Michael, you told me once that anything was possible if you believe? And Susanne said in the story that if you believe in her, you can find her again. Remember, Michael? She said it would look different but it would be the same place."

I took his hand and turned to walk, and as I did I saw my dog Shaman again to the right of us standing in the middle of a path I had not noticed before, staring at me. He turned and began walking briskly into the dark forest. We followed him.

The path changed to the hallway I had walked before. The previous bewildering leader was now Shaman. The screams and shrieks of before were now the birds and insects diving all around me in the visionary nighttime.

On and on we walked through the dense jungle. My body was soaked with sweat from the hot wet air. I held Simon's hand firmly, but I couldn't tell if I was pulling him or he was pulling me. We followed

Shaman dutifully, lost in time and space, with him the only sensible reference.

The flowers began to grow again and the jungle repositioned itself to become a doorway that led to a room. A dusty light was present and a single bed beside it. On the bed was a girl on her back with covers pulled up to her neck and her eyes closed in a peaceful look of submission. I walked closer to her, still holding Simon's hand with Shaman waiting by the door.

"It's Susanne," I whispered to him. I felt that I had been here before at this very spot, staring at this same body on this same bed.

She leaned up and said, "Michael, you have come for me."

"Yes, I've come for you, Susanne."

Simon was leaning over her like a concerned doctor. He was poised to ease her back down, but his reverence for her held him back.

"And who is your friend," she said touching the top of Simon's head.

"He is Simon."

"Shall we go?" she said.

"Go where?" I asked.

"To the Land of Enchantment. To the world of dreams. To the Highlands, the Land of Fathers. I know you, Michael. That is why you've come back."

"I don't know where I am, Susanne, or how I got here."

"Of course you don't know, Michael. You still don't believe there can be a Land of Enchantment. And yet you have been there. Why are you unable to believe in what you know?"

She turned to Simon. "You believe, don't you, Simon?"

"Yes, I do."

"He believes in everything. He is a child." She took my wrist in her hand and said, "But you believe in him, don't you Michael?"

"Yes, I do."

She rose up from the bed. The sun was coming up as we went outside. She continued to hold one of each of our hands and we started down a clear wide path. The forest was no longer frightening but hopeful and bright.

At last we left the road and went into the forest and followed a fast moving stream for a long time. The land became hilly, then almost mountainous. We hardly said a word to each other.

"There it is!" Simon shouted.

We took each other's hands and walked through the waterfall. The whirling spray of colors sounded symphonic and tasted nectarous. I struggled to obtain a clear sense of where I was and what was happening, but like all of the events that day, I couldn't grasp it with reason, so I let myself be taken.

We walked toward the music down a long hill into a valley with many trees. There were no people, no musicians, just surrounding peacefulness. We lay down near some rocks and fell asleep to the beautiful music.

I awoke first. I saw the lake. There were many birds flying above one corner of it and animals running to the center of the activity. I squinted my eyes to focus them clearly and saw a figure in the middle of the activity. It was Susanne!

"Where are your friends, Michael?" she yelled to me from afar.

"They're asleep. Where were you."

"I was here, Michael."

We walked back to the sleepers on the ground in the meadow's sunshine.

"The Land of Fathers always looks different," she said, "because we ourselves are always different and it is we who construct our lives. Absolute is an illusion."

"I don't know which Susanne you are. The Susanne of the story or the Susanne I knew as a boy or the Susanne in Hamburg that I looked for and couldn't find."

"I am all of them. You did find me, Michael."

"All I can remember is walking down the haunted hallway."

I heard sounds in the forest, more than the chatter of the birds and monkeys. The sound of someone sobbing. I followed along the shoreline to a levee which led to a small peninsula. I stopped at a small dark hut and pushed the half-open door slowly and went inside. There was Christiane huddled in a corner with her arms protecting her head.

"Christiane, it's Michael," I whispered.

"Don't hit me again, please." She was crying and trembling. I tried to move her to the bed but she was rigid with resistance.

"I want you to lie down on the cot, Christiane. It's Michael. Don't be afraid."

She looked at me in terror. "You're not Michael." I looked at my arms holding her and they weren't my arms. There was no hair on them and they were dark. I didn't look like myself at all.

"I promise you I'm Michael, Christiane. No matter what I look like. Trust me. I would never hurt you."

She looked up again sheepishly at me and then put her arms around me and folded herself into me. I picked her up and put her on the bed and put a blanket around her shoulders.

I caressed her arms and her white skin felt like silk. I couldn't stop touching her it felt so good. It was making her feel good too.

I leaned down and kissed her cheek and then her lips. She responded deeply and warmly and passionately, and I responded in kind. My loving feelings for her felt bottomless. I couldn't stop the overpowering need I had to convey to her my love and receive the love she reconveyed to me. Her lips, resistant with tension, were absorbent of my lips and moved into them while I moved away from them as I moved into hers in a rhythm like dancing. We entwined in each other's arms and legs like vines around trees, and it felt as if we were a single being from two. We lay like that a long time, she sobbing on my shoulder and my head against hers with our arms and legs tied together as closely as we could unite without entering each other's skin. My thoughts came from her mind and my reflections reflected her; the pleasure that she gave, I felt, and the pleasure that she felt, I gave; the breath I inhaled was expelled from her lungs. It was not possible to distinguish one of us from the other. We were a zygote from two gametes. Night became day in a paranormal morphology of relations, like a word structure turned upon itself, mirroring all facets of understanding simultaneously. I was her father. She was my mother. I was her son and she was my daughter. All permutations of our different sexualities and genders and the ways that they were the same became manifest in a swirling optical pattern of which we were the colors, the textures, the ingredients themselves. We held each other through the fast-moving current of the nighttime revolving past the day, and through each rotation watched our faces change to each other from all we'd been into all we were to be and back again, as if we were sliding together as one through a vortex of realization toward the ultimate expression of transparency, sharing, trust, and vulnerability.

When the maelstrom ended, new day's light shone brightly at last. We looked at each other's faces. They were solid incarnations again.

Our bodies were drenched with sweat, our hair plastered to our heads like sloths emerging from the river. A slight morning breeze evaporated our perspiration and gave us a discrepant chill incompatible with the hot humid air.

We walked outside and saw that the levee which I had come across to the peninsula was a golden bridge. On the other side stood Christiane's father holding his arms out like a shepherd holding a new lamb.

"Hola hijita," he said. "Que bueno volverte a ver."

She looked back at me and I nodded for her to cross over. She took my hand and squeezed it tightly and then began walking over the bridge. At the top she hesitated a moment. Her father gestured with just his outstretched fingertips for her to keep coming. I thought she was going to turn back, and then she walked quickly to his extended arms, and they embraced. Her head was bowed in subservience to his and he lifted it up with his index finger so that they were looking equally into each other's eyes, and he said, "Te amo, Querida Christiane" and kissed her.

Our spells were lifted like shadows in encroaching sunshine while her father slipped away like sunburnt mist. There was Tomas where her father had stood, holding Christiane's chin and kissing her lightly. Simon was beside him.

"Mummy, father has come back to us."

The three of us, Simon and Christiane and I, were in the place where we'd started the ayahausca ceremony, around the fire. The night had been a dream.

Francisco Alvaro was playing music in the background on one of his own instruments. His eyes were closed gently and his face tilted up toward heaven. He looked tired and peaceful. His assistants sat beside him, one was asleep.

The intensity of the ayahuasca diminished hours later, but I knew that a residual of meaning and symbolism would stay with me permanently and that I would never be the same.

Like actors milling around after the show, pleased with their performance but not able to adequately compliment each other, and not wanting the memory of the night or the magic of their presentations to leave them too soon, no one was willing to move to disband, so we continued there together in the early morning comfort of each other.

CHAPTER 21

I didn't want to leave Hamburg. I didn't want to go home. The only plan I had ever had was over. Everything that I had calculated for my lifetime was already computed and spent. There was nothing left.

Our trip was ending. For me its sad melancholy finish was like the finale of a mournful evening tango with long sweeping notes orange and black with sorrow and with slender dancers dancing until dawn steps forward to bring them relief from the dark side of their heartache.

I watched Mr. Seiler meticulously study and pack his bags, placing things perfectly into tiny appropriate spots, as if they would be required to rest that way for eternity. I was fascinated that he could move to the next position of his life, satisfied that this part was over, having made amends with his past and with his soul.

"Michael," he said the day before we left, "I want to go to the place where Katerina and my son are buried. I'd like you to go with me."

The story of the bombing that he had told me many months before on the snowy afternoon in his study would be completed with this final act of forgiveness. How could I refuse?

It was gray the next morning and raining slightly, our first day without sunshine. He wore his long dark coat which I had thought was too heavy, but at the cemetery the wind was blowing hard and cold, and I wished I had had a heavy coat too.

The cemetery was near Uhlenhorst, by itself near a park. It was an old cemetery with huge gravestones and ancient gnarled trees. Some of the dates on the stones were from the 1500's. We wandered slowly among them with no apparent purpose. Mr. Seiler looked tired and slow. He eventually stopped and stared at a stone on which was written, "Katerina F. Seiler...Born, October 14, 1900...Died, July 24, 1943." The stone next to it read: "Fredrich K. Seiler...Born, July 7, 1924...Died, July 24, 1943."

He went down to his knees on the wet ground and tenderly wiped the stone faces clean with the forearm of his coat. With his fingernails he picked out the years of accumulated debris from the etched grooves of writing and then leaned back and folded his hands and closed his eyes. I stood reverently behind him saying nothing. When he struggled to get up, I helped him and felt the strength of his body and its compactness.

"Time passes by, Michael," is all he said.

"Would you like to go by your old house again, sir?" I asked him. His face brightened. "Yes, I'd like that."

We found our way to the avenue where we'd been before and entered it from a different direction. It felt like entering an emerald tunnel, the trees were so thick and the light was diminished by the overcast day. It looked different. Before, I was new to Hamburg and all of my thoughts and expectations had interfered with my vision, but now I had no preconceptions and I was familiar with the city, so I saw it as Mr. Seiler's home for the first time. I saw him as an innocent boy, which in a way he still was, walking down the street of capacious homes with his dog, discovering the world for the first time. And here he was with me, another boy, discovering the world for the first time also. I had an insight that maybe we were the same person at different moments of our lives, arriving briefly together in time as we passed by each other on roads leading to different places.

"Thank you for bringing me here to Hamburg, Mr. Seiler," I said as we stopped near his old house.

He took both of my hands in both of his as he had done that day in his study, and looked at me with soft eyes of age. "You're welcome, Michael. It is you whom I should thank, however. You've helped me to reunite with my self which I had buried long ago and had no intention of revisiting. We cannot merge with ourselves, though, until we have looked homeward, can we?"

"No sir, I guess not."

"Michael, I want you to promise me something. I think you believe you have not accomplished what you set out to accomplish. I can sense it in the sadness upon your face and in your silence. I want to tell you something and I don't want you to forget it, okay?"

"Yes, sir."

"Michael, life does not always occur the way we wish it to. What we thought would make us happy sometimes makes us sad instead. What we were afraid of sometimes turns out to be our friend. However, I believe that what we want will happen eventually, perhaps not exactly as we'd envisioned it happening or at the time we had projected, but in another form. And if we are attentive and faithful to our lives we'll recognize that what we wanted has been given to us. We must plan our lives and we must be organized, but we must also be prepared for things to happen differently than we set forth. You've not failed here in Hamburg, Michael. You have succeeded. You just don't know exactly how yet. Someday it will be clear to you.

"I want you to promise me that you'll go back to school when we return. It's what you should do, Michael. It will give you a great satisfaction in your heart. I think it is a doctor you should become, because a doctor cures the primary source of people's discomfort, and also has great power, first of all from his vast knowledge, and second, because power is given to him automatically by others. So as a doctor you can directly change the well-being of others at their request. Besides, Michael, you have a gift, and to have a gift and not use it is like receiving a present but not opening it, is it not?

"I know that education is expensive and that you don't have much money, so I'm going to pay for your college and your medical school, if you choose to study medicine. You can pay me back after you make money at your profession."

We drove back by a long route to the hotel for a final look at the city. At the port huge ships were coming in and going out, blowing their deep piercing sounds that lingered lonely on the foggy air. We stopped and watched them come and go tirelessly.

A nearby ship blew its horn. It wouldn't let go of the sound and wailed interminably like a crass instructor repeating his point over and over again. I felt as if my ears would crack.

"See, he agrees!" he said.

Horst and Angela met us for dinner south of our hotel in the old city. They were both dressed handsomely in their own unique styles. Simply because their bodies were still so nicely shaped, whatever they wore looked smart and drew others' attention to them, but also they had a flair which derived from an inner gentility. Mr. Seiler had it too.

Angela was charming and full of conversation and humor, as usual. Horst was a bit distant. I think that he was nervous that his father was leaving again. Who knows what emotions prevail at a time like that?

It was amazing how much German I understood by that time. I followed most of their conversation, which was mainly about Hamburg and people from the past. There was a lot of laughter and gaiety, the way it should be before separation.

Then Horst said to me, "What will you do when you return to America? Become a stone mason?"

"I would like that," I said.

It was true, even though I had not given it a moment's thought until then. Working alongside Horst, solving the puzzle made of stone, had given me great pleasure and satisfaction, but perhaps it was just being with him.

"Do you want to come over and teach me?"

"Come to America? That would be different. Sure. I'll come and teach you."

"Okay," I said, flirting back with him halfway seriously.

"He's going to be a doctor," Mr. Seiler interjected. "He already plans to go to school upon returning."

Horst became silent. Then he leaned close to his father and said, "Well, maybe he could build fireplaces on the weekends."

Mr. Seiler took his son's arm and said, "He should be a stone mason if that is what he wants."

"No, you are right. He should be a doctor. He will be a worthy doctor."

I wanted to be both things, a doctor and a stone mason. I wanted to please them both.

The sun was not shining when our plane took off from Hamburg.

Mr. Barlach had accompanied us in a taxi to the airport. How fitting it was that he should be the one to see Mr. Seiler off again. The two men embraced like wounded veterans for the last time ever. As I thought about it later, this was the most prominent feeling I had upon leaving Hamburg – that Mr. Seiler would never see his home again.

Upon returning to the United States I enrolled in the university and was accepted for the fall term. The school was impersonal and massive with thousands of new students. I knew no one and made no attempt to become close with anyone. I had a singular mission in my life: to obtain the credits needed for medical school.

I moved in with Mr. Seiler. There was a room at the back of his upstairs apartment with its own bedroom and bathroom and a separate entrance that went into the alley behind the building, so that I could come and go without bothering him.

My grandfather died that fall and my grandmother was alone, so I visited her often and watched over her. Mr. Seiler and I frequently had dinner with her on Sunday. She liked to cook for us.

I completed undergraduate school in two and a half years, taking a larger course load than my peers and studying in summers as well. I was a total student, obsessed with studying and learning. I surprised myself with what I was able to accomplish and with the copious mental energy I possessed. I remember lying in bed one morning thinking about something and realizing that I had become a thinking machine, that all I did from morning until night was think about the concepts that I was reading. I realized that such deep thinking, like exercise of the body, made me smarter. I had insights all day long every day, flowing like water throughout my hyperactive brain. I couldn't turn them off. Sometimes they kept me awake all night. It was like always being at the cinema watching my intellect create and then perceive its own cognitions.

My grandmother died later that year, and then I had no living relatives. Mr. Seiler was the only person I was close to, and he was beginning to become frail. He still walked every day and his spirit was good, but his strength began to lessen and his body size decrease. Some of the physical conditions for which he had always taken medicine became worse, and he was hospitalized several times during my second year of college. As his strength lessened, mine increased, so that I surprised myself with my capabilities and independence. I did all of the cooking now and all of the shopping. I bought his medicine and took him to the doctor. Our roles reversed.

One day I came home at lunchtime and in the mailbox was a letter from Germany. It was from Horst. He had not responded to many letters from us, and we had given up on hearing from him, disappointed, since our reunion with him had seemed so successful. But that was Horst.

He wrote that he wanted to visit America in the spring and seemed to be asking our opinion. I talked to Mr. Seiler about it, and he was thrilled. I wondered if Angela would come with him. I hoped so.

He didn't respond to our invitation. For many weeks we waited to hear from him, but no letter came.

I came home one day after school, carrying grocery bags and books in both arms. I put them down in the hallway so that I could open the door and as I reached for the doorknob, the door opened and there stood Horst. He was dressed in his usual turtleneck sweater beneath a sport coat and wearing Levis. He had a nice smile on his face and put his hand out to me and when I reached for it he grabbed me and pulled me into his body and hugged me.

He looked much older, and tired. I could see that he was somewhat lame as we walked back into the kitchen where Mr. Seiler was sitting.

"Did you bring Angela?" I asked him.

"Angela's dead."

"Oh, no. What happened?"

"She was in a car accident several months ago. She died instantly."

"Oh, God," I said, "Are you doing all right?"

"I miss her."

"I'm sure you do. I'm sorry, Horst." I felt empty. I had cared for her a lot.

"Hey, we all die! So, you are in school Kurt tells me. About to finish, eh? Then what? Stone masonry?"

We laughed. "No, medical school. I'm applying now. How long can you stay?" I asked him.

"The rest of my life."

He was being sarcastic but the serious look on his face when he said that puzzled me.

"Well, we're happy to have you, Horst." I looked at Mr. Seiler and his face was beaming, having his real son and his "adopted" son together again.

We spent Saturday and Sunday touring the city, going out to dinner, and talking. He was the same old Horst except that he was alone now. I had not realized it at the time I was with them, but Angela had been greatly responsible for bringing forth the qualities in his personality which were so dominant and dramatic, and without her he actually seemed rather shy and unsure of himself. Except when he drank. Then he became aggressive at first followed by a sort of sad resignation that came over him, as if he had suddenly seen himself in the mirror and was disgusted with his own image which he'd seen so many times before. Then he became so quiet he would not talk at all. This pattern repeated itself day after day, until one day I confronted him about it. That I could approach him on this level illustrated to me how much I had matured.

I took him alone to dinner one Friday night while Mr. Seiler was at a friend's house. Horst had been with us almost three months, and indeed it appeared that he was there permanently. He didn't talk of returning to Germany. In fact, he seemed to need us and to almost cling to us. I enjoyed having him but I was worried too. He was still drinking a lot and reading voraciously as always, but there was something about his activities that gave me concern and which I couldn't quite articulate. That interfered with my own work which also gave me concern. He slept late in the morning, read all day, and stayed up all night. He was not as strong or as confident as he had been. Although he had not really been a gregarious person in Germany, he had been one that others were drawn to and wanted to be around. But now he wished only to be alone or with us. I wondered if he felt ill at ease in America and asked him.

"Not at all. I like it here. I don't have a need for friendship right now, Michael. I'm tired of friends and close relationships. I can never explain myself and, frankly, it's harder for me to know who I am now."

This was an unusual statement coming from a man whom I had heard rage for hours in defense of a belief.

Then he said something which shocked me. "I'm dying, Michael. My body is sore and can't work, my eyes are worthless, and my will is gone. I'm haunted by nightmares from my past. I don't see a future that is anything but painful."

I hardly knew what to say. I was afraid that my own silence showed that I didn't care, and when I started to reply my words sounded hollow and solicitous, until I spoke what I truly felt.

"I think that you should stop drinking, Horst."

As soon as I spoke those words he began shaking his head slowly in disagreement. "I can't stop drinking, Michael. It hides the frightening things that are inside of me. It's too late to try to unravel and neutralize them. I don't have the strength to face those things. I have made unpardonable mistakes in my life."

"Nothing is unpardonable, Horst. Why do you think it's too late? If you stopped drinking, I think you would have new strength, and a new will."

He put his hand on my wrist and tightened it. His fingers were so long that they wrapped around my whole forearm. "Michael, listen to me!" he said sternly. "I know what I'm talking about. What I saw in Hamburg as a boy has poisoned my mind and my eyes for eternity. There's no way I can ever be normal. I'm ruined. The decisions I've made since then have taken me to a place from which I cannot escape. I am a defective piece. All of the king's doctors and all of the king's priests cannot put me together again."

I talked to him at length, expressing thoughts and feelings about him and his father and Angela which I had stored for a long time. They were tender and beautiful and sensitive thoughts of love and appreciation and admiration. I told him how much they had all meant to me and what an influence they had had upon my life. It appeared that I had reached him because his face softened as I spoke and a gentle smile formed on it that I thought was an inner pride at hearing my compliments of his unique manhood. My soliloquy was long and articulate. In the end there was nothing he could say to contradict it. He stared at me a long time with a quizzical look on his face, as if what I had said about him did not square with what he thought of himself, as if he were wondering which of us was wrong or if possibly we were both right.

"Let's go," he said and stood up and put his arm around me. "You are a good guy, Michael."

We walked back to our building. It was nighttime and dark in the alleyway where he left me to climb the stairs to our apartment, telling me to go ahead, that he was just going to take a little walk. I climbed a few stairs and then looked back at him staring up at me like a child or a pet afraid that I was leaving him forever.

"Are you all right, Horst?"

"Yeah. I'll see you, Michael. Look after Kurt."

It was a strange statement coming from someone who had promised to come back in just a few minutes. I wrestled with myself whether to go back down and be with him. I could see in the dim light at the bottom of the stairs that he was frowning deeply, as if he were trying again and again to enter something into the calculator of his experience and it wouldn't compute. Then he walked away and I continued up the stairs.

Just before I reached the top I heard a gunshot. I ran down the stairs and turned in the direction that he had walked. There he lay just a few feet away. Dead.

It seemed fitting that Horst should die by his own hand, since he was strong and willful and would never have allowed himself to weaken and wither away. It would have made no difference what I or anyone else could have said or done.

I was devastated and felt an emptiness that was paralyzing, as if something of me had died too. How could I have known, until it happened, that there was a part of me that had come from Horst. He was a part of me that I could never be except in Mr. Seiler's eyes, and I was the part of him that enabled him to receive glory from his father.

I entered medical school in the fall. Even for one as disciplined as I had become and used to working hard all day every day at several different responsibilities, it was still a crushing schedule

Mr. Seiler never fully recovered from Horst's suicide and yet he miraculously continued on. His desire to live, which was all that had kept him from slipping into total physical decline, was badly damaged. I could see him struggle on a daily basis to re-invent his volition. It was a task every bit as demanding as medical school.

One day I came home with an electric wheelchair which I had borrowed from the medical school and presented it to him as a way of becoming more active. At first he resisted it, but he began to spend more time in it and it gave him a new freedom, so I bought him one. I also bought him a small radio with headphones so that he could listen to his music.

As sad as our situation seemed on its face, I gained purpose and wholeness from caring for him. I then had two purposes in my life, which were the same really: to finish medical school and to care for him. Without it being stated by either of us, I knew that he was being nourished by seeing me become a doctor, so through the process of becoming a doctor I was keeping him alive. As a result medical school became even more challenging for me.

I finished school in four years, taking no time off. In that time Mr. Seiler's health failed substantially.

The last months of school were a bittersweet time of celebration and sadness. I had made some good friends whom I was going to leave. I also knew that Mr. Seiler was going to leave me. By then he was feeble and almost silent. However, I knew he had to come to my graduation somehow. It seemed that half of the medical school knew about me and him and many of them were willing to do their part to get him there.

We had stayed in the second floor apartment for the entire time. One of my friends at medical school was a strapping burly man. He came to the apartment to look at the possibility of moving Mr. Seiler down the stairs. "We'll get him out of here," he said confidently.

The day of graduation my friend and three others came by the apartment. It was late spring. The breeze was warm and cool at once, carrying many scents of early spring's new life. It was an important moment at the end of our lives together.

A small Sunday morning crowd gathered and watched my friends carry Mr. Seiler in his wheelchair down the stairs. When they reached the bottom the crowd applauded, not understanding why, just knowing that the event was noteworthy. Mr. Seiler looked like a king appearing before his subjects one last time to reassure them that his leadership was still intact. I could feel my face beaming uncontrollably with pride, and I said to the man next to me, "He used to sail ships all around the world."

I graduated with honors from medical school. Many people were happy for me, people whom I didn't even know. I recognized then that something about my life was blessed. Even though it sometimes felt as if I were climbing a steep hill alone without enough strength to reach the top, someone had always come along to help me or at least be happy for me. At that time I didn't realize why it had happened that way, nor did I have enough wisdom from experience to understand the spiritual dialectics of such things as giving and receiving, of yielding and resisting, of possession and renunciation.

Mr. Seiler died two weeks after I graduated from medical school. I was with him early that morning just after the sun came up above the horizon. No one had to tell me that he was going to die, I knew it. I was holding his hand and he squeezed me hard in a last gargantuan effort to convey to me his feelings for me and his promise for grace.

I didn't have to mourn his passing because his presence never left me.

CHAPTER 22

I observed that Francisco Alvaro went in and out of the two worlds with facility, as if he could see to step over the invisible barrier that separated one from the other. Yet he still clearly identified with that part of himself which stayed behind in the world of illusions.

He appreciated that I was a doctor and that we shared and understood certain traits unique to that profession. One was the awe and reverence with which others approached us and the almost limitless power which they confer upon us. He pointed out to me that all doctors should use this personal power they are invested with to heal their patients. If they understood that healing was in great measure a matter of faith, they would be much more effective, because then they would have a double-edged sword.

It was distressing to him, however, that he was often expected, especially by people coming to him from the USA and Europe, to behave as a mystic involved in the occult.

He invited me to take ayahausca again, with just him. We took only a few items with us, no food or extra clothing, and traveled a long time into the rain forest to a sacred spot that was his.

I watched him prepare the plant for consumption. It was mesmerizing. His hands were delicate like an artist's. They touched all things tenderly, never with anger or haste, always with understanding and care. He took hold of things discerningly, as if on its surface was a code to be interpreted, like braille.

We sat on the ground together meditatively after taking the sacred plant. He began chanting and playing his flute. Gradually visions began to happen in my eyes and in my mind. His eyes were closed and I could see his chest move in and out as he seemed to be sucking the notes from the flute as well as exhaling breath into it, playing it like a harmonica.

I looked at him, hoping to get his attention and talk about what I was seeing when I suddenly realized that it was he who was creating the visions that I was having and of which we were a part. I actually saw these scenes materialize from the notes that came from his flute which were personifying the music. He was completely different than he had been just thirty minutes earlier. He was not attentive in any way to the world which had housed his earlier concerns but was intent upon sculpting our mutual ayahuasca perception with his voice and his music. I realized later that he had largely created my visions that first night, coaxing from inside of me the themes that I needed to treat with awareness, having discerned them from the meetings he'd had with me before.

His music and his chanting stopped and he began smoking, blowing the smoke softly my way with long slow exhalations of his breath and with slow circular outward motions of his hands and arms, until the smoke enveloped me in its wispy white evanescence. I reached out and felt it. It was like soft cotton, cushioning and quiet, so pleasing to my sense of touch that I tried to hold it in my arms like a pillow but it dissipated into separate irretrievable molecules.

I heard him say, "We cannot take into our personal domain that which belongs to everyone or else it will vanish to even us. Be entranced by the world. Do not embrace or possess it." He blew more smoke my way and I simply received its effects and didn't intervene in its mission and it floated me with it on its ride into the breeze.

Now I saw the world from within, from an atomic point of view. I saw the steam of humidity bathing the processes of growth; I saw the light of the sun being converted to chlorophyll; I saw the fundamental microbial core of all of life, the recycling of one nutrient into another, the decomposition of one formerly living thing and its reincarnation into another, the continuation of life made possible by the recycling of life's end.

All is bionomic at its essence, I realized. No matter what we do or the significance which we think our actions have, the actions taking place microscopically in and around us are the final actuaries of our destiny. Our will is their will. We are them. We are all part of the omnipresent inexhaustible factory of animation. All of life resides in all of life. It is inescapable to be born again.

I could not experience Francisco Alvaro's humility without being affected by it. Wisdom is humility. Humility is the result of seeing the microview from inside of life and the macroview from above it, whose overlapping viewpoints testify to the interconnection of all living things, large or small.

We spent the night there together, he sharing with me the brilliant multicolors of his evening's aura.

Christiane and I and Simon left a few days later for Iquitos. The way back seemed different than we had come. The Amazon did not wind as much nor were the waves as high. Halfway there the sky grew dark and cast a fascinating shadow over the land like a spirit. The animals became still at first, an uncanny silence like a city sleeping before sunrise.

The rain forest was still and silent for so long that we wondered if we were perceiving it incorrectly. It seemed that everything was waiting for something to happen, to direct them in the next action.

Then the sky crashed epochally. The boat shook. Long jagged spikes of lightning flashed erratically, racing for the earth. It began to rain torrentially, like a monsoon, inches at a time, so that we could feel the boat rising in the water like an object in a bathtub being filled.

None of us moved. Our instincts to protect ourselves were belittled by our common desire to be part of a great cleansing which was to last until we arrived at Iquitos. Water streamed over our heads and bodies and emblematically washed back to earth the residues that no longer belonged to us but which would leave behind a pure and immaculate freshness of the spirit.

We spent the night in Iquitos, a dreary reminder of what civilization has wrought. We stayed in Iquitos one more day before catching a flight to Lima. After we arrived all of us experienced something like withdrawal or re-entry shock. And although the bold-stroked images of the nights in Cuchari had impressed us for all time, the law of worldly existence commands that the sacred be overcome by the profane.

CHAPTER 23

Christiane had to leave for New Zealand and catch up with her work. She assumed Simon would go with her, but when she mentioned it to him, he was uninterested, so she asked me if he could stay with me while she was gone. He knew that I still had another phase of my healing to finish. He had been there when Francisco Alvaro had discussed it with me. And one day he started a discussion of it.

"What are you going to do next, Michael? Go back to Hamburg? And find Susanne?"

"Yes, I'm going to go back to Hamburg when the time feels right."

"Can I go with you?"

"Yes, I think I would like that. But I don't know if we can find her, Simon. And even if we do, it's possible that we could both be disappointed."

We had to wait until Simon's next long vacation from school. He was thrilled to be going with me, but he no longer expressed happiness in a childlike way. He was far wiser than his peers, and although he didn't disparage what they were doing, he was generally not involved with them.

His compassion for others impressed me. It pleased me that he continued to be a good student and that he read ravenously, seeing the magic of imagination that reading can inspire. He and I talked for hours about many subjects, and he was a wonderful writer who was beginning to transpose his deep thoughts clearly onto paper.

We left the following week for Hamburg. Hamburg had changed.

We didn't stay at Vier Jahreszeiten, but I took Simon there to see it and told him about its magnificence and its history. Seeing the awe on his face as we entered the lobby of that grand hotel, I wished that I had simply booked a room there for us instead, the way that Mr. Seiler had done.

We went into the Condeitori and had an ice cream and watched the swans on the water from the window. The hotel was brilliantly clean and light, sparkling with white marble and gleaming silverware in crisp white linen. I could see the Alsterpavillion in the distance and recalled Mr. Barlach hobbling to embrace Mr. Seiler.

The hotel we stayed at was at the edge of the area where Mr. Seiler and I had first looked for Horst - the artists' colony. As I suspected, it had become popular and there were more tourists there. The moving edge of such places is always an area of fascination to the public, and the old gets transformed into the new.

The last place we went before starting to look for Susanne was the asylum. This was where I had started that first night in Cuchari, when I wandered off on my own into the rain forest, and Simon had followed me. The asylum was closed and there were signs saying it was about to be demolished and to stay out. Weeds, voluntary bushes and trees had taken it over, and my inclination was to obey the signs and go no further, but Simon insisted that we try to enter, saying to me sternly, "You must go in, Michael," the same thing he had said to me at Cuchari.

We had to crawl part of the way beneath an almost impenetrable leafy overgrowth in order to reach the building, which was locked. We made our way slowly around its perimeter, trying each door and window until we found one ajar and climbed through it into the dark sanctuary inside. He led the way to the front room that was lit by the sun through the windows. I realized it was the place where Horst and Angela and I had entered the building and from which I had gone alone into the desolation beyond.

"Which way did you go?"

"Through that door," I said.

He took my hand again and said, "Let's go."

The hallway was dank and dark. The floor was rough with plaster from the collapsing ceiling above. It was sad remembering the howling noises, pleas and screams of the caged people whose lives someone had determined to be unmanageable or not worth the price of their liberty.

What about all of the lives that were spent and ended there, I wondered? What about the mistakes, like Susanne? Could someone who had been abandoned to such a place ever be the same, be trusting, live in a world that is taken for granted?

We walked through the rubble of the building in silence. All of the rooms looked the same to me. I remembered it was a long walk to her room and that the attendant who led me was hunched and lame and dull with ill-refined sensibilities.

I felt anxious and suggested to Simon that we should leave because we were trespassing and that there was no purpose in wandering monotonously from room to empty room.

"I think there is, Michael. I think you will know her room when you enter it. I think we should go on."

I remembered that her room was on the left side of the hallway, so we entered every room on that side and lingered within it a moment or two trying to detect her presence. I felt ill at ease.

"Michael, do you feel as if you let her down in some way?"

"I don't know, Simon. Probably. Those feelings are now just part of who I am, so I have a hard time separating them, but yes, I do remember feeling that way then."

"Why do you think you let her down?"

"I don't know, Simon. I think I was afraid of my feelings for her and maybe I pulled away because of that, which caused her to leave for Hamburg and become lost again. And maybe she became pregnant with my child and I wasn't there to help her."

"But you say 'lost again'. Doesn't that mean she was lost before she met you, and that you found her? Is it your duty to find someone over and over again? And maybe it was someone else's child."

"I was lost too, Simon, and she found me."

"Yes, but who looked after you when she left you? No one. You looked after yourself. You're blaming yourself for things that aren't your fault and you are taking on responsibility alone."

We continued to roam from room to room. Walking and talking with Simon in the place where the meeting had taken place so many years before allowed the truth to come forward which I had hidden from myself for twenty years.

"I should have stayed here in Hamburg and fought to have her released," I said. I told him that I remembered it now as being huge in my thoughts, just before leaving Hamburg, that I was escaping the terrible responsibility of her welfare, as if upon seeing her infirm and impotent, lying pale in this horrible place, I had lost my nerve and my resolve and had chosen the easy exit. I remembered feeling that I was a coward for not insisting upon staying another week or month or whatever time it took to nurse her back to health.

"What could you have done, Michael? You were a boy. You had already lied just to get in to see her. What chance did you have of getting her released, no matter how much longer you stayed?"

"But that's not it, Simon. I gave up on her. I remember now feeling it. I remember clearly having this feeling that my main objective was to escape this place. I was terrified. I had never imagined people could be like this, confined like animals begging for their freedom. I was a coward, Simon. I have spent 25 years seeking pardon from this crime against someone I loved. I can now see the connection between her and every person I saved from dying in the operating room. They were all Susanne, atonements to pay off the debt I owed her.

"Michael, that is wrong!"

We walked into a room just before the end of the hallway, and I felt it. Just as Simon had thought I would. I felt her presence. This was the room.

He must have seen me recognize her spirit for his face lit up and his senses carefully peaked like an animal sensing its prey or its predator.

"Is this the room, Michael?" he asked.

I nodded slowly that it might be, trying to become sure by moving to the corner where I remembered her bed to have been. Ever so slowly I moved about the room trying to position myself to receive confirmation from wherever it comes. I could feel my eyes furrow, trying to focus with the supersense that would give me knowledge. Both of us were so still and so bracingly attentive that I began to pick up tiny apperceptions: the rancid smell of odor and woodsmoke from the attendant's body, the doughlike texture of her swollen face, the single incongruous comfort of soft yellow lamplight next to her bed, all mixing with an intangible taste of fear.

It no longer returned as a memory. It was becoming real, the way that it had been with ayahuasca. In fact, here we were again. My perceptions were blending similarly. I felt as if I could, if I wanted, allow them to cross over into a single hypersense capable of perceiving the very heart of the moment and rendering its meaning.

"I think I see something in the corner, Michael. A small bed made up with covers. And there's a table with a reading lamp beside it. And look! On the floor there, shelves against the wall, with clothes folded neatly upon them. Can you see it, Michael?"

I was amazed! How could he see it just the way it had been twenty years before? As he described it, it re-materialized before my eyes. A chair was pulled up beside her bed, and I was sitting in it, leaning over her. I could feel the clammy perspiration of my nervousness as I picked up her lifeless hand. The attendant was in the doorway like a beast waiting to be told what to do next. I said to her, "Susanne, it's Michael. I've come to take you to the lake and watch the swans and talk." She didn't respond. I wanted to bolt for the door and run back to Horst and Angela. I sat there vapidly, holding her unresponsive hand and staring at her bloodless flesh untouched by the sun for months. I tried to feel the same feelings for her as before, but I couldn't without her participation, and I felt ashamed at my lack of leadership. My feelings for her were hollow and shameful and suffused with fear and something like disgust that life had allowed her to be compromised and dehumanized this way. I turned and looked to Simon for direction, hoping he would say, "Let's leave," but he moved next to me and knelt down and took my hand and tenderly placed it in hers, saying, "This is Susanne, Michael. Now you can tell her what you meant to tell her many years ago. She's just sleeping, Michael. Don't be afraid. Go ahead, talk to her, the way you used to talk to her, the way you did at Cuchari."

Upon Simon's saying that to me, her hand became warm in mine and her face turned red with life and circulation. It was the pretty face that I had first seen over two decades before, and I knew that beneath her gently closed eyelids were the most dazzling blue eyes I had ever seen. With impertinence and selfishness I let go of her hand and reached up to touch her eyelid and roll it back a bit like a doctor checking for life.

By revealing just a slice of the brilliant blue of her eye, the room lit up. I turned around to see if only I was affected and the attendant was shielding his eyes from the glare of her image. Simon's face was lit up like a gleeful blue child in a carnival night. He was laughing. I started laughing. The attendant resumed his deformed attention trying to ignore the blue spotlight upon him, but he couldn't. The light was so powerful it illuminated his inner nature and he ran from the room like a petty thief discovered. I went to the door and locked it and the light faded as her eyelid came back over her eye, like the sun going behind a cloud.

I started to apologize to her for not returning to the asylum to help her, but Simon grabbed my arm and stopped me. "You don't need to do that. Remember, in this world people are what you want them to be. That includes you, Michael. You're what she wanted you to be. That's all you need to know."

She'd not moved an inch. She was like an apparition to which the regular functions of being a body are irrelevant. Her purpose there, I inferred, was only as a repository for the poison self-incriminations to which my mind and heart had given rise for twenty years and which had been putrefying inside of me. So I poured them out to her as fast as they issued forth from me, and she listened like an amulet behind the door of confession.

"They threw me out of here, Simon. That's why I didn't come back. I remember now. They told me it was time to leave and as I walked down the hall with the cripple behind me, I passed a young doctor who looked sensitive and caring. I stopped him and talked in German as fast as I could, but he spoke English. I told him they had made a mistake with Susanne and that she was a brilliant ethereal artist who was put there maliciously by her half-brother. I pled with him to bring her back to life and give her attention and begged him to see for himself. Several other guards descended upon me and pulled me away from him. I can still see his inquiring face looking at me, confused, as they carried me out.

That's how it happened. I remember it now. I remember it clearly, Simon."

CHAPTER 24

Simon and I awoke the next morning and set out to find Susanne. There were no clues for us to follow. No relatives that I knew of. No friends or associates. The city contained over two million people. The only place I knew to go was the Palmaille, where she had lived with her father.

The German I had learned before had almost disappeared. I was relieved when I called upon the new owner of Dr. Ludendorff's home and she immediately switched to English when she heard me stumble through a simple greeting. I told her that I was a friend of a previous homeowner's daughter and wanted to find her.

"Yes, yes, I knew the Ludendorffs. My husband went to the doctor for years," she said.

The home, of course, had been completely changed. The woman was alone and quite talkative. Much of her talk was gossip about the neighborhood. We listened to her frustrations and complaints a long time, and then I said, "What can you tell me about Susanne?"

She placed her palms on her cheeks and bowed her head and shook it back and forth slowly. "Oh, my Lord, isn't that sad what happened to that poor girl?"

"What happened?"

"Oh, don't you know? First she got pregnant and her father disowned her when she wouldn't do something with the pregnancy. They lived together like cellmates in this house. That's why we changed everything when we bought it, to get rid of that atmosphere they created. He had a heart attack, and she had a nervous breakdown. She was never emotionally strong and always very different from the other children. I remember her as a little girl with long blond hair and the bluest eyes you have ever seen. You felt as if you could swim in them.

"Her half-brother put her in Neuengamme. What a terrible place! I knew someone who worked there and they said she laid in bed all day long and never opened her eyes, like a corpse. She was very captivating, you know. Beautiful. And a marvelous musician. But she'd had problems all of her life. This poor girl has had nothing but calamity.

"She inherited some money from father's estate and withdrew to somewhere along the river north of Hamburg. I've not seen her for years. I have heard, however, that she writes music and occasionally plays piano and organ at the Great Room in the Musikhalle."

"Where is the Musikhalle?

"It's in Karl-Muck-Platz, west of the Alster, in Nord."

"Thank you. Have you heard her play?"

"Only once, when her parents were still together. She was just a girl at that time but even then her music was enchanting. Like nothing I'd ever heard, really. People say that her mother was descended from Johannes Brahms, who was from Hamburg himself, you know."

We were on our way. To the Musikhalle. The last time in Hamburg I had delayed even beginning to search for her until the last week, as if I knew intuitively that I would not find her whole. This time, however, it felt different. Upon having a solid place to start, the Musikhalle, and evidence that she was still there, free, in Hamburg, I felt hopeful and energetic about finding her.

The Musikhalle was a lovely brick building, a sumptuous example of Neo-Baroque architecture, built in 1908. Miraculously the building had survived the bombing of Hamburg not just intact, but untouched. In front of it is an amazing bronze sculpture meant to symbolize Brahms's music. It is abstract and impossible to define clearly, but to me it looked like the shape of a piano flowing in all directions but anchored by solid vertical centerpieces advancing towards heaven.

We were told that the director of the museum, Frau Schnitzer, would arrive at twelve hundred. We went to a nearby park and waited for noon to arrive. In Hamburg there is always a park nearby.

I was happy and proud to be with Simon. We found two swings and swung side by side like children.

"You called me your son," he said.

"I'm sorry. I just didn't want to explain everything to the woman."

"You don't need to be sorry. It felt good to be called your son. I wish I was your son."

We waited on a bench with the Brahms sculpture next to us. When the carillon from the nearby church struck twelve times, we walked to the front door and went in. Hamburgers are always on time.

Frau Schnitzer was already behind her desk working hard when we entered. She looked annoyed that someone was bothering her so soon in her day, and I had a sinking feeling that our purpose would not be achieved that day.

"Hello, I'm looking for Susanne Ludendorff. I'm an old friend of hers from the US, and I have not seen her for many years. I've been told that she has a relationship with the Musikhalle."

"Someone has told you wrong then." I knew we would have to penetrate her frozen exterior, and already I felt weary of the task because it was reminiscent of the time before with Horst when we had extracted information from the reluctant doctors on Deichstrasse.

"Do you know Susanne?"

"Oh course I know her. She is a prominent Hamburg musician."

"Can you tell us how to find her?"

She looked at me and resumed her officiousness. "You must understand, sir. We are a patron of the arts and the artists. We are entrusted with their care and cannot simply give out their addresses to anyone who asks for them. Most artists are very private people and wish to remain undisturbed. Their performances are their offerings to the public. Did you say you were a friend of hers?"

"I knew her when I was a boy. We went to school together in the United States and spent a lot of time together before she returned to Hamburg. I lost track of her but I've always wanted to see her again. I visited Hamburg twenty years ago and tried to look her up, but I couldn't find her."

I decided to use my trump card. "I am a medical doctor in the United States." I took my wallet out and showed her my Physician's License.

"Well, I am not sure where Susanne lives, and I couldn't tell you if I knew. It's somewhere along the Upper Elbe. She owns a house and some land in the woods near the river. I have never been there. She's extremely private. This is what I can do. If you give me a business card or write your name down and give me a number where you can be reached, I will call you if she comes in and authorizes me to do so.

I wrote my name and the telephone number of the hotel on the paper. "Will she be performing here soon again?"

"I never know when she will come in here. When she finishes a work, she often stops here to play it on our organ, which is one of the finest in Germany, and at other times she simply comes in to play the piano or the organ in order to 'refresh myself,' as she says. We allow her to do this because her music is so wonderful that we are happy to facilitate it in any way we can. Usually when this happens, crowds wander into the auditorium because she is so popular, which makes it like a concert itself. We charge them a small fee to come in and she donates it to us."

We walked away together into the sunfallen late afternoon. A coolness was coming not far ahead of winter. We walked for miles in the splendid city and ended up far away from our hotel in a beautiful park. We were both so tired that Simon almost fell asleep while walking. I picked him up and carried him in my arms and he fell asleep. The streets were bare and starkly quiet like a moonscape. I sat down on a bench with the boy still in my arms and listened to the abject silence of Hamburg before daybreak. I thought of Mr. Seiler and felt lonely for him too. And Horst. And Angela. What interesting people they had all been for me.

Then I felt the first advance of irresistible tiredness and knew that I could not get up before I fell asleep. The only sound in the hush before the dawn was Simon's slumberous breath upon my shoulder. I placed him on the bench with his head upon my lap and covered him with my coat and I leaned my own head back to sleep beneath what seemed at that moment to be a hardhearted Hamburg sky.

CHAPTER 25

I awakened on the bench to brisk sounds of the city at new morning.
Moment by moment the density of humanity increased, swelling the
streets with movement and sound, until the night's dark tranquility was
entirely replaced by a glaring rush for the heart of another day.

Simon slept through the transition, so I woke him up and we walked
to a restaurant a block away and had breakfast.

We walked back to the Musikhalle. Frau Schnitzer welcomed us in
her office. We had won her approval. She said that Susanne had not
been there yet. I asked her if we could sit in the Great Room.

The hall was plush. Velvety and grandiose, like a house of royalty.
Its emptiness echoed and magnified the slightest sound but did so very
accurately. We sat and enjoyed it a moment.

"Simon, I want to find Horst's house. I think we should rent a
motorcycle."

His face beamed with delight. "Yes, let's do that, Michael. That
would be wonderful."

Horst's neighborhood had changed. The road to his cabin, which had
been almost impassable from neglect when I was last there, was now
paved and lined with expensive new homes. As we made the last turn,
which before had been the end of the road from which we had had to

walk, it was the beginning of someone's asphalted driveway. Apparently they owned all of the contiguous ground, which included Horst's cabin.

There was a doorbell on a half-open gate.

"Let's ring them, Michael."

I rang and no one came at first. Then a young girl wearing a long white dress came and opened the gate as if we were expected.

She turned and walked away slowly and we followed her. After a bit I said to her in German, "Who lives here?" to which she replied in a beautiful Australian English accent: "I'm sorry, I only speak English." I repeated it again in English, and she said, "You are at the Temple of Meditation."

The grounds were beautifully landscaped and all of the trees were still in place the way that I remembered them. I could hear chanting in one of the small buildings we passed on the way to the main house, which was Horst's old cabin that had been added onto many times. What had been his original cabin was now the reception room. This thrilled me to find a piece of his life similar to the way I'd remembered it. The girl introduced us to a man sitting behind a desk and then she left. He had an Indian name which I promptly forgot while thinking that it was not his given name.

"Are you a part of the group for this afternoon?"

"No," I said, "I'm a friend of the person who used to own this cabin."

"The sculptor?" he asked enthusiastically.

"Yes, his name was Horst Seiler."

"Oh," he said coming toward me and taking my arm. "We want to talk to you. What wonderful sculptures he's created. We are so lucky that they were here with the property when we bought it. It's like an art museum."

He let us walk back through the archway and in the opposite direction of the woods. I was in a hurry to show Simon the animals that Horst had sculpted so I walked quickly ahead of him.

"Michael, what is this?"

I turned and saw him next to a sculpture of an old man and a boy standing side by side with their arms around each other. As I came closer I could see who it was. It was Mr. Seiler. And me, twenty years old. Horst must have made it from a picture he took of us the day before we'd left.

"Who is this, Michael? Is this you?"

"Yes, Simon, it's me with Mr. Seiler."

"It's remarkable. Is that what you looked like then?"

"Yes, it is."

"You were just a boy then, Michael. An innocent boy."

Horst had given me a naivete which he must have seen in me, which I myself had not felt at the time but which now pleased me. I could still sense the way Mr. Seiler's arm and mine held each other's waists.

Simon looked closely at the sculpture as if he thought perhaps it was alive in some way. He seemed baffled to see this life-size twenty-year-old Michael alongside the one he knew standing next to it. Maybe he had never imagined me as young.

"Yes, I guess I was innocent. It was so long ago. Horst never told me he made this sculpture."

Simon touched it all over, looking back and forth at me, trying, it seemed, to gain an understanding of the connection between two bodies from two separate times existing at the same time. "A sculpture lives so differently from a painting," I said.

We walked on through the woods until I found the animals that Horst had sculpted. Simon was moved by the extraordinary detail of each piece and also the sensitive placement of them all together in relation to one another.

"This man, Horst, was a genius, Michael. I had no idea he was like this."

By the time we left it was afternoon. We drifted slowly on the motorcycle, riding along the channels of the Elbe. Because of the position of the sun at that time of day and year, the air seemed green and the grass next to the water looked chatoyant, like early rice fields. I thought of Mr. Seiler's description of Hamburg on the day of die Katastrophe, which I had never forgotten: "The sky was the color of yellow it is only occasionally, with a tint of green that makes the world which one views appear to be behind a glass or in a photograph."

That's how it seemed as we drove along the river on our way back to the Musikhalle: like a great Impressionistic painting behind green-tinted glass.

At least once a day we checked with Frau Schnitzer and each day we brought her a little gift.

"She's been here to submit her new composition," she said on the third day. "I gave her your letter."

I must have subconsciously assumed that we would never find her but instead continue the ritual of asking for her each day, because when told by Frau Schnitzer that she had been there and had received my letter and now knew that I was looking for her, I was dumbfounded.

"What did she say?" I asked her.

"She didn't say anything. She just folded it up and put it in her pocket."

"Well, we'll just have to wait for her to respond, I suppose."

"She's coming back to play the day after tomorrow. There will be a crowd here, I am sure, but you're welcome to attend. Perhaps she would see you after she plays."

"Yes. Perhaps she would," I said.

We said goodbye to Frau Schnitzer and told her we would return the day after tomorrow. We got on our motorcycle and looked up at her and waved. She waved back hesitantly, with a questioning look on her face like a mother watching her children leave home alone for the first time. I felt like saying, "We'll be okay."

The two days were special. I felt free to soar, like a grounded bird again given flight. I felt as if the days of my youth were being given back to me to finish out where they had suddenly stopped in front of a chasm. No matter what happens, I thought, just to see her will allow me to resume the journey I'd been on. So the two days were like a free pass because whatever happened I would be the beneficiary: if she was exactly the person I remembered her to be, I would have the good fortune to be in her midst again; if she was entirely other than that, a spell would be broken between the past and the present and would release me from its hold; if she rejected me, that would be the end of the story, there would be no need to seek her out again; if she accepted me, I could maybe become empowered with her new presence.

CHAPTER 26

It was foggy and almost raining, dripping, the night we arrived at the Musikhalle, as if the air of Hamburg were trying to cry but couldn't.

We had forsaken the motorcycle for a taxi which at my request had let us off a few buildings away from the concert hall so that I could walk away some of my nervousness.

In the afternoon we had gone to a tailor and rented for the day wonderful black suits with shiny shoes, ascots and cummerbunds. We were dashing. Simon looked beautiful in black, matching his dark hair and winsome eyes. We had examined each other carefully before leaving our room to make sure everything was perfect. I had combed his hair just right and he had picked the specks of lint from the back of my suit, like two monkeys gratuitously serving each other. The genteel clothing made me feel almost courageous with confidence.

We were thirty minutes early but already a crowd had gathered outside of the hall. Only a few of them were dressed like us and though I felt a bit out of place, it felt good to have honored Susanne in this way.

Hoping to catch a glimpse of her, I kept tripping on things while staring at the stage as we walked into the theatre at ground level. Finally I just put my hand on Simon's shoulder and let him lead me like a blind man through the aisles while I continuously scanned the setting for a sighting of her.

Deep purple velvet curtains hung down fifty feet from the ceiling and their pleats made them look like comforters over tree trunks. On the stage was a beautiful grand piano shining black like our shoes, with a green cushioned seat. The floor below it was polished wood. It looked so lonely out there on the stage, I thought.

I searched the pleats of the massive curtains for a seam from which she might come out onto the stage.

Then I saw her!

Even from the great distance that separated us I could see her lazuline eyes like sapphires staring out to assess the crowd for which she would perform. Our eyes met.

I remembered first seeing those eyes in the school library when I turned around toward her voice, so close behind me, so deep, so bottomless. I remembered sometimes not hearing what she'd said to me, because I had been absorbed in her eyes.

I tripped on Simon's shoe and fell forward into him, but I couldn't take my eyes from her. He caught me, and turning, saw me staring at the stage, unmindful of my own welfare. He stopped and held me up, and then looked where I was looking.

"Is that her?" he asked. "Is that Susanne?"

"Yes," I said. But then she was gone.

"She's beautiful, Michael. She's just the way I imagined her to be."

"Yes, she is still beautiful," I said.

I remembered telling her at the lake near my house that she would always be beautiful like a swan. I was so happy to see that she still was, even though it would have made it easier for me, in a way, if she had been careworn and old-looking.

"Would you like to sit closer so that you can see her better?"

"No, it's fine, Simon. Let's go upstairs. I think the sound is better there."

"She saw you, Michael."

"She did?"

"Yes. She was looking for you and she saw you. She's come here for you."

"What makes you think so?"

"I *know* it, that's all. She knew you would be here."

We made our way to the seats in the high balcony. I sat down with Simon and resumed my inspection of the curtained stage. We were too far away from it by that time to be able to see details but in a way it was more comfortable being at a distance, and I knew from experience that sound is usually better after its waves have first separated and then re-gathered farther away from the source.

I felt ecstatic. The moments before seeing her again after twenty-some years were so full of exhilaration I could not control my expressions. My face felt like a neon sign, broadcasting to the whole auditorium the joy that I was feeling. I was holding my hands together so tightly that white spots appeared around my fingertips and I loosened them and tried to make myself relax. Simon said things to me but I couldn't hear them anymore since all of me was dedicated to the moment that she would appear from behind the curtain. The anticipation of the crowd was palpable. It was clear that she was famous with this group that had come to see her.

Susanne came to the front of the stage. Her posture was erect and proud but she decried arrogance by bowing humbly to the audience from the waist. She said something which I could not hear, and they laughed.

Then she went to the piano and sat down upon the plush green chair. The moment was so still that the quietness had a symphonic character of its own, like a prelude to the piano. She sat motionless and silent for a long moment. It looked as if she were praying, with her head bowed and her hands resting gently on the keyboard.

Then she played a single note and its timbre resonated richly throughout the vast and soundperfect hall. Then another note with the same effect. Then the simplest tune with one hand only. She slowly added complexity to the single cell of music until she had created a whole being which became a family of sounds and then a universe and then an explosion leading in reverse to simplicity again, to the single note sounded in the quiet concert hall.

She bowed to the keyboard again and was silent. And then without her hands apparently moving from the keyboard, the most beautiful music appeared in the air. I strained to see her playing but I couldn't detect a movement of her hands. It was like a water bird moving regally at twilight through the water, presumably paddling with its feet but apparently moving without effort.

I looked at Simon and he seemed enthralled by the music she was creating. I put my arm around his shoulder and he leaned into me and said, "She's wonderful. She's speaking with her hands."

I closed my eyes and leaned back in my chair while my thoughts accompanied the music. Now she seemed to be playing differently, as if we were alone in her mother's living room again and night was falling and the summer sun was rushing to its promise of a lasting contentment. I believed what Simon said: she was here for me. She was speaking to me, picking me out of the huge crowd using encoded musical messages. I could see her long fingers and sensate hands which lived not as an attachment to a wrist and an arm but as separate entities with their own distinct life.

Our bonding to one another had been impossible to explain, even to ourselves. I felt it still, even after only an hour in her presence in twenty five years. It had always felt as if we were perhaps two souls from another galaxy who were mistakenly born on this planet but separated by thousands of miles. And upon finding one another, there was no way to know what to do next, because we were not subjects of this system but of a different way of life which contained no provision for our sensations. So instead of utilizing the powers we possessed, we had to suppress them.

But because we had found each other the world would never be the same for us. We justified each other. We gave each other confidence to bring our true selves out of hiding for the other to see. And then we had to separate again and go back because it was impossible for two of us to interact openly on alien terrain.

The music feathered into its ending just as unnoticeably as it had begun and I resisted the urge to open my eyes when I heard the audience declare its delight by applauding in a crescendo of syncopated claps.

I kept my eyes closed, not wanting the moment to end, afraid that she would stop playing and we would all have to return from her musical realm to our troublesome little worlds. The audience became silent again and I waited for the music to start, but it didn't. I kept my eyes closed nonetheless. Then I heard her speak. She spoke in English.

"This is music that I wrote a long time ago. I wrote it for a friend of mine who was thousands of miles away but who was always in my heart. We have not seen each other for many, many years. I promised myself that I would never play this music in public until he was listening too, because it was for him that I wrote it. Tonight he is here with us. Thank you, Michael, for returning to Hamburg."

People turned in their seats and looked for the subject of her comments, but I stayed sitting motionless. Then she walked to the piano. I could see that some people in the balcony recognized me as the person about whom she was speaking.

The lights dimmed further and the auditorium stilled to a dreamlike silence. The music began and I closed my eyes and let it transport me to another place.

At the end of her playing, I opened my eyes at the sound of the crowd clapping rhythmically, on its feet. She was at the front of the stage, bowing again and again before disappearing behind the curtain. The crowd continued to clap and chant for a long time until they accepted that she would not come out again, and then they left their seats and funneled toward the doors. Some of them stopped at stageside, hoping she would come out and talk to them, but she didn't.

Simon and I continued sitting until all of the balcony had cleared, and then we ourselves left.

"Are we going to see her, Michael?"

"I'd like to see her. Let's walk by the stage and see if she comes out to see us."

I walked slowly, hoping she was watching for us and would come out from behind the curtain, but she didn't. We stopped below where her piano rested. The lights in the theater had been dimmed even further. We waited awhile longer but she still did not come out, so I took Simon's arm and moved toward the exit.

"Michael, you can't leave. We have to see her."

"Let's see if she is waiting for us up ahead," I said, but only an employee of the theater was waiting at the exit. I walked toward him wondering if I should request to see her, when he stepped forward and handed me a note. I opened it and recognized her handwriting: "Michael, I had to leave just after I finished playing, but here are the directions to my home. I would like you to come to see me there tomorrow if it is possible. Susanne."

Frau Schnitzer appeared from the side room and asked us how we liked Susanne's music.

"It was brilliant!" Simon said.

I smiled at her and she smiled back, then she asked if we got the note, and I said yes. "She was very sorry to have missed you, but she had to attend to Arthur."

"Who?"

"Arthur is the man who lives with her."

Even though I had not considered that she might have someone living with her and was startled to find it out, knowing that I would finally see her the next day brought me a great sense of relief and abundant happiness and energy. Outside, in front of the theatre, I picked up Simon from behind under his arms and lifted him high up into the air. He giggled and pretended to struggle for escape.

"Tomorrow we shall finally see her!" I shouted and he echoed my words.

"Let's take the motorcycle to Gluckstadt," he said.

CHAPTER 27

All night long I tossed and turned with strange dreams and mixed up images. Throughout it all I had a petty feeling of jealousy towards Arthur, which I had no right to have. Why should I expect that Susanne would not be involved with another man? What claim did I have to her? Simply because I had never been able to let go of her was no reason to expect her to be the same.

There was another side to it, though. I wondered if it would be impossible to open up to her in the same way I had before, so easily, with Arthur present. After all this time of searching for her, would our tryst be superficial and meaningless? What if Arthur was jealous of us and didn't allow her to talk openly?

I fell asleep again and dreamt of variations on this theme, and in the morning, even though I was tired, I was happy to sense, as always, a feeling of hope given promise by the light of a new day.

We found a small café along the main road with many older people eating midmorning breakfast or early lunch. There was a small stage for performers and a man was sitting in a chair on the stage playing the most beautiful classical renditions of Beatles songs. When we walked in the door, he was playing "Here, There, and Everywhere". It was very quiet and people turned to look at us, a little annoyed. We found a table and whispered what we wanted to a waitress who came to our table. "Who is the man playing?" I asked her. I remembered that the Beatles got their start in Hamburg.

"He's Goran Sollscher. A well-known classical musician from Hamburg."

"He's wonderful," I said.

"Do you know Susanne Ludendorff?" Simon asked her.

"Of course," she said. "She lives outside of Gluckstadt. She has played here with Goran."

"We're going to visit her," Simon said proudly.

The woman look impressed and said something in German like, "Lucky you!" Goran Sollscher was playing "If I Fell" sweetly in the background.

The waitress came with our tea and bread. We ate and listened to "I Love Her" and then "Here Comes The Sun," which I thought was an appropriate time to leave.

The last miles to Gluckstadt were forested and the terrain changed and became rockier as we headed toward the river. We stopped along the roadside and I got out my map to Susanne's house. The directions were clearly written. We took a dirt road to the west just before the town which eventually went along the river. It became wilder as we moved north along the Elbe. I thought that no one lived there because of the swampy nature of the ground or perhaps that it belonged to the government.

Rock outcroppings began to appear as we neared what was indicated on the map as a long lane that went to her house. One of them looked like a tower made of big round sandstone plates or saucers naturally mortared to similar plates above and below, as if they had weathered in some way that mere chance could not account for. More of them appeared and we stopped to examine them since they were so eye-catching. Simon ran ahead of me and climbed on them.

"Michael, Michael, come here, hurry!"

I went to where he was standing on top of a hollowed area in the rocks. He looked as if he had found a treasure. He turned behind him and pointed and said, "Look, Michael" and stood aside for me to see.

It was a cave.

"What do you think? Could this be it?"

The child was full of magic. I thought of how most children believe that anything is possible until their openness to believing is gradually eroded and debunked and then they are adults, never again able to believe that they have found the entrance to the Highlands.

"It very well could be, Simon," I said.

"It looks like the place you described in the story. See below, there is the valley, the meadow. I just don't see the river."

"It's over there, Simon," I said pointing in the opposite direction.

The road to her lane went pathlike through huge trees and thick vines.

It was misty and cool as we motored slowly into the densest part of the woods. The trees towered above us and were so old they had strangled out any chance of smaller ones starting, since they completely blocked out the sun, so it was open at ground level and smelled musty and old.

Halthing Forest, I thought.

At last it opened into a meadow with a lake and beyond the meadow we followed another path through the woods on the other side which ended at a gate. Susanne had given me the combination to the lock and we unlocked and went through it but decided to park the motorcycle there and walk the rest of the way.

We could hear music in the distance that sounded like bagpipes. A woman's lovely voice was singing along with it. There was a very old split rail wooden fence along a charming flower-lined path that went off to the west along the river. We followed it. The music became louder and then we saw the house. It was made of primitive wood and it was rustic-looking but unique and enchanting, two stories tall. On the top floor was a huge balcony which opened into the living room so that the two rooms were really one huge open room. However, the balcony room extended much higher than the living room and had a canopy ceiling like a tent. There was a railing that must have been thirty feet long on one side and twenty feet long on the other. On the balcony I could see a piano and an organ. Two of the walls of the balcony were filled entirely with what looked like speakers and electronic and recording equipment.

As we entered a courtyard with a large brick patio and a spiral staircase that went up to the balcony, I noticed a man in a wheelchair sitting at the top. His body was completely shriveled and he slouched motionless in the chair. Behind him was an elaborate set of computers and monitors. Then I heard a voice and saw her coming next to him. She saw us and she waved diffidently.

"Is that you, Michael?"

I loved her accent. I savored its tone and remembered always wanting more and more of it, often inducing her to talk just so I could have the pleasure of its sound. I had stored her voice perfectly along with all evidence of it in a safe place in my heart because I had known that I would hear it again, so that now as she spoke, a thousand conversations that I had had with her seemed to gather in the air from places they'd hidden for twenty-five years.

I recalled Mr. Seiler telling me that sometimes things do not happen in the framework of time that we envision for them. "Be patient," he'd said, "You will find her again." Because to me he was a great man who did not err about such things, I had believed him.

"Yes, it is, Susanne."

"So you have finally come for me, Michael?" She smiled broadly. "To take me to the lake and watch the swans wake up the day."

"Yes, I have come for you, Susanne. Your mother said you had gone to Hamburg, so I decided to come and find you myself."

"I knew you would come, Michael. I always knew you would come back and find me. I'm so glad you did. Who is your little friend? Is he your son, Michael?"

I looked down at Simon. He was looking at me beseechingly.

"Yes. His name is Simon."

"Oh, what a wonderful name it is. A wise name. You wait there. We'll be down straight away."

In a few moments the floor of the porch beside the staircase opened up and a lift descended slowly to our level. Susanne stood behind the man in the wheelchair and rolled him out in front of herself.

From a distance I appraised her physique. She was a little taller than I remembered, still stately in her carriage, like an athlete. Her hair was long to her shoulders and almost white-blonde from the sun. She wore a simple printed cotton dress that looked soft and loose but still showed the patrician curves of her attractive body beneath it. Finally she looked up at us and smiled a welcoming smile that would have drawn me fully into its allure if not for the other feature of her face which had always stolen my attention: her resplendent blue eyes. The last time I'd seen them so close up, when she was lying mute in Neuengamme, they were lifeless and pallid, but now again they were dazzling like light waves of a higher spectrum. I could feel Simon's hand grip my side tightly and I looked down at him for a second. He was staring at her as one would stare at an exotic animal in a zoo, his eyes agape and his mouth open, as if he had never seen such a creature before. She was just as prepossessing as I'd remembered her, having that rare mystique which only certain persons have which magnetizes attention to them.

"Look at her eyes!" he whispered to me.

She must have heard it, for she went straight to him and extended her hand, saying, "Hello, Simon. It is a great pleasure to meet you. I am Susanne."

I microscopically studied every move that she made and every feature of her body, even to the broad pores and capillary-wide wrinkles on her dark tanned hands, hungrily, as if she might vaporize and be gone for another twenty years and I would only have what I could glean from her in that moment. It felt as if a painting of her which I had been doing as a child and which had been interrupted was now permitted to be reworked and I was filling in the canvas with details as fast as they registered to me.

As she was presenting herself to Simon, I saw myself staring at her almost worshipfully, slack-jawed and dumb-witted, and suddenly I realized something: another person was present whom I had impolitely not even acknowledged yet. The man in the wheel chair. I turned to look at him and his face looked as if it was in terrible pain, distorted and twisted. He was trying to use his mouth to speak but he was only able to grunt spasmodically, as if he were possessed of St. Vitus's Dance. His hands were gnarled and bent back upon themselves and squirming to express themselves, but to no avail. Nothing of him seemed to be able to say what it seemed to be so desperately grappling to say. Neither his real language nor his body language said anything except a twisted complex of efforts. When my eyes met his he tried even harder to communicate something to me. He grunted and snorted until Susanne's attention changed from Simon to us. Still holding Simon's hand in hers, she leaned next to the man and said endearingly and tenderly, "Arthur, this is Simon. Simon, this is my dear friend Arthur." Arthur made a Herculean attempt to raise himself from the chair, enough to somehow swing his arm toward Simon who heroically caught it in mid-air. Simon shook the whole arm up and down with large exaggerated swings like he was an old friend making light of Arthur's affliction. They both laughed, Simon first, and then Arthur followed with explosions of spontaneity like a child.

Then she turned to me and said to Arthur, "And this is Michael, whom I have told you about many times. Michael, this is Arthur."

All I could think to do at that moment, for some majestic reason, was to bow to him humbly and say, "It's my great pleasure, Arthur, to meet a dear friend of my dear friend." I reached forward and took his hand and his face broke into a smile which must have set off a spasm of synapses, because his face literally went to pieces with something like akimbo delight.

"Arthur has cerebral palsy and so all of his movements and his actions come out differently than you are used to, but once you understand him you will see that he is brilliant and funny. He likes to make people laugh. He is free, you know? It is the others who are imprisoned in their expectations. He likes you both."

Then she turned to me and put both arms out wide and invited me into them, to which I moved with disbelief, as if I were entering a fairy tale from my childhood.

"Ah, Michael, and I am Susanne," she said ironically.

We embraced and at once I felt dispossessed of something ponderous like a sickness or an inhibition. I literally felt it vanish through the top of my head, and I could even see its hardened form and ugly face. I thought of Francisco Alvaro, halfway around the world in the Peruvian Amazon Rain Forest, and wondered if he was involved somehow in its divestiture, as if he had shot a dart entipped with curare and killed for all time that menace within me.

I held her two hands lightly in front of us, as if we were dancing. "You look so lovely, Susanne."

She smiled and emblazoned me with her eyes and kissed me on the cheek. "You look lovely too, Michael."

Arthur liked the irony of her calling me lovely and his whole chair rocked expressively.

"Come, let us show you our house," she said, grabbing one of each of our hands and holding us out to the sides of the wheelchair which she deftly moved back toward the lift with her legs, high-stepping like a military person. I reached to help her but she said, "No, no, I want to hold your hand so you don't run away." Arthur loved it. He loved everything. "Besides, I'm accustomed to moving him with my arms full."

Simon asked if he could climb up to the floor above by way of the spiral staircase.

"Of course," she said and let go of his hand and he scrambled up the stairs to beat us to the top.

"What an interesting boy he is, Michael" she said as the lift made its way to the next floor. "How old is he?"

"He is eleven, almost twelve."

"Yes, he is exceptional, isn't he? Most children are afraid of Arthur at first." She squeezed my hand and said, "Well, of course I would know your son would be exceptional."

"Actually, Susanne, he is not my biological son. I just think of him as my son."

"Well, then, Michael, he is your son. That's all that matters."

"Yes, I think that way too. But actually, in some ways he is my friend and at times I think he is older than I."

"Yes, I can see what you mean. He is precocious. Is he musical?"

"I don't know, probably."

"I think he is."

"You do?"

"Yes. Because he watches closely, doesn't he, and sees things clearly. He picks up things with his intuition. I can see that. He has a higher purpose. Music is part of that. Is he good at mathematics?"

"Yes, quite good."

"Well, you will see. He is good at music too. We'll show you." She laughed. "Arthur will bring it out of him.

"Is your wife with you, Michael?"

"I've never married, Susanne. His mother is my friend. She has helped me a lot."

"Is she South American?"

"Yes, how do you know?"

"I can see it in Simon's face and hear the Spanish tongue. But there is something else, something in his accent."

"He has lived in New Zealand a lot. There's that too."

"Yes, I can hear that, but there's also another element. Is it German?"

"Yes, of course, I forgot. His father was German, from Hamburg in fact."

"How interesting."

The lift reached the top and Simon was waiting for us.

The music that had been playing stopped and I asked Susanne if it was a bagpipe.

"Oh no, that's the hardingfele. It's a folk instrument of Norway and Denmark. Arthur and I recorded that music with an old Norwegian. Isn't it lovely? So dark and lonely, full of solitude and longing. The Norwegians are like that, wistful and introspective, waiting forever for the light of day. They love minor keys, as if the long nights aren't dark enough. Their music has a tristequality."

"A what?"

"A tristequality, a predominant theme of sorrow and sadness."

I recalled that Simon had told me his father suffered from 'La Tristeza', from sadness, but I didn't think I should mention it.

"Who is singing?" I asked her.

"It is I."

"I forgot, you sing too."

"Yes, Michael, I sing too. But not always so sadly."

She let go of my hand which she had been holding tightly the whole time. I felt exuberant. The day was still early. It was cool and nice.

"How long can you stay, Michael?"

"We need to return to Peru the day after tomorrow."

"Good, then stay with us tonight, okay?"

"We don't have any extra clothes with us."

"That's all right. Who cares? If they get dirty, we have water or we can go swimming in the river with our clothes on. Or you can wear my clothes, Michael."

"Or he can wear Arthur's," Simon said.

We all laughed. Simon, who had already taken over the steerage of the wheelchair, laughed the loudest and provoked Arthur to compete with him in a volley of laughter that sounded like the howler monkeys of Cuchari.

We turned on the balcony toward the center of the room and there was an elaborate electronic sound and recording system interconnected with the organ and piano and other instruments through hundreds of wires running everywhere. It looked like a gigantic nervous system and felt alive. It covered two entire walls. Everywhere there were instruments, flutes and fiddles and horns and an assortment of primitive noisemakers.

Susanne swept her arm toward the room and said, "This is our studio, Michael. This is where we live and have our being."

The birds, which had been silent before, were suddenly singing wildly outside in the trees and their songs were blown in louder on a strong warm wind from the south. There was a river smell of water creatures. Even though the house felt sunny and open, the trees completely surrounded the house to give us a serene sense of being on an island with no one around.

Another recording of lilting piano tunes started to play. The tunes were jazzy and swinging but with a powerful and aggressive sound, and I assumed it was Susanne, but I had never heard her play that way before.

"So, Michael," she said, "I want to know all about you and what you have done with your life. I want to know where you live and what you do."

"First, let me ask you something, Susanne. Twice you've referred to me coming back to Hamburg. Are you aware that I was here once before?"

"Yes, I'm aware of that, Michael."

"How do you know?"

"Because you came to see me at Neuengamme."

"But nothing seemed to register with you when I talked to you at that time."

"No. But it did. I was aware of you."

"I had no idea."

"Yes. But it was dreamlike. I have told Arthur about it many times. Excuse me, Michael, I have to see where he is."

She left me alone in the living room studio with a light breeze blowing across the balcony and the lovely piano music playing old American standards like "All Of You" and "Love Is A Many Splendored Thing."

She came back. "He's showing Simon the rest of the house. Your son can already communicate with him. Is he good at languages?"

"Yes, he speaks several."

"I thought so. I have to be careful of Arthur or he will overextend himself. He needs to rest often throughout the day, but he refuses to do it on his own, so I have to put him down. Just like a baby. But they'll be all right for a while. He'll have Simon playing Bach Sonatas by midnight."

I laughed.

"Don't laugh," she said. "What is your profession, Michael?"

"I'm a doctor."

"A doctor. That doesn't surprise me. You were so smart in school. My father was a doctor, remember?"

"Of course. You were the first one to tell me I should study medicine."

"Michael, do you know anything about problems of the nervous system?"

"The central nervous system. Not really. Just what I learned in medical school. I've not dealt with it too much. Is that what Arthur has? It's not treatable, is it?"

"Not treatable by ordinary means. Just by miracles."

"Well, I believe in miracles."

"Do you, Michael?"

"Yes, I do."

"Michael, you will see a miracle tonight that you'll not believe. After dinner and after we have rested, I'll ask Arthur to play the piano for us. This man whom you have seen to be completely without the use of his arms and legs can play the piano so beautifully it will bring tears to your eyes. Do you hear this music playing now? It's Arthur. But it's nothing compared to what he can do."

I couldn't see how Arthur could possibly play the piano that I was hearing. I told her I believed in miracles since so many of them had happened to me in the last year. I told her about my illness and meeting Christiane and going to Peru and taking ayahuasca and about Francisco Alvaro and finding her again in my ayahausca experience.

She excused herself and was gone a long time and came back with Simon alone. She had put Arthur to bed. She must have felt, as I did, that we needed to talk, because she suggested the topic. I wanted Simon to hear it too.

For all I knew we would have only one night together, and so I simply asked her straight away why she left and never contacted me.

"First of all, Michael, I left the US because I wasn't happy there, especially with my mother. I hated living with her because of what she had done to my father, whom I adored. But also we were nothing alike. She was totally rigid with me. As you know, I'm not like that. You were the only person who understood that about me. I was in love with you,

Michael. When you withdrew your emotions from me, I felt completely lost. You probably don't think you withdrew from me, but you did.
I have since realized that you had problems of your own and couldn't
be there just for me all of the time as I needed you. Nonetheless, the
things we shared together were extraordinary. It is only with Arthur
that I have felt so close to someone again.

"After returning to Hamburg, I found that I wasn't happy here either. I was so lonely for you. I had no one like you to listen to me and
appreciate me. You see, Michael, I have had problems all of my life
because of my 'imagination'. You and Arthur do more than just accept
it or understand it. You believed in it too, you became a part of it, you
encouraged it. Everyone else has always thought I was mad. 'She's
pretty, but a little odd'; 'She's a great pianist, but as you'd expect, a little
crazy.' I'm tired of hearing that. I know that I'm not mad. And you
knew it, and so does Arthur. I know that what I see in my 'imagination'
is there, is real, and works for me in a totally different world from others. I don't care anymore whether they believe it or not.

"I had been on my own by then. I had been intimate with you and I
couldn't abide my father's strict rules. I made friends in the Reeperbahn
and they accepted me. It wasn't necessary for them to understand me in
order to do that. We all accepted each other. And why not? I moved in
with a girl who was from a good family but who had never been given
love, as so many of the girls there had not. She sought it in a bottomless
search for men's pleasure and approval. It's something which they all
seem to share, a factor of their youth which mercifully plays out after
a while with most of them after they see that they're searching in the
wrong place for the wrong thing.

"The girl had a boyfriend and one day he brought a sailor with him
to her house. The sailor was handsome and quiet, like you Michael. I

liked his gentleness and his good mind. I wanted him to be you. We made love for a weekend, and then he was gone. He never wrote to me, as he said he would, and my letters sent to the address he'd given me came back.

"I became pregnant. I wanted the child to be yours – but I was never sure. I had decided to come back and see you, and I was about to write you, before this happened. I'd obtained money for the plane ticket, but I felt so bad, so full of guilt for what I had done to you, that I couldn't allow myself to affect your life any deeper, so I sold the ticket and moved back in with my father. When he found out that I was pregnant he insisted that I have the baby taken, which I wouldn't do. Our lives together effectively ended then, because a short time later he had a stroke and not long after that he died. I tried to give birth on my own at my father's house after he had died. My friend from the Reeperbahn had assisted other women in giving birth and she helped me, but the child, a little girl, was born dead. I was so awash in guilt and self-hatred that I fell to pieces. I was put into Neuengamme, a horrible place where people are left to die like animals. This place was an unimaginable nightmare of horrors, as you saw, Michael.

"In the middle of it, one day while I lay blocking out the never-ending sounds of people crying and smashing the walls with their fists and heads and feet and moaning and sobbing and screaming, I looked up and there you were! My dearest friend had come to see me from all the way across the sea. I didn't know if what I was seeing was real or not, and I didn't care because seeing what I thought was you made me feel good again. It helped me begin to feel worthy. From that day forward I began to improve. The young doctor, whom you had persuaded, Michael, came in to see me right after you left, and he took special care of me and he believed in me. He got me a room of my own and came in to see me many times a day. There was a piano in the auditorium which was out of tune and which no one ever played. He had it brought to my room and had it tuned. I played it for ten hours a day. I was like the pied piper of Neuengamme. When I played it, the screams and moans stopped, and when I stopped playing they started again. That's when I met Arthur. He was like a stone in a chair. His eyes were dead and his body hardly moved, but when I played the piano he returned to life. I could see what was underneath. I felt as if I knew him from somewhere. He became my goal and my life and my reason for being."

Simon had been staring at her at attention, waiting for an opportunity to speak.

"Did you marry the young doctor?"

"Yes, how did you know that, Simon?"

"Was his name Tomas?"

"Yes, tell me how you know that."

"He was my father."

Together Simon and I had now arrived at the moments of truth we had both been waiting for and which had united us in mutual healing.

"Tomas was your father?" she repeated. She looked as though she were calculating something that would tell her if what he had said was possible. "Is he not alive now?"

"He's dead for almost two years. He killed himself."

"Oh my God! I'm so sorry to hear that." She stood up and walked to Simon and kneeled down and hugged him. "Tell me about him."

"I'd like to talk to you about him when you are done talking to Michael."

"Yes, of course, Simon. He was a lovely man. A very exceptional man."

She left and returned with three glasses of water in tall thin decanters.

She was silent. "Would you like to talk about all this later," I said.

"No, no, Michael. It's not that. I'm just trying to get it clear in my mind how to talk about this. I would like to speak frankly. I think Tomas was in love with the music I played. That's what drew him to me at first. He needed music in his life. You see, we didn't have a typical marriage. How can I say this? Not typical like a husband and a wife."

She looked at me for approval, but I didn't know what to approve. I simply nodded that it was okay to go on.

"He wasn't clear about who he was. He told me he had problems before we got married. We weren't unlike a husband and a wife in many ways, except that the passion between us was hard to express. He was afraid of his own feelings. He wanted to be someone else. He didn't like himself, in that way and in others. He was a brilliant and a wonderful doctor. He treated his patients like they were his family. They loved him and wanted to be around him. They got better just being near him. When I met him in the hospital he was interning in psychiatric medicine for a term because he was fascinated with it. He needed to aid people who were helpless and suffering in this way. I think that was his initial attraction to me. But in a way this love of his was also bottomless and had to be continuously fed with others to save in order to keep him from the deep sadness into which he sank when he was idle. He worked all of the time when he wasn't sleeping and eating, as if he was intent upon curing the world of all sickness and, I always thought, make himself well again too. He had no confidence in himself as a man aside from being a monumental doctor, really almost a hero. I tried to make him more peaceful and contemplative, understanding of why he was the way he was, but he was afraid to face the things inside of himself. We gradually drifted apart from each other, although really our love never ended."

"My father died of 'La Tristeza,' the Sadness they call it. At the end he would be alone in his room for days or else working all day and night for weeks until he collapsed. My mother loved him and was devoted to him. She accepted him just the way he was, even when he was dark and absent. But then other times he was so full of light and life and happiness that he felt like my best friend. He was entertaining and witty and knew many things."

"He was brilliant!" she practically yelled. "Just brilliant! And musical. And funny. I loved those parts of him, but yes, I know what you mean about the Triste." She turned to Simon and put a hand out to him which he took hold of. "I am glad you're here, Simon, thank you for coming. Let me tell you something. I'm sure that you were and still are the light and the joy in your father's life. I'm sure that you made the Tristeza go away and I am sure that he's with you now."

"I saw him in Cuchari."

"You did? Tell me about it."

"It was a vision. But it was real, wasn't it, Michael? We saw you too, Susanne."

"And what did your father say to you when you saw him, Simon?"

"He said that he loved me and, like you said, was available for me if I needed him. I need him now, Susanne. I need him to come back. Everything happened so fast at Cuchari that I couldn't make sense of it until after it was over. I want to see him again."

"Well, he's here, Simon, like he said. You just have to determine how to get to him."

"How do I do that?"

"Let me think about it. Okay?"

"Can you take us to the Land of Fathers, Susanne?"

"I need to think about it, Simon. I will figure out a way."

Then she turned to me and said, "Michael, this is a wonderful day in my life, to see you again. I feel as if the strings of resolution are finally being tied together. Thank you for coming here. You'll stay the night with us, won't you?"

"Of course, Susanne."

"A good spirit has come over our house in the form of Simon and Michael. There will be good things that happen tonight. You will see."

She left the room to awaken Arthur. I looked at Simon and he looked back at me and smiled.

"She's all that you said about her, Michael."

CHAPTER 28

Susanne emerged from the hallway, pushing Arthur. He greeted us
and she sat down beside Simon and me, with Susanne across from
us. She had brought a framed picture from the bedroom and handed it
to Simon. "Would you like to have this picture of your father, Simon?"

"I'd love to have it. Did you know my father, Arthur?"

He nodded and began to talk. I couldn't understand him. Susanne
started to interpret it but Simon said with a slight annoyance in his
voice, "I know what he's saying! He said that he knew my father well
and that without my father's special attention to him he would still be
in the asylum. He says my father was a good man, that he loved him
very much."

"See, Michael, your son already speaks the language of palsy." She
turned to Simon. "Arthur's sad to hear about Tomas. I explained it to
him in the bedroom what had happened to your father. Death is hard
for Arthur to accept - that someone will not be coming back in body
but only in spirit. Because he's crippled in body he is especially sad to
have the body of someone he loved disappear and never re-form in that
same configuration. He thinks that it's too hard trying to figure out
where the spirit went and how it associates and with whom and that it
would be easier to identify if it had the same beautiful body attached
to it. He feels that way about old people. He's sad to see them barely

moving with their wasted bodies. He doesn't see why the spirit of the living can't occupy only a perfect body."

"He thinks that people who have died can come back?" Simon asked.

"Oh yes. But he wants to see them. Not just at séances or visions, but all the time. He's working on that. He'd always hoped he would see Tomas again. Your father had a handsome body as well. Lithe and athletic. He was a dancer."

"You have seances?"

"Well, yes, our own type, probably not the way that most people do."

"And you see people from the dead?"

"Not always. We usually hear them speaking. Only sometimes do we see them. It's only if the spirit chooses to manifest itself in body and only if it can find a body through which to appear."

We sat in a group of four in the comfortable living room that adjoined the studio but back from the light and the breeze. Looking out at the balcony and the railing overlooking the late day-lit courtyard, it felt as if we were staring through a huge camera framed by a wide peripheral angle, so that we were on the edge of the shadow of light from the outside but in the darkness. At night after the sun had set, it reversed, so that the shadow was the outside and the light came from inside.

After a while, when I had stopped thinking of Arthur's speech as grunts and groans and unintelligible noises, I slowly began to understand him myself. I began to see how Arthur could be attractive to Susanne. He was exceptional and lived on a plane above the ordinary. She lived on that plane too and had always lived there and had found someone to live there with her. They were in love.

Simon talked about his feelings for his father and the deep loneliness that still took him over from time to time, but, he said, "Michael has become like a father to me."

I told them that in the last year I had participated in so many myste-rious happenings that I could never be the same but that I was not sure just who I could be or who I was supposed to be, since the awareness I had gained was a mysterious awareness, not amenable to ordinary logic but having to do with faith and intuition.

"Then it's easy to know where to go next, Michael," Susanne said. "Go where your faith and intuition tell you to go."

I asked Susanne if she would play the piano for us and she said that she would in a while after the moon came into view in the window of sky just southeast of the house. She said she would like to play mu-sic that she had written and said its title in German; then she said, "It means in English something like, 'Negotiating With The Moon.'"

Susanne began to clear the dishes from the table and to carry them to the kitchen and when I started to help, she said sternly, "I don't need any help. You stay here, thank you."

I sat silently and listened to her and Arthur conferring together and in time I heard music growing into the conversation. I thought it was a piano but it had an almost nasal falsetto quality like an old-fashioned lute or harpsichord. I could see Arthur's face clearly lighted and I was absorbed in the complexity of his struggle to make words. I turned around and the moon was above the trees shining on his face. Both he and Simon were staring at the moon, and just when I looked at it again, a huge bird was between the moon and us, lingering in the circle of its light. We all watched it disappear into the surrounding darkness, and then Arthur said, "Someone needs to be heard."

"It is an albatross," Susanne said from the other room. "It's believed that he is carrying water in his long beak to someone from the spirit world."

The music became more insistent, not aggressive but more passionate and minor, Mideastern, and haunting in tone. It demanded silence and we fell back to a posture of listening carefully to it instead of using it as a backdrop. I got up and turned off the kitchen light so that there was only the small white light from the piano and opaline light from the moon on the balcony. Arthur was sitting across from me and he began to sway slightly, rhythmically, with control he had not demonstrated before. He closed his eyes and I looked at his face and saw something different than I had seen before. Perhaps it was because his eyes were closed, I thought, and I could examine him more carefully without feeling self-conscious, but it seemed that he was changing and I could begin to see his face as it would be without the palsy.

The transcendental quality of the music that Susanne played evidently helped facilitate the molding of Arthur's body. How can I explain what to me was obviously an interplay between the systems of sounds she was making and the restoration of Arthur's nervous system? All I can say is that over the next thirty minutes, perhaps, Arthur was transfigured. Simon watched it too. Arthur swayed and moaned painfully to straighten himself out, as if he were re-plugging, one by one, thousands of wires that the palsy had disconnected in his body. Susanne's music, like that of a skillful tactician and a secret sweet talker at once, coaxed and implored each tiny re-connection which they together carried out upon him.

The interstices of his palsy-ridden face, deeply inscribed upon by daily colossal efforts to express itself, were straightening out and becoming progressively smoother while the rest of his body was perceptibly emerging from its own debilitating atrophy like a pupa from a cocoon. Each triumphant moment of transmutation, accompanied by Susanne's celestial piano playing, was a duet of prodigious accomplishment at which they labored in tandem. It seemed as if Arthur were trying to step out of his skin while his hands and feet were tied. This went on for an hour, all of us silent. Then Susanne spoke.

"Your father is here, Simon. He wants to speak to you." Susanne spoke to him in a voice of song like a minstrel announcing to the court the arrival of a royal guest.

"He's come from far away and has been riding upon the coattails of the moon. He is seeking entrance to our world. Come next to me and listen for him and help to hasten his arrival."

Simon arose dutifully from the table and went to Susanne's piano. She was no longer simply the gracious and modest hostess that she had been throughout the day but now a powerful and commanding medium intent upon providing the father from the spirit world to his boy in the common world.

Once Simon was beside her she got up from the piano stool and motioned for him to sit down. He did, and then looked up at her, confused, as she stood next to him waiting for him to perform.

"Play for him," she said. "So that he can hear where you are."

"But I can't play the piano."

"Yes you can." She took his hands gently and placed them on the keyboard and spread the fingers out with each one on its own key. "Just play."

He leaned down to study his fingers, and then made a single note, as she had done at the Musikhalle. The note slowly increased in volume until it reached its apogee and then it slowly decreased, like a long slide diminishing without end. Simon was pleased with the sound. He struck another note. And then another and another with different fingers from both hands. Finally he dropped his expectations and let his fingers dance on the keys in whatever melodic or cacophonous way they chose until in time they found their way into a spectacular symphony of sounds. He looked up at her and laughed and she pushed his head playfully. "Keep playing," she said. "I will greet your father's arrival and bring him to you. But you must not stop playing, for your music provides the runway onto which his celestial craft descends."

She walked away, back into the shadows of moonlight. I lost sight of where she went because I was so enraptured with Simon's piano playing. I don't know where the music came from but it had a precise form and direction. It was not just noise. It was a piece composed automatically from memory. A beautiful complex piece with depth and variety, with adagios and allegros and with complex changes in rhythm and wonderful percussive inventions. He was simply recalling it from somewhere within.

From the studio room where we were sitting, I could not see Arthur on the balcony as clearly as I'd seen him before because the moon was behind a tree or a cloud and no longer illuminated his body and face, but I could hear him still straining to get free of his bodily restraints.

I then realized that all three of us were involved with the same event and were all trying to bring together the father lost from his son. Clearly the only way to do it was to think as one. I used all my power of imagination to bring the pair together. I recognized that I was having an influence on them, the same as Arthur, but the variable was Simon and his piano playing. I looked at him and his face was almost touching his hands as he played. He was apparently still in disbelief that he could be producing such sounds. He was not paying attention to the direction that his music was making for the event that Arthur and I were imagining together.

I didn't know how to communicate to Simon that his music needed bearing so that it could deliver his father to him, because I was afraid that

I would break the spell that he was creating. Simon was now pounding the keys with total abandon, completely confident that whatever he did, the music would flow meaningfully from his fingers.

He must have intuitively realized that he was doing something wrong because he suddenly changed the music. It became slow and dramatic, sad with longing, slow like a waltz with long steps. He went back and forth between two chords while Arthur made chilling anguished moans from the darkness.

Simon finally understood that there was a greater purpose to his creation than simply to be delighted with himself. His abandon became studied determination to direct the music that was coming out of his hands, as if he suddenly remembered that Susanne had asked him to play in order to herald his father's arrival.

Arthur, who had been silent for some time, let out a last painful entreaty, and I looked quickly to the balcony where he had been sitting. The moonlight was back but because the moon had moved, he was still partly in shadows. Susanne, who had been silent and uninvolved, reentered the scene from somewhere behind the piano and took Arthur's hand in the darkness. To my utter disbelief he slowly stood up from his wheelchair and made a deep groan, as if his skeleton and musculature were shocked to be supporting him. She held his hand firmly but not with mastery, her wrist bent delicately, the way one might hold a dance partner before a pirouette.

Susanne came first into the music room alone. She stood on the opposite side of Simon and put her hand on his shoulder, and leaned down and whispered, "Your father is here. He would like to enter your presence, but you must keep playing."

Startled by the reality of what she had said, Simon looked up and looked beyond me to the body emerging from the shadows, and so did I. Arthur was moving slowly into the light of the music room. He moved like a newborn fawn, unsteady on new legs but moving inexorably toward the piano.

"Don't stop playing," she again cautioned Simon who was staring in disbelief at the spirit of his father walking unaided into the piano room.

Simon scooted over on the bench and looked carefully at his father and then touched his arm to make sure that what he was seeing was real. They smiled at each other. Then they began playing the piano together.

What they played was so sweet and so tender that it was possible for me to believe that they were actually talking to each other through the keyboard, making an offering of themselves to one another. One of them played a theme and the other answered it. They made affirmative sounds that accompanied the musical dialogue, confirming their communication. I was sure that Tomas was answering all of the bewildering questions which Simon had pondered since his death.

I looked over at Susanne. She was intensely concentrating upon their duet as if she were their piano teacher and they were giving a recital. Or perhaps it was that she could understand the musical language herself and was listening to their statements to each other. Observing her observing them, studying her lovely strong and honest profile, I realized that she had become a mature manifestation of the extraordinary girl who had helped me open my own eyes so long ago. At last I had found her. I had found Susanne. I had found the genie who had given me the wishes and then had disappeared.

CHAPTER 29

In the morning I heard beautiful Brazilian music that accompanied my dream of South America. It was a bossa nova-like piano with, of all things, a harmonica. It was a recording of Susanne playing the piano with a man playing harmonica. I had never heard the harmonica played so gorgeously. He soulfully bent the notes in quick chromatic slides, softly, slightly whimpering, leading the piano.

It felt as if they were playing just for me, as she had played for me when we were children. It was not just music but language, and I could somehow understand it through the process of translation that seemed to inhere to the network of circumstances provided by Susanne's life there. She had told me once: "I must trust that I can express what is in my heart and you must trust that you are able to hear what my heart is truly speaking." I thought that I heard it saying, "Thank you, Michael, for coming here to restore our love, and for believing in me."

I lay there contemplating the phenomenal night before and the extraordinary last year of my life. I recalled what Arthur had said: "You are going where you need to go. Be simple." So I simply listened to the music in the fresh bright stillness of the new morning in Gluckstadt, Germany, where the two rivers joined and where magic seemed to live.

It was hard to leave Susanne because it felt so right to finally be in her presence. She was still the same compelling person I had fallen in love with for eternity when I was a boy, and I knew now the nature of the love I'd had for her and knew that I'd forever feel that way about her. But she was never mine alone and could never be. The projects of her life were lofty and immaterial and took place in a spiritual zone that few of us are comfortable either entering or living within, where she and Arthur lived.

Simon was reluctant when I told him we had to go. He simply did not want to leave. He didn't want to return to school and wanted to stay in Hamburg and live near Susanne and Arthur. He was sure that Christiane would move there with him.

I recalled feeling that way as a boy, knowing positively through my feelings where I belonged and wanted to be but being powerless to ratify my own wishes.

I did my best to talk about that to him, but it did not do much good until Susanne intervened. She took Simon down on the elevator and sat in the courtyard in the shadow of the balcony. I could see them talking to each other but couldn't hear their voices. It was lovely to watch her lips move and her head bob affirmatively, confirming what he was saying. Her gestures were broad and dramatic like a wonderful entertainer. They laughed like great friends telling jokes. At last they returned to the balcony up the spiral staircase. Simon came up to me and jumped onto my lap and put his arms around me and said, "Let's go home, Michael."

I looked up at her with astonishment and she raised her eyes coquettishly as if to say, "I didn't have anything to do with it."

Arthur said goodbye to us at the top of the lift, choosing not to go down with us to ground level. He bid a sad farewell to Simon and me.

"I will miss you, my boy," he said. He wrenched his body to try to put an arm around Simon, so Simon leaned down to him and took his arm and put it around his own neck. He then put his arm around Arthur and tried to pick him up from the wheelchair but couldn't. Neither of them would let go of the other and so for a second they froze together like a strange sculpture whose only sense was that it balanced.

All I could think of was the truly unimaginable sight of Arthur arising dauntlessly from his wheelchair the night before and walking under his own power into the piano room bearing the spirit of Simon's father.

Susanne walked us back through the woods to the motorcycle still leaning against the fence at the edge of the meadow. We had trouble saying goodbye and leaving. We exchanged addresses and phone numbers and hugged each other again and again, promising to stay in touch. I knew that we would.

When I started the motorcycle our voices had to be raised above its roar in order for us to hear each other. It made me feel empty to have to end our visit by shouting. Simon climbed on behind me while he held Susanne's hand. Finally we pulled away, waving and looking back at her until just before she was out of sight. There I stopped the motorcycle and turned off the motor. She was still standing in the distance waving back at us in the same diffident way that she'd greeted us when we'd arrived.

"I love you, Susanne," I yelled with all of my might.

She didn't answer and I debated for an instant whether to drive closer and say it, but it seemed as if it would not have the same effect if I did.

Just as I was about to start the engine again and drive away, I heard her echo. "I love you too, Michael."

I pictured the swans dancing on the moon in the water in the background of the lake near my grandparents' home where we first said that to each other and never uttered it again until then. It was a small round lake with an island in the middle where the ducks and swans took shelter at night. A green grassy hill went down to it and fine brick two-story Tudor houses surrounded it in the distance.

"I love you too, Susanne," Simon screamed.

I wished I could return some day to that lake.

"I love you too, Simon," came her voice from across the meadow. Pershing's Meadow.

We drove slowly southeast to Hamburg with the sun setting warmly behind us and with Simon's cheek pressed against my back and with melancholy in our hearts.

CHAPTER 30

At the airport in Lima there is always a throng of people waiting just outside of the terminal. Simon was so anxious to find his mother's face in the crowd that he walked beside me jumping like a grasshopper to see above the crowd ahead of us. I raised him onto my shoulders. He was full of glee at the prospect of seeing his mother again and made so much commotion that I finally had to put him down for fear that he would fall.

We heard Christiane yelling his name. Then we saw her. I looked at Simon's face as he recognized her. It was the look of every boy seeing his mother's face after a long absence from her and realizing that he is home at last, again.

I felt the same.

CHAPTER 31

I am practicing medicine again. I live in Lima permanently. It has been over seven years since I first came to Peru. But it is longer than that. It is a time beyond calculation.

I am also a writer. I write poetry. And I write about children and about the direction not taken – how to retrieve one's soul, if need be, and to become whole again.

I have a small clinic in an area called Villa El Salvador, the Town of the Savior. My clinic is called Clinica del Dolor, meaning "pain clinic." In a place like Villa El Salvador, one needs no clearer identification of purpose than that. I practice an eclectic medicine, using many methods. I believe that the goal of all medicine is the same: to remove pain and suffering and ideally to restore the body to a condition of wellness. Sometimes pain can only be relieved long enough for the patient to make it through the night. Other times the cause of pain is systemic and widespread and has to be treated holistically. Sometimes surgery is required. Some people need penicillin or morphine to relieve pain, others need someone to love them, and still others need to take ayahausca and completely re-evaluate themselves and their priorities.

When I am in need of a doctor myself or in need of reconstructive surgery to my soul, which has forgotten that magic lives alongside misery, I go to Cuchari and see my friend and fellow healer, Franciso Alvaro.

I have not had an incident of the sickness for nearly seven years.

Christiane comes every Saturday night to my house and we have dinner together and spend the night with each other. I look forward all week long to seeing her again. When she knocks on my door just before sunset each Saturday, I feel as if I have finally arrived at the top of the mountain I had been climbing all week and that now I can view a panorama of the world as a whole and breathe deeply the fresh air which she is to me.

When she leaves Lima to travel with her work, Simon stays with me. He is eighteen years old now. He speaks Quechua fluently and sometimes travels with me back to the rain forest. We have visited Germany together several times.

Simon is also a world class soccer player and is already being recruited by universities as well as professional teams in both North and South America. I attend all of his games at home, not just out of loyalty but because to watch him play is thrilling and even instructive to me. He has instincts of a beautiful graceful animal and can perform feats of dexterity and cunning that demonstrate a rare self-control and confidence, but also an acute awareness of when to let go, when to surrender, when to be used by the underlying process of life's movement.

There is now in my life a sacred place to which I go where there is solitude and to which no one can claim ownership. I am able to find it no matter where I am. It is a place of immense quietness that resides somewhere between the last person who has taken rest and the first person who has arisen dutifully.

Here I can eavesdrop upon scenes that have made up my life. I can see spirits which have passed ahead of me and have joined with the present congregation to prepare for a new inclination. I can assess my life with wisdom and I can envisage the future and understand its identity with both my present and my past.

It is here where the condor soars wingspread to the highest peak of his majesty and invites me to fly with him.

It is a place to which I must go alone.

Here I always give thanks for my blessings and ask for continued strength. I ask that my mind be hopeful and that my thoughts be happy, so that I can help to make the minds and the thoughts of those around me happy and hopeful too.

Upon arriving at this place for the first time, one is startled to realize how easily it could have been found. However, to find it requires a change of heart. Eventually, after years of waiting and miles of searching, when one's point of view has finally aligned with one's part of fortune, it seems as if the change happened effortlessly and that in order to arrive at this place one had simply to step across a line drawn casually in the sand.

ACKNOWLEDGEMENTS

I wish to thank:

- Judith Ludwig Gorham, the lovely German woman who married me, whose eyes are as blue as Susanne's.
- Judy Marquardt, my artistic advisor and my dear friend from birth.
- The impressive team of very talented people who artistically assembled this book and poetically designed its fantastic cover.
- Suzi Johnson Hass, who took the beautiful, ethereal picture of Baileys Harbor on the front of this book.
- Sofia Garavito, my special Peruvian friend, who introduced me to the wonders of South America and translated them for me.
- Hamburg, Germany where I drifted one day accidentally and upon learning about its glorious history was compelled to write this book.

www.ingramcontent.com/pod-product-compliance
Lightning Source LLC
Chambersburg PA
CBHW030911090426
42737CB00007B/158